A Lantern To My Feet

A Lantern To My Feet

Bible readings and comments along a path of faith

John Eaton

Paternoster:
thinking faith

24 23 22 21 20 19 18 17 16 15 14 13   12 11 10 9 8 7 6 5 4 3 2 1

First published 2014 by Paternoster
Paternoster is an imprint of Authentic Media Limited
52 Presley Way, Crownhill, Milton Keynes, MK8 0ES.
www.authenticmedia.co.uk

British Library Cataloguing in Publication Data

A catalogue record for this book is available from the British Library

ISBN 978-1-84227-828-4
978-1-78078-077-1 (e-book)

Scripture translations are the author's own
One quotation from the Authorized Version

Cover Design by David Smart
Printed and bound by CPI Group (UK) Ltd., Croydon, CR0 4YY

Contents

Preface   xiii

1   A World of Meaning   1
God Calls the World into Life   1
Royal Stewards of the Earth   3
An Insight into Love   5
Falling to Temptation and Losing Innocence   7
An End of Life on Earth, and a Sign of Hope   9
High-Rise Building Proves Divisive   11
A World in the Birth of a Child   13
The Terrible Test of Faith   14
Encounters with God in the Night   17
God's Hidden Work   19

2   Formed in the Wilderness   22
The Fire That Does Not Destroy   22
God's Choice Is Hard to Understand   24
Passover and the Start of the Exodus   25
Through the Waters of Death   27
The Fountain Struck from a Rock   29
A Kingdom Where All Are Priests   30
Ten Requirements in the Bond with God   31
Artists Inspired by the Spirit   32
Living Daily with the Reality of God   34
Earth Too Must Have Its Rest   35
The Blessing of Light from God's Face   36

3   Towards a Settled Life: Benefits and Dangers Foreseen   37
The Lord Alone, the Lord Is Everything   37
Land Promised – with Conditions   38
Circumcising the Heart   39

One God and One Temple   40
A King Immersed in Scripture   41
Giving Back to the Lord   42
Moses Dies Short of the Promise   43
The Standing Stone Hears and Bears Witness   44
The Oppressor Slain by a Woman's Hand   46
Blinded Samson's Last Prayer   48
The Foreigner's Faithful Love   49

4   The Lord Works through His Anointed King   52
    A Child Hears the Voice of God   52
    God's Hand at Work in Simple Things   53
    Saul Healed by Music   55
    Saul and His Heir Die in Battle   56
    God's Promise to the House of David   57
    David's Chain of Sin   58
    Lament for Absalom   60
    Ask What You Will: Solomon's Choice   62
    Abundance of Wisdom Given by God   63
    Solomon's Prayer for the Temple   64

5   Struggles for Faithfulness to the Lord of History   66
    The Prophet, the Ravens and the Widow   66
    The Still Small Voice   67
    The Mantle of Elijah   69
    When the Eyes of Faith Are Opened   71
    Judah, the Last Standard-Bearer   72
    The Book That Caused a Storm   74
    The Death of Royal Jerusalem   75
    A Glimmer of Hope   76
    A Great Day for Jerusalem   77
    Nehemiah Defends the Sabbath and Racial Purity   78

6   A Drama on the Mystery of Suffering   81
    The Sufferer Who Wishes He Had Never Existed   81
    Friends Conclude Job Has Brought It on Himself   83
    Job Speaks to God in Bitterness of Soul   84
    Can Death Really Be the End?   85
    God Comes and Speaks to Job   86
    Revelation through the Animals   88
    Job Responds Awed and at Peace   89
    God Openly Sides with Job   90

7   Music of Prayer, Praise and Vision   91
     The Son of God: Victor and Saviour   91
     Not Forsaken in the Land of Death   92
     A Mystery of Suffering and Salvation   94
     God Lets Holy Jerusalem Be Destroyed   96
     Jerusalem to Be Mother City of All Nations   97
     One Who Dwells in the Shadow of God   98
     The Stone the Builders Rejected   99
     The Signs of the Kingdom of God   101

8   Wisdom in Nature and Society   103
     Wisdom as Knowledge of God   103
     Wisdom as Faithful Love and Trust   104
     Wisdom as the Creator's Thought   104
     Happy with a Little   106
     Humility – Awareness of God   107
     Appointed Times of Sorrow and Joy   107
     Remember Your Creator While You Can   108
     When the Winter of Death Is Over   109

9   A Great Prophet and His Disciples   111
     Isaiah Sees the Lord   111
     The Birth of Immanuel   112
     The Birth That Brings Light   113
     When Wolf and Lamb Dwell Together   114
     Good Tidings for the Exiles   115
     The Lord's Anointed Dies for Sinners   117
     An Invitation and an Assurance   119
     A Garland for Ashes   120

10 Messages of Doom and of Love   122
     Reluctant Jeremiah   122
     Forsaking the Lord to Embrace Futility   123
     Darkness Closes in on the Prophet   124
     Promise of the New Covenant   125
     You Shall Live Again   126
     How Can I Give You Up?   127
     The Spirit Poured Out On Young and Old   128
     A Chance amid the Ruin of an Unjust State   129

11 Reaching Out to a New Era   131
     The Wonder of God's Mercy   131

Out of Bethlehem the Second David   132
What God Requires   133
The Rising of the Healing Sun   134
One Like a Son of Man Made King for Ever   135
Awakening of Sleepers in the Land of Death   136

12   What Manner of Man? Perspectives on the Nature of Jesus   138
The Image of the Unseen God   138
The Son through Whom God Has Fully Spoken   139
The Word Come to Dwell on Earth   140
The Word of Life, Made Visible and Tangible   140
The Lord Jesus Christ, Son of David and Son of God   141
The Spirit Descends on Jesus, Messiah and Son of God   142
Mary Conceives Jesus by the Holy Spirit   143
Jesus the Living One Holds Death's Keys   143
Mary's Vocation and Willing Response   144
Mary Visits Elizabeth before the Birth of John   145
The Infant Messiah is Revealed to the Shepherds   146
Eastern Sages Come to the Newborn Child   147
Herod Seeks to Kill the Child Messiah   149
Just One Episode from the Boyhood of Jesus   150

13   Jesus Announces a New Era   152
John's Warning: Repent before the Mighty One Comes   152
The Dove and the Voice at Jesus' Baptism   153
A Contest with the Devil   154
John Points to the Lamb of God   155
Jesus with the Gospel of God in Galilee   157
Jesus Cures Those Who Know Their Need   159
The New That Bursts from the Old   160
A Sign of His Glory   161
Coming to Jesus in the Night   162
Jesus and the Woman at the Well   164
Lessons at the Lakeside; Pictures of the Kingdom   166
Jesus Speaks to the Wind and Sea   167

14   Patterns of Living in the Dawning Kingdom   169
Happiness Not Where the World Seeks It   169
Requirements beyond Natural Strength   170
Doing Good in Secret   172
A Pattern for Prayer   173
Learning from the Birds and Wild Flowers   175

You Will Surely Find Him 177
The Narrow Entrance and Path 178
Prepared for the Storm 178

15 Adventures as the Work of Jesus Unfolds 180
Disciples Sent Out to Preach and Heal 180
Jesus Feeds the Multitude in the Wilderness 181
The Saviour Comes Over the Wild Waters 182
Jesus the Divine Bread 183
Jesus Confronts the Ritual Laws of Clean and Unclean 184
A Trap for Jesus 186
Jesus Crosses a Boundary 187
The Secret of the Servant-King 188
The Shepherd Who Dies for His Flock 190
Jesus Seen Briefly in Glory 191

16 Scenes of Jesus 193
Jesus Indignant to See Children Turned Away 193
How Hard for the Rich to Enter! 193
A Meditation of Jesus 195
Who is My Neighbour? 196
The One Thing Needed 198
God's Joy over One Sinner Who Repents 199
A Father's Love 200

17 Towards the Climax in Jerusalem 203
Premonitions: A Ransom for Many 203
Oh for Eyes to See the Son of David! 204
Jesus Fulfils a Prophecy of the Royal Saviour 205
The Grain That Has to Die to Bear Fruit 207
Upheavals to Come: Keeping Watch 208
An Act of Love for Jesus 209
Jesus Bequeaths a Sign of Humility 210
The Father Known through the Son 212
Last Teachings 213
Jesus Prays That They All May Be One 214
The Last Supper 216

18 The Death of the Messiah 217
Prayer and Betrayal in Gethsemane 217
Jesus Condemned before the High Priest 218
When the Cock Crowed 220

Jesus Condemned to Crucifixion   220
The Mocking and the Procession to Golgotha   222
Jests as Jesus is Crucified   223
Jesus Forgives   224
Jesus Binds Mary and John   225
The Death of Jesus   226
The Burial of Jesus   227

19 The Lord Is Risen   228
The Sun Rises on the First Day of the Week   228
No Ordinary Gardener   229
The Blessing of Faith in the Risen Lord   231
The Risen Lord by the Lake   232
Make All Nations My Disciples   233
Transition to the New Form of Christ's Presence   234

20 The Growing Community Living by the Spirit   237
The Outpouring of the Spirit   237
Great Things Prepared through the Martyrdom of Stephen   239
Philip Baptizes an Ethiopian Statesman   240
An Enemy Reborn to Become a Mighty Apostle   241
Out from the Jews to the Gentiles   243
Planting in the Capital of Syria   244
Overcoming a Controversy in the Church   245
Paul's Work in Corinth   246
Paul's Witness in the World's Centre   247

21 The Life of the Spirit   249
Nothing Can Part Us from God's Love in Christ   249
God's Foolishness?   250
Differing Gifts, from the One Spirit   251
The Supreme Gift   252
The Strength of Weakness   253
Clothed with Christ   254
The Spirit's Law of Love   255
A Prayer to Know the Depths of Christ's Love   256
And Again I Say, Rejoice   257
Hidden with Christ in God   258

22 Messages for the Churches   260
Eyes Fixed on Jesus   260
Receive the Word and Act Accordingly   261

New Birth and Living Hope 262
God is Love 263
Buy from Jesus Gold from the Furnace 264
When All is Made New 265

Preface

John Eaton was a distinctive as well as a distinguished figure in Old Testament Studies. He was a humble and reclusive researcher, never one to flaunt his scholarship at big international conferences, though he appreciated quiet friendships with colleagues in the Society for Old Testament Study. Yet he was widely recognised as immensely learned in the biblical and related languages, acquired not only in Cambridge and other academic contexts but in three years spent in the Middle East in the 1950s. To this he added a profound spirituality and a gentle holiness that resonate in a special way with the content of the biblical literature whose study he made his life. In a world of academic fad and fashion and of professional ambition, John stood out as a beacon of sanity and wisdom.

What we have here are approximately two hundred excerpts from across the whole Bible, newly translated and provided with brief expositions, intended by the author to introduce beginners to the significance of the whole biblical narrative, the richness of the poetry and the insights that emerge from an attentive reading with the eyes of faith.

John Eaton devoted his life to understanding the Hebrew Bible in its original language and, simple though it is, this collection reflects not only his linguistic and historical expertise but also his insights into the way modern critical reconstructions can facilitate the reclamation of New Testament perspectives on the foreshadowing of Christ in what became, for Christians, the Old Testament. Thus his comments on the passion story take up many resonances with Psalms and Servant Songs not usually noticed, amplifying traditional insights into the Gospel fulfilment of the prophetic vision of a Servant-King suffering for his people.

It is perhaps telling that the final sentences commenting on Revelation 21:1–8 and written just a few days before John's death, read as follows:

Sometimes people say they cannot believe in God because of the state of the world. But scripture after scripture has shown God himself as anything but content with the world as it is. In Christ he dies to change it. And still, his name is yet to be hallowed, his glory to be manifest, his reign come. And God's own words ring in the prophet's ear: 'Behold, I make all new.'

Christ is at the heart of this work, for, daring to move from his specialist terrain, John here takes on the New Testament as well as the Old, selecting and translating key passages from the Gospels and then other New Testament writings that illuminate the way of faith through Jesus Christ.

So in its own quiet way, this is a very important book for contemporary theology. It demonstrates how the Bible may be read as Christian Scripture in a postmodern era indelibly marked by the biblical criticism of the modern period. Implicit, and occasionally explicit, is the perspective of the scholar informed by archaeology and history, form criticism and literary analysis, yet primarily this work probes biblical passages to illuminate the human condition in general, and in particular the perspectives of Christian theology on the way the world is. These brief studies of discrete selections, quoted in fresh translations by this eminent Hebraist, constitute in combination an overarching narrative of the Bible. What is thus presented emulates the vision of the scriptures found in the traditions formulated by the Church Fathers, while at the same time being earthed in the new insights demanded by modern biblical scholarship. Altogether this adds up to a profoundly contemplative expression of the path of faith mapped by the Bible.

In the relevant chapter the Proverbs are described as 'gleams of truth gladly received from a mysterious world' – that constitutes an excellent description of this collection of brief but telling Bible studies, 'gleams … given to light up a fruitful path of life'.

As colleagues and friends of John, who were privileged to work closely with him and to learn from him at many different levels, we are proud to commend this special collection to its readers.

Paul Joyce, Professor of OT, King's College, London
Frances Young, Professor Emeritus, University of Birmingham

1.

A World of Meaning

God Calls the World into Life

Genesis 1.1–23

When God began to create the heavens and the earth, while the earth was yet in chaos, and darkness was over the face of the deep, and the breath of God drove against the face of the waters, then God said, 'Let there be light.' And there was light. And God saw the light and found it good. And God divided the light from the darkness. And God called the light Day, and the darkness he called Night. So evening had come, then morning, a first day.

Then God said, 'Let there be a vault through the middle of the waters to divide the waters in two.' And God made the vault and divided the waters below it from those above it. And so it was. And God called the vault Heaven. So evening had come, then morning, a second day.

Then God said, 'Let the waters under the heaven be gathered into one mass and let the dry land appear.' And so it was. And God called the dry land Earth, and the gathered waters he called Seas. And God saw that it was good. And God said, 'Let the earth green over with growth, plants on the earth that sow seed and fruit trees that yield fruit containing their seed, according to their kind.' And so it was. And God saw that it was good. So evening had come, then morning, a third day.

Then God said, 'Let there be lights in the vault of heaven to divide between day and night and let them be for sacred seasons, days and years . . .' And so it was . . . So evening had come, then morning, a fourth day.

Then God said, 'Let the waters swarm with swarms of living creatures, and let birds fly across the face of the vault of heaven.' And God created the great sea-monsters and all the living creatures that glide and swarm in the waters according to their kind, and every winged bird according to its kind. And God saw that it was good. And God blessed them, saying, 'Be fruitful and

multiply and fill the waters in the seas and let the birds multiply on the earth.'
So evening had come, then morning, a fifth day.

Looking back through the mists of time with inspired imagination, the bards and priests through whom traditional stories were developed taught not only about the beginning of the world, but silently also about meaning and value in present life. The two great stories found in Genesis 1 – 3, so different from each other, each contain a wealth of interpretation of existence, and in the end complement each other.

'When God began to create . . .' or 'In the beginning of God's creating . . .' – what a challenge at once to *our* imagination! To leave the order and beauty of the natural world we know, and sense that horrifying void, formlessness, cold and chaos! A heavy darkness lies on the ocean of chaos called *Tehom*, the Deep. A wind of colossal force beats over the murky waters. It is a terrifying scene – but the story has spoken already of God. No need is felt to explain who or whence he is. He is. He purposes. He acts and achieves. Life and meaning come from him.

And so, through God, the scene is changing. It moves decisively towards a world of beauty and delight. That awesome wind now appears as his Spirit or Breath, the outgoing of his creative power which takes effect as he utters his word: 'Let there be light.' This is a light that floods the chaos with a spirit of goodness, a radiance of hope. The Creator, Father of all those skilled in craftwork, looks carefully at what he has made and sees that it is good. Like true craftspeople also, he works in measured stages, unhurried, thoughtful and with pleasure.

The first day's work is completed, a day measured from evening to morning and full daytime. Giving light and darkness their names, God awakens them into his service and care. He affirms their difference – each has a particular character and role. But each is valued, and the daylight complements and crowns the useful darkness of the night. A complete day must hold them both.

On following days God disposes the waters to do their vital work. Through the middle of their mass he inserts a plate or arch (its Hebrew name *raqia* means something 'hammered out') and calls it Sky or Heaven. The waters held above it form the heavenly ocean, storing aloft the rains. The waters below it drain into low-lying and underground stores, allowing dry land to appear. Before the end of the third day God calls into existence earth's plants and trees, with seeds that will continue the distinctness of the various species.

Only on the fourth day is he said to make the sun and moon and set them in the sky-vault. They are valued especially as markers of holy seasons, days and years, giving order and regulation to the life of worshipping God. Light as such, night and day, evening, morning, plants and trees are not thought to have needed them. They are not even named, and it seems there is care not to encourage the worship of sun and moon common among some populations.

The story passes to the fifth day. We see the waters made to teem with living creatures, and the skies with the many kinds of birds. God sees the beauty of them all and gives them his blessing. This blessing makes them fruitful, able to multiply and fill the waters and skies.

Two important days remain in this first week. But already we have been invited to a vision of a good and beautiful world, full of creatures with their own distinctness, but united in looking to God for their existence and continuance. His eternal reality, goodness and power permeate the vision. There is no speaking of them, let alone analysis. They are taken instinctively as the foundation of everything.

Royal Stewards of the Earth

Genesis 1.24 – 2.4a

Then God said, 'Let the earth bring forth the living creatures according to their kinds – cattle and creeping things and wild animals according to their kinds.' And so it was. And God made the wild animals according to their kinds and cattle according to their kinds and everything that creeps on the ground according to its kind. And God saw that it was good.

And God said, 'Let us make humankind in our image, after our likeness. And let them rule over the fish of the sea, and over the birds of the air, and over the cattle, and over all the wild animals, and over every creeping thing that creeps upon the earth.' So God created humankind in his own image. In the divine image he created them. Male and female he created them. And God blessed them, and God said to them, 'Be fruitful and multiply and fill the earth and order it. And rule over the fish of the sea and birds of the heaven and over every living thing that moves on the earth.'

And God said, 'See, I have given you every plant yielding seed that is on the face of the earth, and every tree with seed in its fruit, and you shall have them for food. And to every beast of the earth and to every bird of the air and to everything that creeps on the earth, everything that has the breath of life, I have given every green plant for food.' And so it was. And God looked on everything that he had made, and see, it was very good. So evening had come, then morning, a sixth day.

Thus heaven and earth were finished, and all their multitudes. When the seventh day came, God had finished the work he had been doing, so he ceased on the seventh day from all his work that he had done. And God blessed the seventh day and consecrated it, for on it God ceased from all his work that he had created and made. Such were the stages in the origin of heaven and earth when they were created.

Here we come to the creation of land animals and humanity. The story has kept both for the sixth and last day of the Creator's work. These species are thus linked to each other, as they are also in the matter of their diet. For each of them, and indeed for all living creatures, the food appointed by God is plants and fruit. God's will is that among all the creatures there shall be peace and trust and no harming. The ideal will come to be obscured, but it will shine through again in great prophecies of a perfect age to come.

The making of the human species, however, is distinguished by some special features. Speaking with a royal 'we' ('us', 'our') as though for a solemn moment, God expresses his profound intention – to make this species, males and females, in his own image and likeness. They will thus be able to enjoy close communion with him and share in his work. The practical effect mentioned here is that they are appointed to rule over the other creatures. As images and likenesses of a great king were distributed to show his presence in all provinces of his empire, so the sovereignty of God will be represented and enacted through this species that he has made in the divine likeness. By his word, and ever answerable to him, they will have power to maintain good order, to rule – it goes without saying – for the benefit of all the earth and every creature.

With this commission to the human race, the series of God's creative acts is finished. For the complete pattern, however, a seventh day is needed, a day without work. And now we see why this story of creation has taken the form of carefully demarcated days. The common round of life should follow the good pattern of God. Our days of work and our time of rest will be in the likeness of that first week, crowned by its holy time, the day specially his. Most modern people have moved far from a strict Sabbath observance, but still on that day blessed of God our hearts should return to him in new devotion, our energies wait upon his re-creation. And so a pool of light, restful and refreshing, is made around us for the good of the earth and of its creatures.

In our time it has become ever clearer that this story is far from being a satisfactory account of the world's beginnings. Its obvious shortcomings as a scientific account can, however, be taken as signposts pointing us in another direction. They point us away from searching here for science and point us rather towards the discovery of deeper truths, the meanings which are best expressed in the unfathomable simplicity of poetic imagination. Only along this way shall we allow the story to bring us before God, to receive his blessing and command.

An Insight into Love

Genesis 2.4b–25

On the day when the Lord God made earth and heaven, when there was yet no wild shrub on earth and no wild herb had sprung up – for the Lord God had sent no rain on the earth and there was no one to till the ground – a flood began to well up from the earth and water all the face of the ground. Then the Lord fashioned the earth-man out of clay from the earth, and he blew into his nostrils the breath of life, and the man became a living creature.

And the Lord God planted a garden in Eden over in the East, and there he placed the man that he had fashioned. And out of the ground the Lord God made to grow up every tree that is pleasant to the sight and good for food, with the Tree of Life in the centre of the garden, beside the Tree of the Knowledge of Good and Evil. And there was a river rising from Eden to water the garden, and as it left the garden it branched into four streams.

So the Lord God took the man and put him into the garden of Eden to tend and care for it. And the Lord God commanded the man, saying, 'Of every tree in the garden you may eat freely, but of the Tree of the Knowledge of Good and Evil you shall not eat, for on the day you eat of it you will surely die.'

Then the Lord God said, 'It is not good that the man should be alone. I will make for him one that matches him and brings him succour.' So out of the earth the Lord God fashioned every animal of the field and every bird of the air and brought them to the man to see what he would call them. And whatever the man called each living creature, that was now its name. Thus the man gave names to all cattle, to the birds of the heaven and to every wild animal. But for the earth-man there was still not found one that matched him and brought him succour.

So the Lord God caused a deep sleep to fall on the man, and he slept. And he took out one of his ribs and closed up the flesh in its place. And the rib which he had taken from the man he built up into a woman and brought her to the man. And the man said, 'Now *she* indeed is bone from my bones and flesh from my flesh. She shall be called Woman, because she was taken out of man.' That is why a man leaves his father and his mother and clings to his wife and they again become one flesh. And they were both naked, but felt no shame together.

There is quite a different style and perspective in this second story of origins. We find it less comprehensive in regard to the emerging world. We just have to follow the thread of meaning which is there to lead us on, and enthralling it certainly is. The Creator is here referred to with a personal name, 'Yahweh' (probably meaning 'He Who Is', the absolute, eternal, not derivative; in most English Bibles 'the Lord'), and this is combined here with the word for 'God' used in the preceding story, 'Elohim' (in form a plural expressing majesty or plenitude). His actions are described picturesquely (he 'moulds/shapes', 'builds', 'plants') and he even proceeds experimentally. The story has a childlike quality, charming, resonant and profound.

We are invited to imagine a day on which earth and heaven have been made, but the earth remains an empty, dry desert. And then a source wells up and waters all the ground. The dusty surface is now changed to mud, and the Lord, like a potter, shapes from it a human figure. He blows into its nostrils and the divine breath animates it to become a living 'soul' (*nephesh*), a living being. The thing of clay now lives from and for the Holy One.

Then the Lord plants and makes grow a 'garden' (an area walled off from the wilderness). This place in the east is called Eden ('Delight'). The river from its spring not only waters the garden, but then divides into four streams to bring life to all the corners of the earth. Eden is thus a place at the heart of things, a fountain of life and meaning for the world. And in that very place the Lord puts the human being, who is thus for ever destined as the tender and carer of God's creatures.

The Lord observes with compassion the man's loneliness and sets about providing for him a veritable salvation, a bringer of succour who is complementary, 'corresponding' to him. To this end he works again at moulding and fashioning the clay. Persevering in his quest, he makes the whole range of animals and birds, introducing each one to the man, who names each one, entering into a relationship of mutual knowledge and respect. But still that matching, complementary companion is not found.

So the Lord goes further. From near the man's heart, the seat of love, he takes out a rib and 'builds' it into a woman. The man awakes from the deep sleep, his side closed up again, only to see before him the woman brought to him by the Lord. He knows at once that she is the one he has yearned for, 'bone from [his] bone, flesh from [his] flesh'. And now it is a true match. The two in love become one, for one they were in the beginning of time.

Falling to Temptation and Losing Innocence

Genesis 3

Now the serpent was more subtle than any other animal that the Lord God had made. And he said to the woman, 'Has God really said, You are not to eat from any tree of the garden?' The woman answered the serpent, 'We can eat the fruit of the trees of the garden, except the fruit of the tree in the middle of the garden, for of that God has said, You must not eat of it nor even touch it, or you will die.' And the serpent said to the woman, 'Oh no, you will not die. Rather, God knows that on the day you eat of it your eyes will be opened, and you will be like the divine ones, knowing good and evil.'

As the woman saw that the tree was good for food and that it was a delight to the eyes and desirable for gaining wisdom, she took some of the fruit and ate it. And she gave some also to her husband beside her, and he ate it. Then the eyes of both of them were opened and they realized that they were naked. So they stitched fig leaves together and made themselves loincloths.

And they heard the sound of the Lord God walking about the garden as the heat of the day declined. And the man and his wife hid themselves from the face of the Lord God among the trees of the garden. And the Lord God called out to the man and said to him, 'Where are you?' He answered, 'I heard the sound of you in the garden and I was afraid because I was naked.' And he said, 'Who told you that you were naked? Have you eaten of the tree from which I forbade you to eat?' And the man answered, 'It was the woman you gave to be with me – she gave me from the tree and I ate.' Then the Lord God said to the woman, 'What is this you have done?' The woman answered, 'It was the serpent – he beguiled me and I ate.'

So the Lord God said to the serpent, 'Since you have done this, accursed are you above all cattle and wild creatures. On your belly you shall go and dust shall you eat all the days of your life. And I will put enmity between you and the woman and between your offspring and hers. They will strike at your head and you will strike at their heel.'

Then to the woman he said, 'I will greatly increase your pangs in your childbearing; in pain you will give birth. Your desire will be for your husband and he will rule over you.'

And to the man he said, 'Because you have listened to the voice of your wife and eaten of the tree from which I commanded you not to eat, cursed is the ground because of you. With toil you shall eat from it all the days of your life. Thorns also and thistles it shall bear for you, and you shall eat the plants of the wild, and by the sweat of your brow you shall eat bread, until you return to the ground. For out of it you were taken. Dust you are and to dust you shall return.'

Now the man called his wife's name Eve [*Hawwa*, 'Abundant-in-life'], for she was the mother of all living. And the Lord God made for the man and his wife garments of skin and clothed them. Then the Lord God said, 'See, the man has become like one of us, with knowledge of good and evil. Now therefore, for fear he reaches out his hand and takes also of the Tree of Life and eats and lives for ever' – therefore the Lord God sent him away from the Garden of Eden to work the ground from which he had been taken. So he drove out the man and placed in front of the Garden of Eden a guard of *kerubim* and the flame of a whirling sword to keep the way to the Tree of Life.

The story continues from our previous passage. The dramatic developments are set in motion by one of the animals, the snake or serpent, who till now walks in the common manner, speaks and is remarkably clever – and wily. Why it should want to draw the couple away from obedience to the Lord is not explained. The story needed an embodiment of temptation, and the serpent was selected because of many ancient ideas about its knowledge and its sometimes sinister character.

Temptation is indeed vividly represented. It suddenly intrudes into a pleasant and comfortable life. The wily serpent picks on the woman as his first target, draws her into conversation, uses her sense of beauty, her instinct for knowledge, and even her satisfaction in preparing a fine repast for her husband. And the serpent adds the deadly ingredient of doubt in the truth of God's word. Approached through her, the man falls easily. And at once the time of childlike innocence is ended.

The footsteps of the Lord now prompt only fear. Questioned by God, the man blames the wife who was given by God, and the woman likewise blames the snake. The sentence pronounced by God mirrors the hard facts of life in much of the world – women suffering in childbearing and from male domination, men toiling to wrest a living from the unsparing ground right to the day of death, the snakes with their legless life in the dust, especially hated and feared by humankind.

The hardest fact reflected in the story is the estrangement from God. Yes, knowledge of a kind has come – and continues to come – in abundance, but it has multiplied the ways and the scale of doing evil. While access to the greater tree, the Tree of Life, gave no concern in the happy beginning of the story, now the thought of the fallen race living for ever is alarming to God. They must be driven from the paradise garden and the way of return must be securely barred.

More tales of primeval times are to follow, showing how the estrangement mars the continuing race and its role as the world's carer. But one can just hear also a hopeful theme which is never lost, and indeed grows stronger – the hope of return and reconciliation.

Even before the expulsion from Eden there are instances of the Lord's continuing care, as when he makes better garments for the man and woman. Continuing love and respect for the woman are reflected in the mention of her naming – 'Eve', the mother of the race. The *kerubim* guards (winged heavenly beings) and the whirling sword ensure that the fallen race cannot return at their will to the garden and plunder the tree of eternal life. But these are still early days in the Bible's greater story. The symbolic tale has expressed the tragedy of earthly life, but not revealed all the counsel of the Lord Creator. His good purpose is not so easily destroyed. Long and hard will be the ages of estrangement, but hope will not die that one will be sent at last with the keys and the right to open the way again to the garden and the Tree of Life. Not wholly lost are the Light, the Beauty and the Love.

An End of Life on Earth, and a Sign of Hope

Genesis 6 – 9

[6.5] And the Lord saw that the wickedness of humankind across the earth was great, and that every product of the thoughts of their heart was evil all the day long. And the Lord was sorry that he had made humans on the earth and he grieved in his heart. And the Lord said, 'From the face of the earth I will now wipe out earth-man that I created, and beyond humankind the animals also and creeping things and birds of the air, for I am sorry that I made them.' But Noah found grace in the eyes of the Lord . . .

[6.13] And God said to Noah, 'The end of all flesh has come before me, for the earth is filled with violence through them. So now I will destroy them from off the earth. Make for yourself an ark of wattle and daub. With woven reeds you must make the ark and daub it inside and outside with pitch . . . [6.17] For I myself am about to cause the ocean above to flood the earth and destroy all flesh that has the breath of life from under heaven. Everything on earth will die. But I shall establish my covenant with you, and you shall enter the ark, you, your sons, your wife and your sons' wives with you. From every living thing of all flesh you must bring two into the ark to keep alive with you, a male and a female. And be sure to collect all kinds of suitable food and lay it in store, and it shall be food for you and for them.' And Noah did all that God commanded him. So he did . . .

[7.17] And the flood lay over the earth for forty days, and as the waters rose, they bore the ark up and lifted it high above the earth. Then God, having regard for Noah and for all the wild animals and cattle that were with him in the ark, sent a wind to sweep over the earth, and the waters diminished . . .

[8.6] After forty days Noah opened the window he had made in the ark and sent out a dove from his hand to see if the waters had abated from the face of the ground. But the dove found no place to rest its foot and returned to him to the ark, for water still covered the face of all the earth. And he stretched out his hand and took the bird and brought it to him in the ark. And he waited another seven days and then sent the dove out again from the ark. And the dove came back to him at evening time, and see, in its mouth an olive leaf freshly plucked! So Noah knew that the waters had abated from the earth. And he waited another seven days and sent out the dove, and it did not return to him again . . .

[8.15] Then God spoke to Noah, saying, 'Go out from the ark, you, your wife, your sons and your sons' wives with you, and bring out with you all the living creatures of all flesh that are with you, birds, animals and every creeping thing that creeps on the earth, and let them spread over the earth to be fruitful and multiply' . . .

[9.12] And God said, 'This is the sign of the covenant which I set between me and you and every living creature with you for all generations: my bow I set in the clouds, and it shall be a sign of covenant between me and the earth. And when I becloud the sky with cloud, the bow shall be seen in the cloud, and I will remember my covenant which is between me and you and all living creatures of all flesh. And the waters will never again become a flood to destroy all flesh.'

From a great wealth of primitive stories the inspired authors select, adapt and weave to continue their greater story. They tell of the spread and increase of the human family, the great progress of skills and techniques, and with it all, increasing manifestations of sin. They tell of the sons of Adam ('Man', father of the race) and Eve (Genesis 4): Cain murders his brother Abel, and when the Lord seeks Abel, Cain affects ignorance – 'Am I my brother's keeper?' But the very earth cries out against him, earth that has received the innocent blood. In a subsequent generation we are shown a violent and boastful spirit in Lamech.

Soon a terrible overview of the ways of the whole race is given as the prelude to the flood story (Genesis 6.5). Wickedness has become so general that the Lord is grieved at heart, sorry that he ever made human beings. Childlike but profound, the story of Noah's ark unfolds from this tragic sentence. Versions of the story more than a thousand years older than our account have come to light from clay tablets in the river plains of Iraq, and it is clear also that in the biblical story two Hebrew versions have been woven together. But still, from all the strands of tradition, one of the world's best-known stories has emerged, with deep insights and truths to give to the patience and humility of meditation.

Striking is the bond seen between animal and human life. Both together suffer the destruction. But for both too a way of salvation is found and an eternal promise is given. God brings back the waters with their old chaotic force, killing all the creatures of the earth, except that remnant in the ark which represents male and female of every species. Ancient mariners employed birds to locate land, and this cooperation of the species is evident in the beautiful detail of Noah and his birds. It is the dove who brings first the message of hope and then gives the confirmation that all is well. How carefully Noah reaches out for the bird! And what a symbol it becomes of peace and salvation, and indeed of the Spirit of God!

Beautiful too is the sign of the rainbow. Once the chaotic waters are drawn back again and the nucleus of new human and animal life is joyfully back on the open land, God makes a solemn promise, undertaking an everlasting obligation, a covenant with all living creatures: never again to release those waters of destruction. His bow appearing against the rain-clouds is to be the sign and reminder of his covenant. This war-bow is a beautiful thing, the sure protector, the power of the Merciful One. And still we can see the bow and recognize the sign of divine beauty and goodwill which shines in the natural world, a blessing for the creatures of all species, which all have their place in the heart of the Creator.

The story of human corruptions is not ended. Much will yet be told, after the flood, of greed, debauchery, cruelty, of ravaging the good earth and its species. Judgements again will fall. But a rhythm of life and beauty through the seasons will continue through God's goodwill. Working through the few who love and fear him, he will effect his mercy. Their deeds of care and conservation he will take up into his. The ravagers will not have the last word. That belongs to his tender heart and to the eternal covenant he made with all his creatures.

High-Rise Building Proves Divisive

Genesis 11.1–9

> Now all the world was yet of one language and used the same words. And as people migrated from the east, it happened that they found a plain in the land of Shinar and settled there. Then they said one to another, 'Come on, let us make bricks and bake them hard.' And so they used bricks for stone and bitumen for mortar. 'Come on,' they said, 'let us build a city and a tower with its top in the heavens, and so make a name for ourselves and not be scattered all over the face of the earth.'

Then the Lord came down to see the city and the tower which the descendants of Adam and Eve were building. And the Lord said, 'See, they are one people, all with one language, and this is just the beginning of what they may do. And now, nothing they set their mind to will be beyond them. Come, let us go down and there confuse their language, so that they do not understand one another's words.'

And the Lord scattered them abroad over the face of the earth and they ceased to build the city. So its name was called Babel, because the Lord had made a babble of the speech of all the world and scattered them all over the earth.

Stories within a story! Beads in a necklace, each with its own value, but joining with others to form the treasured string. As we consider these 'beads' in Genesis, it becomes ever clearer that they are threaded to form a wonderful row – nothing less than the long purpose of the Creator, his work to guide his creation through vast ages to its destiny of final goodness.

Incidents after the flood, alas, reflect a continuing struggle with evil. Killing for food now becomes permitted, though with rules of respect for the life poured out (9.3–5). The first drunkenness is related, and the subsequent debauchery (9.20–27), and then the story of a pride that would usurp God – the tale of the Tower of Babel.

The wandering nomads settle in a watered plain. Cleverly they invent bricks baked from the mud and find how to build them into walls bonded with bitumen. No longer need they be wandering nonentities. Security, power, riches and fame can be theirs in a grand city with a tower reaching to the heavens. Alarm bells ring in heaven. The story in its own way is depicting that drive in human society to be its own god. Skills and rich resources are misused. The consequence is failure in the grand plans and the race divided into sections no longer able to 'hear' one another. The babble of different languages is a sign of estrangement, rivalry, even hatred.

Considering how once again we have a deeply suggestive story formed from earlier elements, we catch echoes here of the wonder felt by simple traders visiting the great city of Babel (Babylon). They were astonished at its vast brick buildings and great sacred tower, and the babble of languages in its tumultuous markets. While a Hebrew word *bilbel* meant 'confused', 'Babel' really meant to its own citizens 'Gate of God' and the tower was intended for the leaders in prayer. The impressions of the amazed visitors have thus been re-created in our story to become an insight into the estrangement and war that result from the drive for fame and power. So our authors trace the deterioration of our race a step further.

Could there now follow an impulse from a counter-force? Will the divine mercy move towards the long way of redemption? Will a communion of prayer indeed rise high above the city, and will the Gate of God be opened at last for the creatures to enter their true home?

A World in the Birth of a Child

Genesis 18.1–16

The Lord appeared to Abraham by the oaks of Mamre, as he sat in the opening of the tent at the hottest time of day. He raised his eyes and looked, and see, three men were standing over against him. As soon as he saw them, he ran from the tent door to meet them. He bowed low to the ground and said, 'Lord, if I have now found favour in your eyes, do not pass by your servant. Let a little water be brought and wash your feet and rest yourselves under the tree. And I will fetch a morsel of bread that you may recover strength. After that you can go on your way, since you have come to your servant.' And they said, 'Do as you have said.'

So Abraham hurried to Sarah in the tent and said, 'Quickly, knead three measures of fine meal and make cakes.' Then over to the herd he ran and took the best calf and gave it to the servant, who hastened to prepare it. And Abraham took curds and milk and the calf which was prepared and set it before them, and he waited on them himself under the tree, and they ate.

Then they said to him, 'Where is Sarah your wife?' And he said, 'There, in the tent.' 'Without fail I will come back to you in the spring,' came the reply, 'and see, Sarah your wife shall have a son.'

Now Sarah was listening at the tent door, standing just behind it. And Abraham and Sarah were old, well on in years, and Sarah was past the age of childbearing. So Sarah laughed to herself, saying, 'Old as I am, shall I have pleasure again, and my lord also being old?' But the Lord said to Abraham, 'Why did Sarah laugh, saying, Shall I indeed bear a child, and I so old? Is anything too wonderful for the Lord? At the due time I will return to you in the spring and Sarah shall have a son.' Then Sarah denied it, saying, 'I did not laugh', for she was afraid. But he said, 'No, you did laugh.'

And the men set off from there and looked down on Sodom. And Abraham went with them to bring them on their way.

The race has been broken up and scattered in groups that no longer share a language; they no longer 'hear' each other (Genesis 11). The next chapter relates God's countermove. The Lord calls Abraham to leave home territory and people and take a way with the Lord which will result in great multitudes of descendants, in their becoming settled, and most significant of all, in blessing for all the families of the earth. Here and in the following chapters these great promises are given for the future descendants of Abraham – yet he and his wife Sarah have no children of their own and are already well on in years!

Such is the background, as our story now begins in the heat of the day in southern Palestine. Drowsy, no doubt, the elderly nomad Abraham is squatting at the opening of his tent where there is shade and air and also a view, though nothing is likely to be happening. Looking up, he sees three travellers suddenly before him. His only thought is to do to his utmost the Bedouin duty of hospitality – to do unstinting kindness to the travellers who would have been toiling through the wilderness since early dawn. The 'morsel of bread' that he offers turns out to be a feast. And then it is time for a little talk. The mysterious visitors come at once to the heart of Abraham's need – he that is promised such great things in his descendants is in fact a childless old man. From the travellers comes the assurance that next spring Sarah will bear him a son.

Sarah's ironic laughter is a significant feature of the story as it would be heard in Hebrew. Four times the word 'laugh' is used, in Hebrew echoing the name of the coming child Isaac (*yishaq*[*-el*], 'God laughs'). The divine grace and power will act beyond what reason can imagine. The laugh of disbelief will give way to the rejoicing in heaven.

The story values self-effacing kindness to the stranger in need. The generous reaching out in kindness to the hungry and weary of another tribe turns out to be a service to the Lord himself. But the Lord's appearing is a great mystery. In some way unexplained, he appears in the three, the one in three persons. The greatest of all Russia's icon paintings, Rublev's *Trinity*, springs from centuries of meditation on this aspect – the Three gathered over the sacrifice of Christ encompass the world in love and grace.

And we may well think the challenge of Christ's birth to human reason is foreshadowed in the story. How could such a birth be? And how could the world's blessing turn thus on the birth of one little child? This story of promise to Abraham holds to its way of homely simplicity and faith: 'Is anything too wonderful for the Lord?'

The Terrible Test of Faith

Genesis 21.8b–21; 22.1–13

> Now Abraham made a great feast on the day that Isaac was weaned. And Sarah saw the son of Hagar the Egyptian, the child Hagar had borne to

Abraham, playing with her son Isaac. And she said to Abraham, 'Drive out this bondwoman and her son. The son of this bondwoman shall not be heir with my son Isaac.' This request greatly troubled Abraham on account of his son. But God said to Abraham, 'Do not be distressed on account of the boy and your bondwoman. In all that Sarah says to you, agree to her request, for it is through Isaac that your line shall be established.'

So Abraham rose early in the morning and took bread and a skin of water and gave them to Hagar, and he lifted the boy on to her back and sent her away. And she went and wandered in the wilderness of Beersheba. When the water in the skin was all gone, she thrust the child under one of the bushes and went and sat down opposite him, but about as far away as a bowshot, for she said, 'I cannot watch the death of the child.' And as she sat opposite him, the child cried out and wept.

But God heard the voice of the boy. And the angel of God called to Hagar out of heaven and said to her, 'Why do you despair, Hagar? Have no fear, for the Lord has heard the boy crying where he lies. Rise, take him up and hold him in your arms, for I shall make of him a great nation.' Then God opened her eyes and she saw a well of water. And she went and filled the skin with water and gave drink to the boy.

And God was with the boy, and he grew up and dwelt in the wilderness. He was skilled with the bow and lived in the wilderness of Paran. And his mother took a wife for him out of the land of Egypt . . .

Now after these things, God put Abraham to the test. He said to him, 'Abraham,' and he answered, 'Here I am.' Then he said to him, 'Take your son, your only son, whom you love, your Isaac, and go to the land of Moriah, and there offer him up as a sacrifice on one of the mountains which I shall show you.'

So Abraham rose early in the morning and saddled his donkey, and he took two of his young men with him and Isaac his son. He chopped wood for the sacrifice and then set off and went to the place God had told him of.

On the third day Abraham raised his eyes and saw the place far off. Then Abraham said to his young men, 'Stay here with the donkey, and I and the boy will go yonder and worship and then come back to you.' And Abraham took the wood for the sacrifice and laid it on Isaac his son, and he took in his own hands the fire and the knife. And the two of them walked on together.

And Isaac spoke to Abraham his father and said, 'My father', and he answered, 'Here I am, my son.' And he said, 'See, the fire and the wood, but where is the lamb for sacrifice?' And Abraham said, 'God himself will provide the lamb for sacrifice, my son.'

And the two of them walked on together. And they came to the place God had told him of. And Abraham built the altar there and laid the wood in order.

And he bound Isaac his son and laid him on the altar upon the wood. And Abraham reached out his hand and took the knife to kill his son.

Then the angel of the Lord called to him out of heaven and said, 'Abraham, Abraham!' And he answered, 'Here I am.' And he said, 'Do not lay your hand on the boy or do anything to him, for now I know that you fear God, since you have not withheld from me your son, your only son.' And Abraham raised his eyes and looked, and see, a ram caught by its horns in the thicket. So Abraham went and took the ram and offered it up as a sacrifice in place of his son.

At the feast for his weaning Isaac may be as much as three years old, and the other boy, Ishmael, only a little older. This Ishmael was the son of Abraham and Hagar, as related in Genesis 16. In a case of childlessness it was a recognized practice for the wife to appoint her own maid to bear a child to the husband, as it were on the wife's behalf. Thus Hagar the maidservant had borne a son for Abraham, but then exalted herself, seeming to threaten Sarah's position. The difficulty flared up at Isaac's weaning. The whole procedure of Ishmael's birth has been narrated as a purely human initiative, whereas Isaac's (chapter 18) is all of God's purpose and gift.

All the same, the idea of expelling Hagar and her child is repulsive to Abraham, but at God's express command he obeys without question. He is shown personally helping Hagar at her departure. He gives her food and a water-skin to carry and lifts the little boy on to her back. Perhaps he alone trusts that God will save them. And save them he does, when all seems lost. The child becomes the ancestor of the southern Bedouin, the aristocracy of the wilderness.

All the more now, Abraham depends on Isaac for that promised future when his numerous descendants will be settled and become the source of great blessing for all earth's families. But in a supreme test of his faith, he is required by God to offer up the beloved child as a sacrifice! Here the story moves beyond the plane of ordinary human life. True, it gathers up elements from ancient times when children might be sacrificed and when the practice of redeeming them by substituting an animal was accepted. But from such fragments of ancient tradition a profound story has been developed, with many layers of meaning in its depths. Read in a spirit of awe and meditation, it is found to be a drama of the challenge to trust God utterly even in the darkest place, to give back into his hands what he has given of comfort and delight, to hold on to his faithfulness and his wisdom for what is best against all that cries against it, even when he seems to take from the world his own work of salvation. And deepest of all, the drama becomes a prophetic symbol of God the Father and his only Son. Here we discern the heart of the Father who so loves the world that he will give in sacrifice his only begotten Son, and we discern the Son who walks on quietly together with his Father, walks on his way to death, and in obedience and trust lets himself be bound and laid on the wood. So against the sins of human presumption, jealousy and heartlessness is raised a mighty power of trust, a harmony with God's heart.

In its Genesis setting the story has taken us only a step further on the long way of God's redeeming work, but already the climax of that work is prefigured in the unearthly light of prophecy. Already we begin, from afar, to behold the Lamb of God.

Encounters with God in the Night

Genesis 28.10–19a; 32.22–31

Then Jacob set out from Beersheba and took his way towards Haran. And he came upon a certain place and settled there for the night because the sun had gone down. And he took one of the stones of the place and put it under his head as he lay down in that place to sleep.

And he dreamt, and see, a stairway set on the ground with its top reaching to heaven, and see, the angels of God going up and down on it! And there above it stood the Lord, and he said, 'I am the Lord, the God of Abraham your ancestor and the God of Isaac. The land on which you lie I will give to you and your descendants, and they shall be like the dust of the ground, and you shall spread out to the west and east and to the north and south. And through you and through your descendants shall all the families of the earth be blessed. And see, I am with you and will keep you wherever you go, for I shall not leave you but shall accomplish all that I have promised you.'

Then Jacob awoke from his sleep and said, 'Surely the Lord is in this place and I did not know it.' And he was afraid and said, 'How terrible is this place! This is none other than the house of God, and this is the gate of heaven.' And Jacob rose early in the morning and took the stone that he had put under his head and he set it up as a standing stone and poured oil over its head. And he called the name of that place Bethel . . .

[Returning years later] Jacob arose in the night and took his two wives, his two maids and his eleven children to pass over the ford of the River Jabbok. And he took them and got them over the stream and sent across all that he had. And Jacob was left alone, and a man wrestled with him until the break of day. And seeing that he could not overthrow Jacob, he grasped him by the hollow of his thigh and strained it as he wrestled with him. And he said, 'Now let me go, for day is breaking.' But Jacob answered, 'I will not let you go unless you bless me.' So he said to him, 'What is your name?' And he answered, 'Jacob.' And he said, 'No longer shall you be called Jacob, but Israel, for you have struggled with God and with other people and have won through.'

Then Jacob asked him, saying, 'Tell me, I pray, your name.' But he answered, 'Why do you ask for my name?' And then he blessed him. And Jacob called the name of that place Penuel ['Face of God'], for he said, 'I have seen God face to face and my life has been spared.' Then the sun rose upon him as he passed over Penuel, limping because of his thigh.

Isaac's wily son Jacob fears the wrath of his twin brother Esau whom he has outwitted and deprived. In haste he has left the family camp in the southern wilderness and set off north on a long and lonely journey towards kinsfolk in a distant land. We join him as he reaches a stony hill in central Palestine and night is falling. Taking a long stone for a pillow, he falls asleep and dreams. But unawares, he has put himself in a holy place, a 'thin' place of spiritual presence. In his dream he encounters God.

He sees a stairway rising from this place to the very floor of heaven. Angels hurry up and down it in God's service. And above it the Lord appears and carries his promise to Abraham forward and on to Jacob. This fugitive nomad, in the person of his descendants, will one day be given this place and they will multiply and spread in all directions, and through him blessing will come to all families of the earth.

When morning comes, Jacob takes his stone pillow and sets it up as a sacred standing stone, and he calls the place Bethel, 'House of God'. Centuries later a great sanctuary will flourish here, and pilgrims no doubt will hear this story of Jacob and see the stairway of a prayer-tower and a standing stone. And some may sleep there, praying for a visitation of God in the night to comfort and guide them.

In John's gospel 1.51 Jacob's dream foreshadows the work of Christ, himself the stairway, the way of communion: 'You will see heaven opened and angels of God ascending and descending on the Son of Man.' And some have taken the story as a poetry of spiritual experience – the lonely and fearful soul that, stumbling on Bethel unawares, sees the way to God and hears his 'I will not leave you'. In a well-known hymn the angels beckon the wanderer 'nearer, my God, to thee', and the stone-like suffer-ings are raised as an offering that finds God near.

Our second extract finds Jacob returning years later, rich in family and flocks, but fearful still of encounter with Esau. Under cover of night he carefully gets his people and animals across the ford of the River Jabbok, east of the Jordan. But as he now stands alone in the darkness, a myste-rious figure, as it were the guardian spirit of the ford, grapples with him. They wrestle together until, with the first sign of dawn, the Unknown would depart. But Jacob holds on until he has obtained a blessing from his opponent, now recognized as a manifestation of God.

So he crosses over at last, limping but lit by the sun. His new name marks a new phase of his life before God. In its pre-Hebrew language the name meant 'God reigns'; the Hebrew ear now catches the sense 'He struggled with God'. Under this name he will live on in his 'seed', the ancestor one with his descendants – 'Israel'.

These and other stories of Jacob maintain, indeed increase, the mystery of the purpose of God. The promise of God to Abraham is here carried forward in a man who strives both with God and with other people, a wily, controversial character who, however, knows what is good and perseveres to have it – the blessing of God. And through him the Lord directs his own purpose for the blessing of all the families of the earth. The long struggle in the night has often been seen as the struggle of faith. In his hymn 'Come, O thou Traveller unknown', Charles Wesley wrestles to know the secret of the Crucified, whose name, the heart recognizes at last, is Love.

God's Hidden Work

Genesis 45.1–20,25–28

Then Joseph could not keep his composure before all his attendants and he called out, 'Cause every one to depart from me.' So none of them were present when he made himself known to his brothers. And he sobbed aloud, and the Egyptians heard it and the house of Pharaoh heard it. And Joseph said to his brothers, 'I am Joseph. Is my father still living?' But his brothers could not answer him, for they were utterly dismayed before him. So Joseph said to his brothers, 'Come close to me, I pray you.' And they came close. And he said, 'I am Joseph your brother, whom you sold into Egypt. And now do not be grieved or full of recriminations that you sold me here, for it was to save lives that God sent me before you. For the famine has been in the land these two years and there are yet five more years when there will be no ploughing or harvest . . . So then, it was not you that sent me here, but God. And he has made me a father to Pharaoh and lord of all his house and ruler over all the land of Egypt.

'Make haste then and go up to my father and say to him, "Thus says your son Joseph: God has made me lord of all Egypt. Come down to me without delay. You shall dwell in the land of Goshen and be near to me, you and your children and your children's children and your flocks and herds and all you possess. And there I will provide all you need. For there are still five years of famine to come, and you would otherwise be impoverished, you and your household and all that you have."

'And now you see with your own eyes, my brother Benjamin also, that it is my mouth that speaks to you. You must tell my father of all my glory in Egypt and of all that you have seen. Then make haste to bring my father down here.' And he fell upon his brother Benjamin's neck and wept, and Benjamin wept on Joseph's neck. And he kissed all his brothers and wept on them. And after that his brothers talked with him.

When the news that Joseph's brothers had come reached Pharaoh's house, it pleased Pharaoh and his servants greatly. Pharaoh told Joseph to say to his brothers, 'This is what you must do: load your animals and go back to the land of Canaan. Then bring your father and your families and come to me. And I will give you the good things of the land of Egypt and you shall eat the finest of the land. And be sure to tell them: Do this, take for yourselves from the land of Egypt wagons for your little ones and for your wives, and bring your father and come. Do not be sorry to leave your possessions, for the good things of all the land of Egypt will be yours' . . .

So they went up from the land of Egypt and came into the land of Canaan to their father Jacob. And they told him, 'Joseph is alive and is ruler over all the land of Egypt.' And his heart fainted and he could not believe them. But when they spoke to him all the words that Joseph had said to them, and when he saw the wagons which Joseph had sent to carry him, the spirit of their father Jacob revived. And Israel said, 'It is enough. My son Joseph is still alive. I will go and see him before I die.'

The enthralling story of Joseph has begun in Genesis 37 and will fill twelve chapters in all (37; 39 – 48; 50), a little book in itself, rewarding a complete and sympathetic reading. It makes the link between Jacob and Moses – Israel in Canaan and then in Egypt, carrying forward the faithful promise of God to Abraham. But the artistic story in itself brings forward such great themes as the power of forgiveness, the patience in suffering that at last finds great happiness, the people saved through the one they had rejected, and the work of God which is mighty even when hidden. Only a few details are not clear, due to the combining of two versions of the story.

Jacob had deeply loved his wife Rachel, who had borne Joseph but died in bearing Benjamin. His particular attachment to these sons aroused the jealousy of their ten elder half-brothers. They thought to murder Joseph, but in the end sold him into slavery in Egypt. There he became a slave of the captain of the royal guard, and rose to become a trusted steward in the house. But a false accusation by his master's wife landed him in the dungeons. Even there God prospered him and he won respect and trust. His fame for interpreting dreams led him beyond more setbacks to the highest rank, for the grateful pharaoh made him ruler of all Egypt, charged especially with the task of averting the effects of the famine he had foreseen in Pharaoh's dreams.

In all his glory and power Joseph comes face to face with the brothers who so misused him. They have come down to Egypt in the famine to buy grain. While they do not recognize him, he keeps it that way, being only concerned at first to have his full brother Benjamin come down to him – the apprehensive father having kept the lad at home. After much drama, the brothers do make a second visit, this time with Benjamin. Joseph's scheme to retain Benjamin now brings matters to a head. In all the tension and distress, it becomes clear to Joseph that the brothers repent of their past conduct, also that his father's heart will break if Benjamin does not return to him. He is therefore moved to reveal his identity and to forgive them and trust them in a reconciliation.

'Come close to me,' he says to the astounded and fearful brothers – already showing his trust by abandoning the protection great rulers needed. He knows also that God had him suffer at their hands to save them and many peoples also. The humiliations and pain, the deliverances and honours, all took him God's way in God's purpose. Joseph clearly forgives, but is too kind to speak of it. They embrace with tears and talk together, reconciled. With every consideration for the old father and with the pious pharaoh's encouragement, the whole family is brought to the safety of Egypt and its wise ruler Joseph, there to stay and become a numerous people.

Some years later when Jacob dies, the brothers' fears return, but Joseph reassures them with affection and humility, pointing to the secret working of God which has brought good out of evil (50.20).

2.

Formed in the Wilderness

The Fire That Does Not Destroy

Exodus 3.1–15

Now Moses was tending the flock of his father-in-law Jethro, the priest of Midian, and he led the flock to the west of the wilderness and came to Horeb, the holy mountain. And the angel of the Lord appeared to him in fire that flamed from the midst of a bush. As he looked, he saw that the bush blazed with fire yet it was not consumed. And Moses said, 'I will turn aside and look at this great sight, to see why the bush is not burnt.'

When the Lord saw that Moses had turned aside to look, he called to him from the midst of the bush, 'Moses, Moses.' And he answered, 'Here I am.' God said, 'Do not come near. Take off your sandals, for the ground under your feet is holy.'

And further he said, 'I am the God of your father, the God of Abraham, the God of Isaac and the God of Jacob.' Then Moses hid his face, for he was afraid to look upon God. And the Lord said, 'I have seen all the suffering of my people in Egypt and heard them cry out because of their taskmasters. Well I know their sorrows, and I have come down to rescue them from the grasp of Egypt and bring them up from that country to a good and spacious land, a land flowing with milk and honey, the country of the Canaanites, Hittites, Amorites, Perizites, Hivites and Jebusites. And now the cry of the Israelites has come to me and I have seen how the Egyptians oppress them. So come, and I will send you to Pharaoh and you shall lead my people the Israelites out of Egypt.'

But Moses said to God, 'Who am I to go to Pharaoh and lead the Israelites out of Egypt?' And God said, 'But I am with you: And this will be the sign confirming that I have sent you: when you have led the people out of Egypt, you will all worship God on this mountain.'

Then Moses said to God, 'If I come to the Israelites and say to them, The God of your ancestors has sent me to you, and they ask me, What is his name?

what shall I say to them?' God said to Moses, I AM WHAT/WHO I AM.' And he continued, 'Say this to the Israelites: I AM/I WHO AM has sent me to you.' And God said further to Moses, 'Say this to the Israelites: The Lord [he who is], the God of your ancestors, the God of Abraham, the God of Isaac and the God of Jacob, has sent me to you. This is my name for ever, and with this name you shall call to me throughout all generations.'

The book of Exodus picks up the story of Jacob/Israel's descendants long after his death and the death of Joseph and his brothers. The setting is still Egypt, where the immigrants have multiplied and are called, according to tribal custom, 'the children of Israel', and also 'Hebrews', a name for marginal or semi-nomadic folk throughout the Near East. The king (or pharaoh) tries to curb them by using them as forced labour for his building projects and even by infanticide. Their cries rise to heaven and God prepares a deliverer.

A Hebrew child has been adopted in wondrous circumstances and named Moses by none other than the king's daughter. As a grown man, however he intervenes against a cruel taskmaster and kills him, and then has to flee to the desert. Among the desert people, the Midianites, he finds hospitality and marries a daughter of their chief priest.

In our present extract, then, we find him serving as shepherd of his father-in-law's flock. As sometimes happens in biblical stories, the animals play their part in a great deed of God. Their needs take Moses to the region of Horeb (also called Sinai), a great holy mountain.

There he is drawn to a bush which appears to be ablaze, yet is not consumed, and from the fire he hears the voice of God. He has indeed been drawn to a place filled with the divine presence. The very ground is 'holy', especially possessed by God. The mountain is a chosen place for his appearing on earth, a place for worship.

Moses hears the words that identify the revealed God and convey his awesome power. Here the link with the ancestors is stressed: this is the God who has been at work with Abraham and his descendants and has a purpose to fulfil through them. So he has come to rescue this oppressed generation. But Moses already has the gift of an intercessor to press upon God. So he pleads to know the divine name which will be the key to the way of prayer and praise. This most solemn and holy knowledge is not given without mystery, but we may interpret God's answer to mean that the name for them to use in worship is 'Yahweh' (for which English Bibles usually put 'the Lord' throughout the Hebrew Scriptures) and that it means 'the One Who Is'. It is an echo of God's own mighty utterance of self-expression, 'I AM' and 'I AM WHO I AM'. The words express the unique being of God, who alone 'is', existing independently in his own right.

Moses is to lead the people out to this very mountain to confirm them as the worshippers of God as thus revealed – God who is linked to their tribal history, shaping and guiding them for a special purpose, yet God also high above all beings, himself the only full Being, and the source of all other existence.

God's Choice Is Hard to Understand

Exodus 4.10–16

> Moses said to the Lord, 'O my Lord, I am not a good speaker, neither in the past, nor since you have spoken to your servant for I am clumsy in mouth and tongue.' Then the Lord said to him, 'Who made people's mouths, and who makes someone dumb or deaf, seeing or blind? Is it not I, the Lord? Now then, go, and I will be with your mouth and teach you what you must say.'
>
> But Moses persisted, 'O my Lord, I beg you, choose someone else to send.' At this the Lord became angry with Moses and he said, 'Is not Aaron the Levite your brother? I know that he can speak fluently. See, he is already on his way to meet you, and when he sees you his heart will rejoice. You shall speak to him and put the words into his mouth. And I will be with your mouth and also with his, and will teach you both what you must do. So he will be your spokesman to my people. He will be as a mouth for you, and you will be as the spirit inspiring him.'

The Lord has continued speaking with Moses and has explained how he is to confront the pharaoh, the king of Egypt. But Moses sees possible snags and persists in putting his objections to God. His final objection is his inability to speak fluently and persuasively. He has never been and is not now 'a man of words'. A remarkable choice then by the Lord, picking out the man who is to be the chief teacher of ancient Israel! But such, it seems, is often the way, 'that no one should boast in the presence of God' (1 Corinthians 1.29). If Moses could trust, he would find that God would be with him and all would be accomplished. Yet Moses is not convinced and in Hebrew words of great tact pleads that God should choose someone else.

It may seem childlike or primitive that the story now tells of God losing his patience. His anger kindles, and yet he makes a concession, appointing the partnership of Moses and his eloquent priestly brother Aaron for the task. On reflection we find something profound and wonderful here. The infinite and almighty Creator is willing to listen to human anxieties and objections and, as it were, to meet them halfway.

In his grace, stooping to us, he will work with us in a partnership where greater trust can grow.

All the same, it is not intended that we should find in Moses a model of how we should ever be objecting and contesting God's will for us. Moses is regarded as exceptionally called to the highest office of mediator and intercessor. His ability to wrestle with God and obtain concessions is in the end a gift, an endowment from God (for who would dare to do it of himself? – Jeremiah 30.21). His calling foreshadows the interceding of Christ and the Holy Spirit, whereby human needs and cares are taken up with great tenderness and brought into the full light of the divine pity.

Passover and the Start of the Exodus

Exodus 12.21–36

Then Moses summoned all the elders of Israel and said to them, 'Go quickly and take lambs from the flocks and slaughter them for Passover. And take a bunch of hyssop (marjoram] and dip it in the blood in the basin and strike the lintel and the two doorposts with that blood from the basin, and not one of you must go through the door of the house until the morning. For the Lord will pass through to strike Egypt, and when he sees the blood on the lintel and the two doorposts, he will pass over that door and will not let the destroyer enter your house to strike you.

And you shall keep this as a regular custom for you and for your children for ever. Then when you come to the land which the Lord will give you as he has promised, you must keep this service, and when your children ask you, 'What is the meaning of this service?' you shall say, 'It is the sacrifice of the Lord's Passover, for he passed over the houses of the Israelites in Egypt, when he struck Egypt but spared our households.' And the people bowed their heads and worshipped.

And it came to pass at midnight that the Lord struck all the first-born in the land of Egypt, from the first-born of the pharaoh who sat on his throne to the first-born of the captive held in the dungeon, also all the first-born of the cattle. And the pharaoh rose in the night and all his servants, and all Egypt, and a great cry went up from the Egyptians, for there was not a house without one dead. And he called for Moses and Aaron in the night and said, 'Arise and go out from among my people, you and the Israelites, and go and worship the Lord as you have asked. Take your flocks and cattle as you have said and be gone; only ask a blessing for me also.'

And the Egyptians urged the people on and hurried them out of the country, saying, 'Go, before we are all dead!' So the people picked up their dough before it was leavened, wrapping their kneading troughs in their cloaks, putting them on their shoulders. Also the Israelites did as Moses had told them, asking the Egyptians for jewellery of silver and gold and for clothing. And the Lord gave the people such favour now with the Egyptians that they let them have what they asked for. In this way they took spoil from the Egyptians.

With his wife and little son on a donkey, Moses has left the desert people and set off for Egypt. Near the sacred mountain he meets his brother Aaron and together, back in Egypt, they meet the elders and explain the Lord's intentions. But when they go to the pharaoh, they meet only a hostile refusal to let the people go. The oppression indeed is increased, and so the Lord begins to strike Egypt with a series of plagues. In this battle of wills, the pharaoh (considered by his people as a god) seems to do well, for he is unmoved by the first nine plagues (the Nile turned to blood, the frogs, mosquitoes, horse flies, murrain, boils, hail, locusts, darkness). But the story explains that the Lord had strengthened the pharaoh's resistance so that the revelations of God's power might be more fully unfolded. It has all been told and retold in ancient celebrations of the Passover and become a narrative of mounting excitement, rather in the manner of folk tales. The climax is reached with the tenth plague, as related in our extract.

The final plague, the death of the firstborn, is linked to the institution of the Passover observance. The blood of the lamb or kid smeared above and around the door wards off destruction for Israelite homes. It may be that a more ancient custom of pastoral folk to ward off danger underlies this application in the exodus. At all events, the observance of the sacrificial meal here becomes a way of preserving through countless generations the experience of a salvation which rescues from oppression and opens the way to a new life with God.

The church came to make much use of imagery from the Passover. St Paul speaks of Christ as the Passover lamb sacrificed for us, and teaches that we must therefore be rid of every scrap of the old leaven (meaning evil deeds) and, as in the festival, have only the unleavened bread (meaning sincerity and truth, 1 Corinthians 5.7). In baptism Christians see a new exodus, with deliverance from the waters of death into new life in Christ.

Through the Waters of Death

Exodus 14.5–31

Thus the king of Egypt was told that the people had fled. And the heart of Pharaoh and his ministers was changed towards the people and they said, 'What have we done, letting Israel go from slaving for us?' And he made ready his chariot and took his army with him, 600 picked chariots with the rest of the chariotry, each with its commander. And the Lord made the pharaoh's heart determined so that he pursued the Israelites as they went out in high spirits. And the Egyptians came up with them as they camped by the sea at Pi-hahiroth opposite Baal-zephon. And as the pharaoh drew near, the Israelites raised their eyes, and there were the Egyptians marching after them, and they feared greatly . . . [v. 13] But Moses said to them, 'Do not be afraid. Stand firm and see the salvation of the Lord which he will work for you today. For as surely as you see these Egyptians today, you will never see them again. The Lord will fight for you, while you have only to be still.'

Then the Lord said to Moses, 'Why this crying to me? Speak to the Israelites so that they go forward. Lift up your staff and stretch out your hand over the sea to cleave it in two, so that the Israelites can go through the sea on dry ground . . .' [v. 21] So Moses stretched out his hand over the sea, and the Lord drove the sea back with a strong east wind all night and made a dry path through the sea, for the waters were divided. And the Israelites went through the sea on dry ground, and the waters made a wall for them on their right hand and on their left. And the Egyptians pursued them through the midst of the sea, all the pharaoh's mounted troops with chariotry and cavalry.

Then in the morning watch the Lord looked out on the host of the Egyptians through the pillar of fire and cloud and threw them into confusion. For he clogged their chariot wheels till they could scarcely drive them. And the Egyptians said, 'Let us flee away from Israel, for the Lord fights for them and against us.' Then the Lord said to Moses, 'Stretch out your hand over the sea so that the waters flow back over the Egyptians, their chariots and their cavalry.' So Moses stretched out his hand over the sea and it all flowed together as morning appeared. And the Egyptians were fleeing right into it. Thus the Lord overwhelmed them in the midst of the sea. Not one of them survived . . . [v. 31] And Israel saw the mighty work which the Lord did against Egypt. And they feared the Lord and believed in him and in his servant Moses.

Historians have much difficulty in agreeing on the period and places of the marvel underlying this great story. But the event, they think, is likely to have been on a smaller scale than what is now presented – a clan-group of Hebrews fleeing perhaps along the treacherous coastline, which effected the doom of the heavily equipped Egyptian pursuers.

As we read the story now, our concern should be to hear what it has to testify from many centuries of experience of the faithfulness and power of the Lord. Yes, many centuries, because the telling and retelling in the commemorative festivals, as also the growth and editing of written versions in various sanctuaries, have made the story a focus for faith and testimony through several eras.

The obdurate pharaoh is never named. He has come to symbolize the powers that exalt themselves against the Lord. Head of the greatest of states and himself worshipped as a god, considered indeed to be essential to the world's life and prosperity, he is shown in direct combat with the Lord. But he is found powerless to frustrate God's purpose, and if he can prolong his opposition, it is only because that, too, is God's will. Of his great army it is especially the chariotry and cavalry that suffer in the waters, for these were the weapons of the superstates, rich and highly organized. But they flee from the harmless crowd of fugitives in panic and their doom signals the futility of worldly might.

The universal supremacy of the Lord is shown again in the behaviour of the sea. Ancient lore of creation took the original sea as a symbol of opposition to the Creator. In combat with the monstrous sea, he was said to cleave it in two and then make it serve his purpose of life. The exodus sea might still have been a force of chaos and death, but the Lord is its master and uses it for his work of salvation and judgement.

The Lord's goodness in saving the Hebrews is shown as undeserved. Quick indeed they are to blame Moses for bringing them out – were there not enough graves for them in Egypt (14.11–12)? But the Lord saves them because of his compassion and his work of promise given long ago – his everlasting purpose. Nor could the Israelites by any means save themselves. Their part is to 'stand still', to be quiet and trustful, while the Lord alone defeats the tyrant.

Yet there was a mediator, a 'servant' of the Lord. In obedience to God he must confront the pharaoh and he must take the people forward on their hazardous pilgrimage as their earthly guide, ruler and teacher. His hand is used to cleave the sea and again to restore its flow. He has to bear rebukes from the Lord and grumblings from the ungrateful people. But at their best the people have faith in the Lord and in Moses – he is their true link to God.

With such themes the story aims to nourish its people and speaks still to their successors today. Fundamental for the ancient people, these insights into the divine working have been found also to illuminate the salvation celebrated in the church.

The Fountain Struck from a Rock

Exodus 17.1–7

Then all the congregation of the Israelites moved on from the wilderness of Sin in stages directed by the Lord, and they pitched camp in Rephidim. But no water was found there for the people to drink. So they clamoured against Moses, saying, 'Give us water to drink.' And Moses said, 'Why this clamour against me? Why do you put the Lord to the test?' But, driven by thirst, the people continued to blame Moses and said, 'Why did you bring us out of Egypt only to kill us with thirst, and kill our children and cattle also?'

So Moses cried to the Lord, 'What shall I do for this people? Very soon they will stone me!' The Lord answered, 'Go on ahead of the people, taking with you some of the elders of Israel, and take in your hand the staff with which you struck the Nile. Go on till you see me standing before you on a rock in Horeb. Then smite the rock, and out of it will flow water for the people to drink.' And Moses did so in the sight of the elders of Israel.

And he named the place Massah and Meribah, because of the querulous disputing of the Israelites, and because they put the Lord to the test saying, 'Is the Lord among us or not?'

The wilderness journey continues. Various places are named, but we have little sure knowledge of them. Yet in a deeper sense the journey is very familiar to us, for we too are inclined to be so wholly taken up with difficulties or sufferings that suddenly come upon us that we lose the greater and wiser perspective.

The narrative has been telling of a crisis due to hunger and how, by God's grace, that was overcome. Now they have reached a place where no water can be found, and the people quickly turn against Moses and are near to stoning him. But the long-suffering mediator, obedient to God's direction, is able to strike open an abundant fountain from the least likely place, a great rock.

The crisis is overcome. But the naming of the place by Moses remains a warning against the angry discontent that can so quickly take the place of failed trust.

Yet more mighty, and for all generations, is the sign of the fountain struck from the rock. From the hardest places on our way, from depth of pain and from the peril of death, the Lord can bring the water of new life. The flinty rock he turns into a springing well for those who, like Moses, turn to him, listen to him and trustfully follow his guidance. And from the hard rock of Christ's sufferings, it was to be revealed, flows a fountain of eternal life, and those who drink of it will never thirst again.

A Kingdom Where All Are Priests

Exodus 19.3–6

> Then Moses went up the mountain of God. Then the Lord called to him from
> the mountain, saying, 'This is what you must say to the House of Jacob, yes,
> tell the Israelites, You have seen all I did in Egypt, and how I carried you as on
> eagle's wings and brought you here to me. Now if only you will listen to me
> and keep my covenant, then out of all peoples you shall be my special posses-
> sion. For all the world belongs to me, but you shall be for me a kingdom
> where all are priests, a nation where all are holy. These very words you are to
> speak to the Israelites.'

By now the people have come to the region of the holy mountain, Sinai,
and are encamped before it. Moses ascends the mountain and receives
from the Lord a message of great significance to carry down to his people.
The remote and lofty head of the mountain is regarded with the greatest
awe as the place of sacred presence where heaven touches earth. No one
is worthy to penetrate into that mystery. The chosen mediator, Moses,
alone is called to make the ascent and be entrusted with the words of
God.

To this people who have already received the grace of rescue from
slavery there is now given a clear word of their calling, the divine
purpose which lies at the heart of their bond or 'covenant' with God. This
is the God to whom all the world belongs and whose power embraces
all nations. But he makes this people, the offspring of Jacob/Israel, his
special or personal possession, specially close to him. This people as a
whole, all of them, are to serve him as a kind of priesthood. Their intimacy with the Lord is to enable them to be mediators between him and
all nations. Like priests, they are to draw the peoples to the Lord, and
bring them gifts of the Spirit from him.

In this sense they will be 'a kingdom consisting of priests', the whole
nation (rather than one class or profession) being 'holy', dedicated to this
service of priestly mediation. A privilege, yes, but also a responsibility.
For of great importance is the word 'if'. The wonderful calling, with all its
gifts, is to be fulfilled only if the people listen to the Lord and stay faithful
to his will.

The words, here entrusted to Moses, in a new era will illuminate the
calling of Christians (1 Peter 2.9). They too are to be a kingdom of priests,
a people where all are holy, so that they may show to the wider world the
great deeds and truths of the Lord who has called them out of darkness
into his marvellous light.

Ten Requirements in the Bond with God

Exodus 20.1–17

Then God spoke all these words, saying, 'I am the Lord your God who brought you out of the land of Egypt and its slave camps.

[1] 'You shall have no other gods before my face.

[2] 'You shall not make for yourself a carved image or any likeness of anything in heaven above, or on the earth below, or in the waters under the earth, to bow down and worship them. For I the Lord your God defend my right as God, holding the wrongdoing of the parents against the children down to the third and fourth generations of those who scorn me, but keeping faith to a thousand generations of those who follow me and keep my commandments.'

[3] You shall not misuse the name of the Lord your God, for he will not acquit anyone who abuses his name.

[4] Observe the Sabbath day as a holy day. Six days you shall labour and do all your work, but the seventh is a Sabbath rest offered to the Lord your God. On that day you shall not do any work, you, your son, your daughter, your servants, your animals, or any foreigner living in your household. For in six days the Lord made heaven, earth and sea and all that lives in them, but on the seventh day he rested, so he blessed the seventh day and made it holy.

[5] Honour your father and your mother, so that your days may be many on the portion of land which the Lord your God allots you.

[6] You shall not murder.

[7] You shall not commit adultery.

[8] You shall not steal.

[9] You shall not give false evidence against your neighbour.

[10] You shall not covet what is your neighbour's – his wife, servants, animals – or anything that is his.

As part of continuing revelations from Mount Sinai come these ten 'commandments' or 'words'. God speaks to the end of the second commandment and then the rest is indirect 'reported speech'. But here we have a strong sense that the Lord reveals himself, the awesome 'I AM', but also the compassionate Saviour. He has come to a people he has already saved and is showing them how they are to live with him. All is spoken to a singular 'you', the people as one body and also each individual, responsible before the Lord.

The first requirement is for worship of the Lord alone, worship of other gods being forbidden. This at once gives the Israelite faith a distinctive character. This is an essential and powerful drive to love the Lord with a whole and undivided heart.

The second commandment forbids the worship of images of other beings. The Lord is 'jealous', absolutely determined that none should usurp his claims as God and his lordship over his people. Such false worship brings harm affecting several generations, but faithful worshippers find the faithfulness of God which lasts for ever. This second requirement seems now to overlap the first, but originally it probably had a terser form and simply forbade the worship of images of the Lord. This again would be something very distinctive, showing a profound sense of God's mystery, uniqueness and transcendence.

The third commandment forbids 'using' God for human ends, such as by taking up his name in false oaths or in magic spells. There are no doubt modern equivalents of such abuse.

The fourth commandment concerns the seventh day, our Saturday, which becomes a kind of offering, a day without work. It is 'holy', dedicated to him. In Christian tradition the first day, Sunday, takes the honoured place, being the day of Christ's resurrection. But a whole society refraining from work seems now an unattainable goal. The Sabbath, however retains its importance. Human beings are the servants of God, not the slaves of work, and rest is a blessed gift of God to humans, animals, and all the living earth. Sabbath indeed is enjoined as an imitation of God's own way of working, and in the similar account in Deuteronomy 5 it is motivated by compassion for employees and animals.

The fifth commandment teaches respect for elderly parents. Let there be no haste to take over their rights to the family land.

Commandments six to nine remain in the original terse form, two or three words in the Hebrew. Social laws, but still part of the life with God. The 'stealing' probably referred originally to stealing, or kidnapping, people, often to sell as slaves. Other stealing was originally covered by the tenth commandment, where 'covet' meant 'covet and steal'. Now the eighth has become more general, as the tenth became focused on greedy desire.

So the Lord commands who has already rescued his people from slavery. This is to be the pattern of their new life of freedom, their life of devotion to him.

Artists Inspired by the Spirit

Exodus 35.21–35

And so they came, all whose heart lifted them and whose spirit made them eager, and they brought offerings to the Lord for the making of the Tent of

Meeting and for all its services, and for the holy vestments . . . [v. 25] And every woman whose heart had the wisdom spun with her hands. And they brought what they had spun, blue, purple and scarlet stuff and fine linen. And all the women whose heart lifted them in wisdom spun goat's hair, while the chiefs brought cornelians and other stones to be set in the priest's ephod and breastplate, also spices and oil for the light and for anointing oil and for sweet incense . . .

[v. 30] Then Moses said to the Israelites, 'See, the Lord has called by name Bezalel son of Uri, son of Hur, of the tribe of Judah. He has filled him with the Spirit of God, giving wisdom for understanding and knowledge in all kinds of craft, to devise skilful work in gold, silver and bronze, and for cutting stones to set and for carving wood in all kinds of skilful designs. The Lord has put it in his heart to teach, along with Oholiab son of Ahisamach of the tribe of Dan. He has filled both of them with wisdom of heart to work in all kinds of artistry . . .'

During the revelations on Mount Sinai, God commands Moses to make him a sanctuary, a kind of tent-shrine foreshadowing the later temple. In chapters 25 – 31 he specifies the details for its construction, furnishing and functioning.

Our passage covers similar ground. We notice how the materials and artistry are all offerings to the Lord. For him and for his worship is offered all that can be given of beauty and dedicated work. But the impulse for all this spinning and weaving, woodcarving, work in precious metals, and cutting and setting of precious stones, is inspiration. The heart uplifts the artist or craftsperson, and the spirit impels with eagerness. The source of this inspiration is the Spirit of God, the Holy Spirit.

The names of the two chief figures in all this work are significant here. 'Bezalel' (*b-sal-el*) means 'In the shadow of God', while 'Oholi-ab' can be understood as 'The Father is my tent/home'. These great artists and craftsmen are thus seen as very close to God, and only so could such beautiful and skilful work be accomplished.

So we hear a message from ancient times and from the wilderness: nothing is more important than the worship of God where we meet God and meet each other in his presence. Nothing is more deserving of our offerings, our gifts, our capacity to make beauty. And all that we offer, all the beauty we make, all our dedication, love and inspiration, comes from the work of the Holy Spirit, an uplifting and filling of our souls granted by God in his grace.

Living Daily with the Reality of God

Leviticus 19.1–37

Then the Lord spoke to Moses and said, 'Speak to all the congregation of the Israelites and say to them: You shall be holy, for I the Lord your God am holy.

Every one of you shall respect your mother and father, and you shall keep my Sabbaths – I am the Lord your God.

Do not turn to idols or make for yourselves gods of metal – I am the Lord your God . . .

And when you reap the harvest of your land, you shall not reap right into the corners of your field, and you shall not glean your vineyard or gather its fallen grapes. You shall leave them for the poor and foreigners – I am the Lord your God.

You shall not steal or cheat or lie to one another. And you shall not swear falsely by my name and so profane the name of your God – I am the Lord.

You shall not oppress your neighbour or rob him. The wages of a hired servant shall not remain with you all night till the morning. You shall not curse the deaf or put an obstruction in the path of the blind, but you shall fear your God – I am the Lord . . .

You shall not hate your brother or sister in your heart, but you shall reason with your neighbours and not be at fault because of them. You shall not take revenge or bear any grudge against your kinsfolk, but you shall love your neighbour as yourself – I am the Lord . . .

[v. 32] You shall rise up before the hoary head and honour the face of the old man or woman, and you shall fear your God – I am the Lord.

And if foreigners reside with you in your land, you shall not do them any wrong. They must be treated as those born among you and you shall love them as yourselves. For you were once foreigners in the land of Egypt – I am the Lord your God.

You shall not cheat in measures of length or weight or quantity. You must have true balances, weights and measures for dry and liquid – I am the Lord your God who brought you out of the land of Egypt. You shall keep all my laws and teachings and do them – I am the Lord.

The rules of conduct set out in this passage give some idea of what is meant by the broad command, 'You shall be holy.' We have already met some of these rules in the list of the Ten Commandments. Additional commands reflect compassion for the disadvantaged and the importance of kindness in the heart, overcoming impulses of resentment and vengefulness. Before you are tempted to take advantage of someone's blindness or deafness, remember that God sees and hears what you do, and fear him.

The poor labourers need their wages that very day, so do not put off payment. The 'brother or sister', neighbour or kinsfolk is someone you work or live with. With such daily contact, how important to maintain 'love' – goodwill and kindness. But if you are dealing with someone from another people seeking shelter or work near you, the same rule of kindness applies – love them as yourself. It is a golden thread of conduct which runs through into the teaching of Jesus (Mark 12.31, etc.).

Of great importance is the reverberating 'I am the Lord'. The good conduct is done in the awareness that the Lord is present. His mighty reality, his holy and infinite being, is over and above every situation of your daily living, and in every creature that needs your compassion and kindness. So fear this God, reckon with him in all you do, and this will be for you the way of holiness, a life in harmony with him.

Earth Too Must Have Its Rest

Leviticus 25.1–7

> The Lord spoke to Moses on Mount Sinai and said, 'Speak to the Israelites and say to them: When you come into the land which I give you, the land shall keep Sabbath to the Lord. For six years you shall sow your fields, and for six years you shall prune your vineyard and gather its fruit. But in the seventh year the land shall have a Sabbath of holy rest to the Lord. You shall neither sow your field nor prune your vineyard. Whatever grows of itself by harvest time you shall not reap, and the grapes of your unpruned vine you shall not gather. It shall be a year of solemn rest for the land. But what grows of itself in that Sabbath of the land, all its yield, shall be food for you – for your servant, your maid, your hired servant and for any foreigner settled with you, also for your cattle and for the wild creatures living on you land.'

The rhythm of times of rest is not a benefit for humans alone. Our extract shows the Lord solemnly commanding that there must be sabbatical years for the land and its plants. Every seventh year the field and vineyards are to be left fallow and they must not then be systematically harvested, though their natural yield is to be freely available to the household, its cattle, and the wild creatures.

Such rest for the land would obviously be beneficial, countering the driving impulse of the owner to extract the maximum growth without let-up. But Sabbath rest is something more. It is a rest 'to the Lord', done at his command, done before his face. The land and its creatures are then specially open to his blessings of healing and restoration, re-gathered under the wings of his care.

The Blessing of Light from God's Face

Numbers 6.23–27

> And the Lord spoke to Moses and said, 'Speak to Aaron and his sons, saying: This is how you are to bless the Israelites. You shall say to them, "The Lord bless you and guard you. The Lord make his face to shine upon you and be merciful to you. The Lord lift up the light of his face upon you and give you peace." In this way they will put my name upon the Israelites and I will bless them.'

The Lord through Moses gives to the priests the words of blessing they are to pronounce over the assembly of worshippers or over individuals. It is a blessing to give protection and 'peace' – wholeness. The divine name is spoken early in all three sentences, putting already the power of God's presence over each worshipper, while all the words, God-given, are strong in grace.

Prominent also is the image of light from God's face. Light, again, signifies fullness of life. And the face of God, lifted attentively towards the worshipper, signifies closeness to him, the merciful and the life-giver. To be thus in his presence through the days of one's life and in all activities is indeed the fullness of blessing, the perfection of peace.

3.

Towards a Settled Life: Benefits and Dangers Foreseen

The Lord Alone, the Lord Is Everything

Deuteronomy 6.4–12

> Hear, O Israel, the Lord is our God, the Lord alone. And you must love the Lord your God with all your heart and with all your soul and with all your strength. And these commandments which I give you this day shall be on your heart, and you shall teach them to your children. And you shall talk of them when you sit in your house and when you walk on the way, and when you lie down and when you rise up. And you shall bind them as a sign on your hand, and they shall be as frontlets between your eyes. And you shall write them on the doorposts of your house and on your gates.
>
> And when the Lord your God brings you to the land which he promised to your ancestors, Abraham, Isaac and Jacob, to give you, with its fine towns which you did not build, houses full of all good things which you did not fill, cisterns hewn out which you did not hew, vineyards and olive trees which you did not plant, and when you eat and are satisfied, then beware that you do not forget the Lord who brought you out of the land of Egypt, out of the slave camps.

The eloquent book of Deuteronomy is formed as exhortations given by Moses to the people, whose long journey has brought them to the threshold of the Promised Land, still east of the River Jordan. The speeches gather up ancient laws, look back over the eventful journey and put a tremendous stress on the need for loyalty if possession of the land is to be retained. It seems that some circles in sympathy with the great prophets have been inspired to make the voice of Moses sound again, drawing from ancient tradition a powerful message of burning relevance to the troubled years near the end of the monarchy.

In this famous passage Moses urges utter devotion to the Lord. 'Love' here is a dedicated obedience to God. It is a practical love shown in the doing of what pleases him, in the keeping of his commands. Moses calls for a total love, a devotion driven by all one's capacities, all one's might, excluding attachment to unworthy goals and powers harmful to the bond with the Lord.

Borne along by passionate eloquence, the preacher may have been speaking figuratively when he says that his words should be put as signs on hand and brow and on doorposts, just as it would be figurative to say they should be written on the heart. In Jewish piety, however, the requirement is taken literally.

The call to love God with all one's might is warmly endorsed by Jesus as the first and supreme commandment (Mark 12.29). And still today, for both Jews and Christians, the concluding caution is timely – in prosperity not to 'forget' the Lord, not to slip into an attitude where his awesome reality is not respected, where other claims and desires have precedence, and faith in the true Saviour has faded.

Land Promised – with Conditions

Deuteronomy 8.1–20

> You must carefully observe all that I command you this day so that you may live and multiply and go in and possess the land which the Lord promised to give your ancestors. And you must remember all the way which the Lord your God has led you these forty years in the wilderness to humble you and test you, to know whether it was in your heart to keep his commandments.
>
> He humbled you and made you hungry, then fed you with manna which neither you nor your ancestors had known, to teach you that human beings do not live on bread alone but live on every utterance of the mouth of the Lord. Your clothes did not wear out on you, and your feet did not swell these forty years. And you must consider in your heart that as a parent disciplines their child, so the Lord disciplines you. So you shall keep the commandments of the Lord your God, walking in his ways and fearing him.
>
> The Lord your God is bringing you into a good land, a land of brooks of waters, of fountains and depths springing out in valleys and hills, a land of wheat and barley, of vines and fig trees and pomegranates, a land of olive trees and honey, a land where you will eat bread in plenty and lack for nothing, a land whose stones are iron and in whose hills you can dig for copper. And you shall eat and be full and shall bless the Lord your God for the good land that he has given you. Then beware of forgetting the Lord your God by not

keeping his commandments and his laws and his statutes which I give you this day. When you have eaten and are full and have built fine houses and dwelt in them, and when your herds and flocks multiply, and your silver and gold and all you have is multiplied, beware that your heart is not lifted up and you forget the Lord your God who brought you out of the land of Egypt ... [v. 17] Take care not to say in your heart, 'My power and the might of my hand have gained me this wealth.' But you shall remember the Lord your God, for he it is who gives you strength to gain wealth, as even this day he is fulfilling his covenant as he promised to your ancestors.

For if you should forget the Lord your God and go after other gods and serve them and bow down to them, I bear witness to you this day that you will surely perish. Just like the nations which the Lord makes to perish before you, so you shall perish, because you would not listen to the voice of the Lord your God.

On the brink of the Promised Land the exhortations continue. The land itself is depicted in glowing terms, justified by comparison with the howling wilderness and before the ravages that many generations of incomers and inhabitants would inflict over the centuries.

The message is hammered out clearly and persuasively. The land is to be a place to live with the Lord, alert and obedient to him, the Saviour who has provided it. If through comfort and prosperity the people grow indifferent to him, congratulating themselves, worshipping other powers or gods, they too, like the nations before them, will be driven out and will perish.

Against that catastrophe they must guard by remembering, staying mindful of all God has done for them – all his marvels of deliverance along that way of hardship and testing.

Circumcising the Heart

Deuteronomy 10.4–22

See, the Lord your God owns all the heavens, and the heaven of heavens and the earth and all that is in it. Only the Lord delighted in your ancestors and loved them, and he chose their descendants after them, you yourselves, out of all peoples, as you are this day. So you must circumcise your heart and be no longer obstinate. For the Lord your God is God of gods and Lord of lords, the supreme God, the mighty and terrible one who is no respecter of persons and takes no bribe. He sees justice done for orphans and widows, and he loves the foreigners who live among you, giving them food and clothing.

So you, also, love strangers, for you were strangers in the land of Egypt. You shall fear the Lord your God. You must serve him and cleave to him and in his name swear your oaths. He it is that you praise, for he is your God who has done for you these great and terrible things, as you have seen with your own eyes. Your ancestors went down into Egypt numbering seventy persons, and now the Lord your God has made you like the stars of heaven for multitude.

Still they roll on, the speeches ascribed to Moses on the threshold of the Promised Land. The twin convictions are held together: the Lord is God of all, utterly supreme, and yet he is the God of the Israelites – in special bond with them. So a great responsibility lies on this people, to fear and serve him, to cleave to him, ever to praise him in vivid remembrance of the marvellous deeds that have opened to them a dedicated life.

The circumcision of every male child was a practical way of keeping the consciousness of a whole people in covenant with the Lord. But like all 'external' ceremonies, it would come to be taken as adequate and effective in itself and so nurturing a false pride, a smugness in the vocation. So the preacher calls for circumcision of the heart, a conforming of the whole person, mind and soul, to the calling of the holy people, the 'priesthood' destined to serve God towards the world. This is the true circumcision. It would come to be seen as something only God himself could bring about, a radical conversion (Deuteronomy 30.6).

One God and One Temple

Deuteronomy 12.2–7

You must utterly destroy all the sanctuaries where the nations you shall dispossess worshipped their gods, on the high mountains, on the hills and under every spreading tree. You shall pull down their altars and dash in pieces their sacred pillars and burn their sacred poles with fire, and you shall hew down the images of their gods, and so you shall destroy their very name from that place.

You shall not worship the Lord your God in such ways. But you shall make your way to the place where the Lord your God will choose from all the tribes to put his name for his habitation. There you shall come, bringing your whole offerings, sacrifices, tithes, contributions, your votive and freewill offerings and the first-born of your herds and flocks. There you shall eat before the Lord your God, and so you shall rejoice in all that you put your hand to, you and the families with which the Lord your God has blessed you.

The actual history of the Israelite tribes in Palestine, as far as we can tell, was generally a story of finding space among older inhabitants. And for many centuries the older religion persisted, being firmly wedded to concerns for cultivation and fertility. A severe, uncompromising religion of Yahweh, the Lord, irrupted from time to time, but it was not until towards the end of the Israelite kingdoms (almost the seventh century BC) that the programme expressed in our passage was fully formulated. Under the blows of great invading armies, reformers concluded that laxity towards the old fertility-centred cults was to blame.

Their key proposal, as in our passage, was that there should be only one sanctuary for the worship of the Lord – and so a tighter control. All other sanctuaries were to be abolished and their furnishings and symbols destroyed. When it became possible to enforce this rule of one sanctuary, there were major consequences for worship itself. Local faith-activities of some kind there had to be. And so the synagogues developed all over the country and in many surrounding countries – places not of altars, sacrifices and priests, but of prayer, Scripture reading and teaching, and religious administration.

The earnest voice of Moses – or rather, the voice of reformers seeking to save the tottering kingdoms – what message does it carry beyond those far off crises of history? Now, as then, all turns on worship of the Lord alone. The disciples of the Lord have ever to consider whether their priorities and energies are all for God. Is it the Lord who is relied on, whatever channel or instrument he works through? Is trust really in him? Or is reliance placed elsewhere, downgrading and fatally weakening the love, worship and trust that are due to him? With such an application, this message from the threshold of the Promised Land is surely still to the point.

A King Immersed in Scripture

Deuteronomy 17.14–20

When you come into the land which the Lord your God is giving you and you take possession and dwell in it and you say, 'We will set a king over us like the nations round about us', then you must set as king over you one whom the Lord your God will choose, one from among yourselves. You may not put a foreigner over you who is not of your people.

And he must not multiply horses for himself or cause the people to return to Egypt to get more horses. For the Lord has said to you, 'You shall never go back that way.' Nor shall he multiply wives for himself lest his heart turn away. And he must not amass for himself silver and gold.

Once he becomes king, he must write himself a copy of this law in a book, taking it from that kept by the Levite priests. He shall have it ever with him and he shall read from it every day of his life, so that he may learn to fear the Lord his God, keeping all the words of this law and obeying all these statutes. Then his heart will not be lifted up above his compatriots and he will not turn aside from the commandments to the right hand or to the left, and he will reign many years, his children also, in the midst of his people Israel.

The preacher acknowledges the need for a king provided he is chosen by the Lord. Also he is to come from the Israelite people, accustomed to their sense of right and to the path of the Lord. He is not to 'multiply horses', building up a huge military machine with chariots and cavalry, for that would make him so independent of the people that he would be inclined to dictatorial rule. Nor is he to 'multiply wives' in polygamy, a mark of outstanding wealth, and a way of making alliances with foreign states, but sure to bring in the influence of other gods. And wealth itself is not to be amassed for personal gain.

He must be especially devoted to the Lord, as keen as any dedicated disciple. So he must make himself his own copy of these commandments, have it always with him and meditate in it every day.

Brought close to God in this way, he must not be arrogant towards his people, but live and work among them in humility and the fear of the Lord. It is an ideal which has inspired many good leaders who, however, have often been torn by conflicting considerations. The Israelite monarchy itself could not be saved and hope rested on the promise of a Messiah – the Lord's Anointed and Chosen One. In the fullness of time Jesus will take his royal way without possessions, humble among his people, wholly dedicated to the Father's will, and destined to reign for ever.

Giving Back to the Lord

Deuteronomy 26.1–11

When you have come into the land which the Lord your God is giving you for your own and you have taken possession of it and settled there, then you shall take from the first of all the produce of the ground which you bring in from your land which the Lord your God gives you. And you shall put it in a basket and go to the sanctuary where the Lord your God has chosen to make his name dwell. And you shall come to the priest who is there in those days and say to him, 'I declare this day before the Lord your God that I have come into the land which the Lord promised to our ancestors to give us.' Then the priest shall take the basket from your hand and set it down before the altar of the Lord your God. And you shall recite before the Lord your God, 'My ancestors were but Syrian nomads when they went down into Egypt and resided there with a small band. And there they became a great nation, strong and numerous. Then the Egyptians were cruel to us and afflicted us and laid on us hard bondage. And we cried to the Lord God of our ancestors. And the Lord heard our voices and saw our affliction, our labour and oppression. And the Lord brought us out of Egypt with a mighty hand and an outstretched arm, with fearsome deeds and with signs and wonders. And he brought us to this place and gave us this land, a land flowing with milk and honey. And see, I have brought the first of the produce of the ground which you, O Lord, have given me.' And you shall set it down before the Lord your God and bow down before him. And then you shall rejoice in all the good things which the Lord your God has given you and your household, you and any Levites or foreigners who may reside among you.

The typical crops of the land are mentioned in Deuteronomy 8: wheat, barley, figs, vines, pomegranates and date honey. The best of the first fruits of particular harvests are to be carried in a basket to the sanctuary and laid at the altar, as a sign that to God, the giver, all belongs.

The force of the ceremony described in our passage is in the uniting of the processes of nature with historical experience of God's care. The Lord has guided and saved his people, given them land, and food from the land. He is the life-giver, active in all circumstances and experiences, in nature as in history.

The ceremony of the first fruits is thus a practical expression of the rich meaning in the belief that from God is the life that embraces the fullness of experience.

Moses Dies Short of the Promise

Deuteronomy 32.48–52

And the Lord spoke to Moses on that same day and said, 'Go up this moun-tain in the Abarim range, Mount Nebo in the land of Moab opposite Jericho, and look out over the land of Canaan which I am giving to the Israelites as their own. And die on the mountain that you go up and be gathered to your father's kin. For you were unfaithful to me both at the waters of Meribah in the wilderness of Zin and you did not regard my holiness among the Israelites. So you shall see the land before you, but you shall not enter that land which I am giving to the Israelites.'

On that eventful day Moses is shown as giving his final words to the people. He has taught them an extensive song of warning and testimony. And now the Lord bids Moses climb Mount Nebo east of Jericho to have a wide view of the territory west of the Jordan. Thus the veteran mediator, servant of the Lord, will glimpse the Promised Land and then die. And so it was, as related in Deuteronomy 34, and the Lord buried him still in Moab east of the Jordan, and the grave was never to be found.

The judgement on Moses and his brother is referred to in several other places, but the nature of their offence is never clarified. In one place indeed (Deuteronomy 1.37) Moses says it was because of the people that he incurred the Lord's anger. At all events, we are left wondering about an offence which could not be forgiven so faithful a servant and about which the records are vague in the extreme. And in the end the testimony stands that Moses surpassed all the old prophets in his face-to-face knowledge of God (Deuteronomy 34.10).

There is something profound in the tradition that could not say what Moses had done wrong or where his tomb was, and could only record that he came within sight of his goal but never reached it, alive or dead. It seems a parable of human hopes and ideals. The earthly fulfilment eludes us, though we may get near. The way leads into the beyond. Centuries later, it was to be said that Moses and other heroes of faith did valiantly, but did not receive what God had promised, for they were not to reach perfection without the redeemed whom Christ was yet to bring (Hebrews 11.39–40).

The Standing Stone Hears and Bears Witness

Joshua 24.14–28

[Joshua speaks to the assembly in Shechem] 'Now therefore, fear the Lord and serve him wholeheartedly and faithfully. Put away the gods which your ancestors served beyond the River Euphrates and in Egypt, and serve the Lord. And if you do not want to serve the Lord, choose this day whom you will serve, whether the gods your ancestors served beyond the Euphrates or the gods of the Amorites in whose land you dwell. But as for me and my household, we will serve the Lord.'

And the people answered and said, 'Perish the thought that we should forsake the Lord to serve other gods, for the Lord our God it is who brought us and our ancestors out of the land of Egypt, from the slave camps, and did those great signs in our sight, and preserved us all the way we went among all the peoples through whom we passed. And it was the Lord who drove out before us all the peoples, the Amorites who dwelt in the land. Therefore we also will serve the Lord, for he is our God.'

But Joshua said to the people, 'You cannot serve the Lord for he is a holy God and a God of zeal. He will not forgive your rebellion and your sins. If you forsake the Lord and serve alien gods, then he will turn and bring misfortune on you, and make an end of you after having done you good.' To this the people answered, 'No, but we will serve the Lord.'

Then Joshua said to the people, 'You are witnesses against yourselves that you have chosen to serve the Lord.' And they said, 'We are witnesses.' And he said, 'Then put away the alien gods that are among you and incline your heart to the Lord, the God of Israel.' The people answered him, 'The Lord your God we will serve and to his voice we will listen.'

So Joshua made a covenant for the people that day and he drew up a statute and an ordinance for them in Shechem and wrote it in the book of the law of God. And he took a great stone and set it up there under the oak in the sanctuary of the Lord. And Joshua said to all the people, 'See, this stone shall be a witness against us, for it has heard all the words of the Lord which he spoke to us. It shall therefore be a witness against you if you are false to your God.' Then Joshua sent the people away to their own homes.

The tribes have assembled at the great central sanctuary of that time, Shechem. Joshua, successor of Moses, addresses them and challenges them to make a formal decision, ratified by witnesses and recorded in a book kept in the sanctuary – a decision to choose to worship the Lord alone. The people readily make such a decision. Their profession of faith cannot be faulted. Yet it is evident that other gods are still honoured among them, up to that very moment. It is not so surprising, for it remains the case even to our own day, that excellent outward profession may be combined with an underlying farrago of conflicting loyalties and values.

Joshua writes up the proceedings in the form of a covenant, an agreement with promises from both parties, and he sets up a great natural stone to be a standing stone under an oak in the sanctuary as a witness. The stone, he says, has heard all the words of the Lord spoken to them.

Such a sacred stone, common in world religions, was banned in later reforms. But here we have the older view where the standing stone is one instance of the sensitivity of the natural world to the ongoing work and will of God. Mountains, skies, trees, animals are often shown as living before God, responding to him no less than humans. It is not exceptional, for example, when a great prophet speaks at length to the mountains and says to them, 'Hear the word of the Lord' (Ezekiel 36).

The Oppressor Slain by a Woman's Hand

Judges 5.19–31

> Kings came, they fought,
> Then fought the kings of Canaan
> At Taanach by Megiddo's waters,
> But had no profit from it.
>
> From heaven above they fought
> Stars in their courses fought against Sisera.
> The torrent Kishon swept them away
> The rushing torrent, the Kishon torrent.
> March on my soul, with might.
>
> Oh the hammering hooves of the horses
> As they gallop, his mighty ones gallop away!
>
> 'Curse Meroz,' says the angel of the Lord,
> 'a deadly curse on its folk,
> for they gave no help to the Lord,
> they were not at his side in the battle.'
>
> Of all women blessed be Jael,
> wife of Heber the Kenite,
> of women in tents most blessed!
>
> When he asked for water she gave him milk,
> A fine bowl of curds she brought him.
>
> She reached out her hand for a tent peg,
> Her right hand for a labourer's mallet.
> And she hammered Sisera, she pierced his head,
> She struck and drove through his temple.
>
> By her feet he bowed, he fell,
> he lay, by her feet he bowed, he fell,

where he bowed there he fell down, dead.
Through the window she peers, she gazes,

The mother of Sisera, through the lattice.
'Why is his chariot so long in coming,
why tarry the hoofbeats of his chariots?'

Her wisest princess answers her,
As already she answers herself:
'Are they not finding and sharing the spoil,
for every man a girl or two,
spoil of dyed stuffs for Sisera
of dyed stuffs with embroidery,
two pieces of dyed work embroidered,
spoil for my neck . . .?'

So, Lord, let all your enemies perish,
but those who love you be like the sun
when he rises in his might!

Our passage is the climax of a very ancient ballad-like hymn composed soon after the event in the twelfth century BC – one of the world's oldest poems and very skilful. As it happens, there is a prose account of the dramatic event in the preceding chapter.

The song takes us into the heart of a tribal society in the highlands of Palestine that lived in constant fear of attack. Especially in the north, the tribes have suffered from powerful kings in the lowlands, and now Deborah, prophet-leader and national mother, has summoned them to a war of the Lord. At her call ten thousand men leave their occupations and families and muster on Mount Tabor. The enemy, commanded by Sisera, gather below, professional troops with an overwhelming force of nine hundred chariots.

Confident that the Lord is at their head, the tribesmen charge down the slopes. Suddenly the river bed in the plain is engulfed with a torrent from the mountains, and conditions for the iron-clad Canaanite army are appalling. They are routed, and Sisera, fleeing on foot, seeks refuge with a Bedouin clan that has been at peace with him. But they are Kenites, zealous worshippers of the Lord and not likely to be neutral in his war.

Exhausted, Sisera is led by Jael to rest in her tent. She seems hospitable and brings him a splendid bowl of *leban* (like yoghurt). He relaxes and sleep beckons. But the hardy nomad woman means to strike the final blow in the Lord's battle. Taking up a mallet, she drives a tent peg through his head.

The singer gives her the highest praise. But we, far removed from that ancient life and death crisis, may condemn her deceitful hospitality and violent deed. For the ancient folk the main point was that the Lord had worked through the circumstances to answer the cry of his people. He used the very powers of heaven to defeat the great army, and he used the hand of a Bedouin wife to kill their commander and show that military might was nothing before him.

A third woman comes into the ballad. We see her gazing out through the palace window, straining to see the victorious return of her son, to hear the distant thud of his mighty chariotry and horsemen. She is the mother of Sisera, and as she thinks up reasons for his delay, the awful truth is dawning.

'So perish all your enemies, O Lord' – yes, and perish all that makes for enmity and war.

Blinded Samson's Last Prayer

Judges 16.23–30

Now the lords of the Philistines had gathered to make a great sacrifice to their god Dagon and to rejoice, for they said, 'Our god has given Samson our enemy into our hands.' And when the people saw him they praised their god and chanted, 'Into our hands our god has given our foe who has laid waste our land, and multiplied our slain.'

And when their hearts were merry they said, 'Call for Samson that he may make sport for us.' And they called for Samson out of the prison and had their sport with him. And when they put him between the pillars, he said to the boy who held him by the hand, 'Let me feel the pillars on which the temple rests, so that I may lean on them.'

The temple was full of men and women and all the lords of the Philistines were there, and on the roof there were about three thousand men and women watching the sport they made of Samson.

Then Samson called to the Lord and said, 'O Lord God – remember me, I pray, and strengthen me just once more, that I may be avenged on the Philistines for one of my two eyes.' And Samson took hold of the two central pillars on which the temple rested, grasping one with his right hand and the other with his left, and he bowed with all his might. And the temple fell upon the lords and all the people who were in it, so the dead he slew at his death were more than those he slew in his life.

The legendary exploits of Samson had been recounted in a series of localized folk tales marked by a crude humour. At some stage there was woven into them a religious element, with Samson being consecrated from birth and his marvellous strength being linked to that consecration. In the end Samson can perhaps be seen as a man of high calling and gifts who proved unworthy of them and yet could still turn to God in his last moments and be used by him. The setting is the period of tribal life beginning to be disturbed by the pressure of the Philistines, an efficient people who may have come from north of Greece via Crete and settled on the coastal plain. The mighty Samson has caused them much trouble in single-handed exploits, but in our extract has come to his tragic end. They have captured him, put out his eyes and set him to turn the grinding stone in the prison.

At a great feast of the Philistine god Dagon, Samson is brought to the temple to be made sport of, to the delight of the drunken worshippers. It has every appearance of being a celebration of Dagon's triumph over the Lord, the God of Israel. But the fallen hero, blinded and tormented, yet managed to pray, and the mocking revellers fall in the ruin of Dagon's temple under the dramatic judgement of the Lord.

It is a moving and dramatic story. Yet it calls to mind a very different occurrence, its very opposite. For the dying Christ will also stretch out his arms and bow with his last strength and last prayer. But those he will save by his death will outnumber by far the many he saved in his earthly life. The prayer of vengeance has not the strength of the Christ-prayer of forgiveness.

The Foreigner's Faithful Love

Ruth 1.1–19

Once in the days when the judges ruled there came a famine in the land. And a man from Bethlehem in Judah went with his wife and two sons to stay a while in the territory of Moab. His name was Elimelech and his wife's name was Naomi, and his sons were called Mahlon and Chilion. While they were there, Elimelech the husband of Naomi died and she was left with her two sons. These married Moabite women, one named Orpah and the other Ruth. They had been living there about ten years when both Mahlon and Chilion died, leaving Naomi bereaved of her two sons as well as her husband.

And now she arose with her daughters-in-law to return from the territory of Moab, for the news had reached her that the Lord had acted for his people and given them food. So she set out from the place where she had been living, accompanied by her two daughters-in-law. They had gone some way on the road back to Judah, when Naomi said to her two daughters-in-law, 'Go, return each to your mother's house. May the Lord show you faithful love as you have shown faithful love to the dead and to me. The Lord grant that you each find a home with another husband.' Then she kissed them and they wept aloud.

And they said, 'No, but we will return with you to your people.' But Naomi persisted, 'Go back, my daughters. Why would you go with me? Can I bear more sons to be your husbands? Go back, my daughters, go your way, for I am too old to marry again. If I should claim to have hope, even if I had a husband tonight and should bear sons, would you wait for them to grow up? Would you forbear to marry? No, my daughters, it grieves me greatly for your sakes that the hand of the Lord has gone out against me.'

And they lifted up their voices and wept again. And Orpah kissed her mother-in-law, but Ruth clung to her. And Naomi said, 'See, your sister-in-law has gone back to her people and to her gods. You too must go back as she has done.' But Ruth answered, 'Do not beg me to leave you and return from following you, for where you go I will go, and where you stay I will stay. Your people shall be my people and your God my God. Where you die I will die and there will I be buried. The Lord do so to me and more also if even death parts you and me.'

When Naomi saw that she was determined to go with her, she said no more to her. So on they went, the two of them together, until they came to Bethlehem.

We feel the poignancy of this opening to the story of Ruth when we take account of the ancient attitude to family continuance. There was great joy in the birth of a son because it was felt he would ensure the survival of the family line. The worst tragedy, it seemed, was the death of a husband before a son was conceived. But even then a last hope remained – the custom of a kind of proxy marriage (described in Deuteronomy 25). The dead man's brother, or another close relative, was encouraged to marry the widow, as it were on the dead man's behalf, and if she bore a son, he would be counted as the child of the late husband, continuing his family line. But in several stories we see that the dead man's relatives were often reluctant to enter such a proxy marriage, perhaps for economic reasons. A lot would depend on the fidelity of the widow, persevering in her late husband's cause with courage and, if need be, ingenuity.

In our story tragedy centres on Naomi, for she has passed from being the happy mother of two sons to being a childless widow, now too old to hope for a proxy marriage. It seems that her late husband's line will die out and her role as wife end after all in failure. 'Naomi' means 'My sweet one', but now she experiences a bitter fate.

As she sets off without hope to her own country, her two daugh-ters-in-law start with her, a gesture at least of fidelity. But these Moabite women have no real prospects in leaving their own people for an almost hopeless cause and soon Naomi declares them free of obligation and urges them to return to their own mothers. With many tears Orpah kisses her and departs. But Ruth will not swerve from her fidelity. Come what may, she will keep faith with her late husband and with Naomi.

They reach Bethlehem in springtime as the harvesting of barley begins. Ruth joins the poorest of the people in gleaning scraps in the fields, toiling from early morning to have something to take to Naomi. But now the blessing that was on her begins to appear. Where she toils on the open hillside turns out to belong to Boaz, a relative of Naomi's husband and so a possible partner in a proxy marriage. He learns who she is and of her faithfulness, and he protects her through the weeks of barley, then wheat harvest, and ensures she has plenty. 'The Lord recompense you for what you have done,' he says, 'and a full reward be given you by the Lord, the God of Israel, under whose wings you have come to shelter' (2.12). Naomi recognizes the hand of God and senses that the bitter time has passed. Hearing of Boaz she exclaims, 'Blessed be he by the Lord whose faithful love has not forsaken the living or the dead' (2.20).

The harvesting nears completion as Boaz and his men winnow the grain, working with the late evening breeze and then sleeping in the open to keep guard. Naomi plans to bring him to a decision, and Ruth follows her instructions as she creeps beside him in the night as though for a wedding night. The worthy man turns and wakes. Surprised, but with presence of mind, he explains to Ruth that first he must approach another relative with a better claim to her. She steals away before light, laden with a gift of barley, and that new day Boaz ascertains that the other relative does not wish to take up his right. So Boaz marries Ruth, who duly has a son counted as saviour of the family line of her late husband. The local women put it like this as Naomi cradles the baby in her arms: 'To Naomi a son has been born! Blessed be the Lord who has not left you this day without a protector. He shall be to you a restorer of life and a nourisher of your old age. For your daughter-in-law has borne him, she who loves you and is more to you than seven sons' (4.17,14–15).

Ruth's faithful love has reflected and expressed that of the Lord who does not forsake the living or the dead. It turns out to be important for the whole biblical story, for her son becomes the grandfather of King David and she has her part in the line leading to Jesus (Matthew 1.5; Luke 3.32). A law stated that Moabites should be forever excluded from the congregation of the Lord (Deuteronomy 23.3). But the faithful heart of Ruth, the young woman from Moab, brings a fuller revelation of the divine grace at work in all peoples.

4

The Lord Works through His Anointed King

A Child Hears the Voice of God

1 Samuel 3.1–12

Now the boy Samuel was ministering to the Lord under Eli's guidance. In those days the word of the Lord came seldom and no vision was disclosed. One night Eli, whose eyes were dim and his sight failing, was lying down in his place, and the lamp of God had not yet gone out, and Samuel was lying down in the temple of the Lord where the ark of God stood. And the Lord called Samuel and he answered, 'Here I am.' He ran to Eli and said, 'Here I am, for you called me.' 'I did not call you,' said Eli. 'Lie down again.' So he went and lay down. And the Lord called again, 'Samuel.' And Samuel rose and went to Eli and said, 'Here I am, for you called me.' 'No, my son,' he said, 'I did not call you. Lie down again.'

Now Samuel did not yet have direct knowledge of the Lord, and the Lord's word had not been revealed to him. And the Lord called Samuel the third time, and he rose and went to Eli and said, 'Here I am, for you called me.' Then Eli realized that the Lord had been calling the boy. So he said to Samuel, 'Go lie down, and if he calls you, say, "Speak, Lord – for your servant hears."' So Samuel went and lay down in his place, and the Lord came and stood and called as at other times, 'Samuel, Samuel.' Then Samuel said, 'Speak, for your servant hears.' And the Lord said to Samuel, 'See, I shall do something in Israel and both ears of everyone who hears of it will shudder. For on that day I will carry out against Eli all that I have spoken concerning his household from beginning to end.'

A vivid story has told how Hannah, long childless, came to have her son Samuel and how she dedicated him to be brought up in the service of the Lord at the central sanctuary of that time, Shiloh. Every year, making pilgrimage to the shrine, she would see her growing son and bring him a little coat she had made him. And God's blessing brought her three more sons and two daughters.

At the time of the present incident, Samuel may have reached a significant age – 12, according to tradition – and his lying through the night in the sanctuary near the ark (symbol of the divine presence) may have been in accordance with a custom of seeking a revelation. This would initiate him into a prophetic life. It was a time in his people's history when revelation was rare, and certainly Samuel and his guide Eli did not at first recognize it when it came. The boy, we can understand, was especially anxious for his blind tutor, and his first thought, on hearing his name called, was for him.

The message is of immense moment for the nation and the great sanctuary and its priests – Eli's indulgence of his evil sons is about to result in disaster. Entrusted to a child, the tragic word of the Lord announces a purging of corruption which in the end will bring good. Striking is the patience of the Lord in this coming to Samuel. He does not overwhelm but stands humbly waiting for the moment of recognition.

The passage has been treasured as a lesson in hearing God's voice. In times of godlessness such hearing will be rare. But when there is a child-like heart and the will to wait and watch at the Lord's threshold, he will come and he will speak. To the heart that will truly hear, in the spirit of willing service to the Lord, the message will unfold. As an old hymn has it,

> Oh give me Samuel's ear . . . quick to hear each whisper of thy word.
> Oh give me Samuel's heart . . . that still moves at the breathing of thy will.
> (James Drummond Burns, 1823–64)

God's Hand at Work in Simple Things

1 Samuel 9.1–16

There was a man of the tribe of Benjamin whose name was Kish . . . a man of substance. He had a son named Saul, a fine young man. Among all the Israelites there was none more handsome than he. He stood head and shoulders above any of the people. Now the herd of female donkeys belonging to Kish had strayed, and Kish said to his son Saul, 'Take one of the servants with you and set off to look for the donkeys.' So they went through the hills of Ephraim and then through the region of Shalishah, but did not find them. Then they went through the region of Shaalim, but still no trace. All through the territory of Benjamin they went but still no sign of them. When they came to the region of Zuph, Saul said to the servant who was with him, 'Come, let us go back, or my father will give up worrying over the donkeys and start worrying about us.'

The servant answered, 'But see, there is a man of God in this town, a prophet who is highly esteemed because all he says comes true. If we go up there he may advise us about the search we are making.' Saul said, 'But if we go, what can we bring for the man of God? There is no bread left in our packs and we have no present to bring him, nothing at all.' The servant answered, 'See, I have in my hand a quarter of a shekel of silver that I can give to the man of God to guide us on our way . . .' [v. 10] Saul said to his servant, 'Good, let us go to him.' So they made for the town where the man of God was.

Just as they were going up the ascent to the town, they met some girls coming out to fetch water, and they asked them, 'Is the seer in the town?' They answered, 'He is. See, he is just ahead of you. Hurry now because he has come today to the town as the people have a sacrifice at the hill-shrine. Just as you enter the town you will meet him before he goes up to the shrine for the meal. The people, you know, will not eat till he comes. He blesses the sacrifice, and only then the people who are invited begin to eat. Go up now, for this is the moment to find him.'

So they went up to the town, and just as they were entering it, Samuel was coming out towards them on his way to the hill-shrine. Now the day before Saul came, the Lord had revealed the event to Samuel, saying, 'Tomorrow about this time I will send to you a man from the territory of Benjamin, and you shall anoint him to be leader over my people Israel. He shall save my people from the hand of the Philistines, for I have seen the suffering of my people and heard their cry.'

Our story brings us to the threshold of a new era in the nation's history, the rule of kings. The loose tribal society guided by leaders called 'judges' is about to give way to a more authoritarian and efficient system, able to withstand attack from without, but still recognizing the overarching rule of the Lord, the true King. Samuel, the last of the judges, is now old and his sons are corrupt, and he is guided to make Saul the first king.

Some chapters show the development as driven by the people's desire rather against the wishes of the Lord and of Samuel, who in the end conceded. But our extract is the opening of a more favourable account where the initiative is said to be God's and the development is seen as welcome. Here the story is told in a charming style and as it was experienced on the ground. So the events happen naturally – donkeys stray. Search is made, Saul wearies, the servant has a good suggestion, the excited girls burst out of the town gate at the right moment, and so on

– but we grow aware that guiding these ordinary human events is the hand of God. It is he who begins and steers the development that in the fullness of time will lead to the anointed Saviour-King, the Christ. The anointing itself is understood to be done by God acting through his minister. With it comes soon the gift of the Spirit, changing Saul's heart, so that he becomes 'another man' (10.9) – we might say, born again.

Pondering, we wonder about the ordinary events we move in daily. Is the hand of God at work in them? Has he a purpose in the frustrations and obstacles that redirect our way? Does he still work through animals? Is there still a man or woman 'of God' – someone dedicated to the Lord, close to him – who can sense his purpose and give true guidance?

Saul Healed by Music

1 Samuel 16.12–23

Now the Spirit of the Lord had left Saul and a harmful spirit from the Lord would sometimes trouble him. Saul's servants said to him, 'Let our lord now command your servants who attend you to find a man skilled in playing the lyre. Then if the harmful spirit from God comes on you he will play with the hand and you will be well again.' So Saul said to his servants, 'Find me such a man who can play well and bring him to me.' At this, one of the attendants spoke up: 'Now I have seen a son of Jesse of Bethlehem who is skilled in playing, and also a brave man, experienced in war, wise in speech and a handsome man, and the Lord is with him.'

So Saul sent messengers to Jesse, saying, 'Send me David your son who is with the flock.' And Jesse took a basket of bread and a skin of wine and a kid and sent them with David his son to Saul. So David came to Saul and attended on him. Saul thought well of him and made him his armour-bearer. And Saul sent word to Jesse, saying, 'Let David continue to attend me, for I think highly of him.'

So it came about that whenever the harmful spirit from God came on Saul, David would take up his lyre and play softly, and Saul would grow calm and at ease and the harmful spirit would leave him.

Saul has come to a difficult time in his reign. It seems as though God has withdrawn the power that enabled him to do great things and sometimes sends instead a spirit of depression. And so it comes about that the young David is brought to serve him, ready as need be to comfort the king with his playing of the lyre – playing softly with the hand, rather than with the bolder plectrum.

Such music was thought of as communion with the other world, like an angel carrying prayer up to God or blessing down from him. So Saul finds relief and is not wholly cut off from the grace of God. He will continue valiantly to defend his people from the powerful Philistines, and all the while the hand of God is at work, raising David gradually towards the royal succession.

Saul and His Heir Die in Battle

1 Samuel 31.1–13

Now the Philistines were fighting against Israel, and the men of Israel fled before them and fell slain on Mount Gilboa. And the Philistines pursued Saul and his sons closely, till they slew Jonathan, Abinadab and Malkishua, sons of Saul. And the troops pressed on hard against Saul, and the archers hit him and he writhed with the wound. And Saul said to his armour-bearer, 'Draw your sword and thrust it through me, or these uncircumcised men will come and pierce me and make sport of me.' But his armour-bearer, fearful of the sacrilege, would not do it. So Saul took his own sword and fell on it. And when his armour-bearer saw that Saul was dead, he also fell on his sword and died with him. So, on that one day, they all died together: Saul, his three sons, his armour-bearer and all his men.

When the Israelites who lived by the side of the valley and across the Jordan saw that their army fled and that Saul and his sons were slain, they fled, abandoning their homes, and the Philistines moved in and occupied them. Next day, when the Philistines came to strip the dead, they found Saul and his three sons as they had fallen on Mount Gilboa. They cut off his head and stripped him of his armour, and they sent runners through the surrounding Philistine areas with victory tidings for the temples of idols and for their people. Saul's armour they put in the temple of Astarte, and they fastened his body on the wall of Bethshan.

But when the inhabitants of Jabesh-Gilead heard what they had done to Saul, their valiant men set off and went all night and recovered the bodies of Saul and his sons from the wall of Bethshan. They returned to Jabesh and burnt them there. Then they took the bones, buried them under the tamarisk tree in Jabesh, and fasted seven days.

Saul resolutely continues his main duty of defence against the Philistines to a bitter end. In this his last battle he sees his army annihilated and his three sons killed in the pursuit, including his heir Jonathan, beloved friend of David. Gravely wounded by an arrow, he commits suicide, since his bodyguard and armour-bearer refuses to strike the Lord's anointed, though neither will he go on living without him.

But the final humiliation, when the royal corpses are hung on the walls of Bethshan, is suddenly relieved. Across the Jordan valley and southwards, within view of Bethshan, lies the town of Jabesh-in-Gilead, and its people have never forgotten how the young king Saul came dramatically to their rescue from a cruel tyrant (1 Samuel 11). So now some brave men of Jabesh set off to rescue those bodies, going hard all through the night to traverse some 20 miles and a river crossing and take the Philistines by surprise. Back again in Jabesh, the unusual cremating of the bodies may be intended as a purification after the ill-treatment. The sacred burial of the bones and the week's fasting mark their grief and deep respect for Israel's first king.

In spite of all, then, Saul is not left without love and honour. He is one of those tragic figures who cannot fulfil early promise. But to the end he tries to do his duty, and he has at least made a necessary and important beginning on which David and Solomon can build.

God's Promise to the House of David

2 Samuel 7

When the king dwelt at home and the Lord had given him respite from all his enemies round about, he said to the prophet Nathan, 'See how I live in a house of cedar while the ark of God dwells within the curtains of a tent' . . . [v. 4] That same night the word of the Lord came to Nathan, 'Go and tell my servant David: Thus says the Lord, "Do you think to build a house for me to dwell in?" . . . [v. 11b] The Lord promises that he will make you a house, for when your tally of days is full and you lie at rest with your ancestors, I will exalt your child after you. It is he who shall build a house for my name, and I will establish the throne of his kingdom for ever. I will be his father, he my son. If he does wrong I shall punish him with blows, but never will my faithful love leave him as I took it from Saul. So your house and kingdom will be made sure for ever before me. Your throne shall be established for ever"' . . . [v. 18] Then King David went in and sat before the Lord and said, 'Who am I, Lord God, and what is my house that you have brought me thus far? . . . [v. 28] And now, O Lord God, you alone are God, and your words will come true, and you have promised this great thing to your servant. May it then ever please you so to bless the house of your servant that it may indeed continue for ever before you, for you, O Lord God, have spoken it and with your blessing shall the house of your servant be blessed for ever.'

In the unsettled period following the death of Saul, David becomes settled at Hebron as king of the southern tribe Judah. Seven years later he is welcomed as king by the other tribes also, and he loses no time in capturing the ancient non-Israelite city of Jerusalem to be his capital, standing neutrally between the two blocks of his kingdom, which David has united only with great tact and patience. In his new peace and prosperity, David turns his thoughts to the building of a temple. He has already brought the ark, symbol of the Lord's presence, to rest in Jerusalem, but to make Jerusalem the centre in the hearts of all his subjects he needs to build a worthy sanctuary. But the message from the Lord through the prophet Nathan is that this building will be accomplished by David's successor, one of his sons – Solomon, it turns out. However the theme of house-building is now turned about. As though in appreciation of David's intention, the Lord promises to make David a house for ever in the sense that the reign of his family line will continue for ever.

This promise is repeated in later years and becomes central to the biblical story. History will show a great reduction in the domain of the dynasty after Solomon's death, for the northern block of tribes breaks away and forms its own kingdom. Even more dramatically, the Babylonians (from present-day southern Iraq) put an end to the dynasty's reign of over four centuries amid great destruction and displacement. Yet the promise of God is never forgotten and it becomes the basis for the faith that he will one day fulfil it by sending a greater David, the Lord's Anointed or Messiah, to reign in God's name for ever.

In world history many dynasties rise and fall, as do nations themselves. A few show great persistence, and such was David's. But our extract points to a treasure beyond historical fortunes. It witnesses to the birth of a hope that the Lord himself will one day establish his own reign of joyful peace. This he will do by sending a Servant-King who will truly represent him, truly mediating the divine power and love worldwide and to eternity.

David's Chain of Sin

2 Samuel 11.1–15

At the spring of the year, the time when kings go on campaign, David sent Joab, the royal guards and the whole muster of Israel, and they brought destruction to the people of Ammon and laid siege to their capital. But David himself remained in Jerusalem.

One evening David rose from his couch and was walking on the roof of the palace when he saw from there a woman bathing, and she was very beautiful to see. He sent servants and inquired about the woman and was told, 'Is not this Bathsheba, daughter of Eliam and wife of Uriah the Hittite?' Then David sent messengers and brought her, and she came in to him and he lay with her, for she had purified herself from her uncleanness. And she returned to her house. In time she conceived and sent and told David, 'I am with child.'

So David sent word to Joab, 'Send me Uriah the Hittite.' And Joab sent Uriah to David. David asked him how Joab fared, and the army and the campaign. Then David said to Uriah, 'Go down to your house and take your ease after your journey', and as Uriah went out a present from the king was sent after him. But Uriah slept at the outer door of the palace with all the servants of his lord and did not go down to his home. And when this was told to David, he said to Uriah, 'Have you not come from a journey? Why have you not gone to your home?' And Uriah answered, 'The ark and Israel and Judah dwell in tents and my commander and the guards of my lord are camping in the open. Should I then go to my house to eat and drink and sleep with my wife? By your life and soul I will not do this.'

David then said to Uriah, 'Stay here today and tomorrow I will let you go.' David invited him to eat and drink at his table and made him drunk. But in the evening he went out again to lie on his couch with the servants of his lord and still did not go home. Next morning David wrote a letter to Joab and sent it by the hand of Uriah. And in the letter he had written, 'Put Uriah at the front where the battle is fiercest and then withdraw from him so that he may be struck down and die.'

This is part of a narration centred on David's court and the question as to which of his sons would succeed him. This vivid account of events in the tenth century BC is one of the treasures of world literature and is unsurpassed in the Bible for its style and dramatic skill. We see David drawn down by his comforts. While he has dispatched his loyal guards and the whole muster of Israel to campaign in hardship across the Jordan, he remains in his palace, eating well and taking his siestas in the heat of the day. When the evening breeze gets up he rises from his couch and walks about on the flat roof of the palace, enjoying the views over the huddled houses to the surrounding hills and valleys.

But one evening he looked no further than the little courtyards of the houses, for he could, from his vantage point, see Bathsheba washing herself. Struck by her beauty, he makes enquiry about her, and although he learns that she is the wife of one of his faithful warriors, now dutifully risking his life for David at the front, his desire drives him to commit adultery. When Bathsheba becomes pregnant, he follows a plan of deceit.

He tries to get Uriah to go to his wife, only to be thwarted by the good man's faithfulness to his duty and his commanders. So David abuses his position as supreme commander to contrive Uriah's death. In trustful ignorance Uriah has carried to his commander his own death warrant.

The story will continue, relating how Uriah died, Bathsheba mourned, and David then took her to be his wife. He will be condemned by the prophet Nathan and be penitent, but many troubles will beset him, especially the tragic misconduct of his sons, which seems to flow from his own bad example.

But David is a sinner who yet holds on to the Lord. Psalm 71 seems to express well his prayer and praise:

> O God, do not stay far from me,
> Do not forsake me now that I am old and grey.
> Though you have shown me great troubles and ills,
> you will turn and revive me
> and bring me up from the depth of the earth again.

Because he can humble himself and weep for his sins, so the Lord's promise to his dynasty can remain.

Lament for Absalom

2 Samuel 18.9–33

Now Absalom found himself in the path of David's troops. He was riding on his mule, and as it ran under the thick branches of a great oak, he was caught up and left hanging in midair while the mule went on from under him. A man who saw it told Joab, 'I have just seen Absalom caught up in an oak tree.' Joab exclaimed, 'You saw him! Then why did you not strike him to the ground? I would have given you ten pieces of silver and a belt.'

'Though I should receive a thousand pieces of silver,' rejoined the man, 'I would not raise my hand against the king's son. For in our hearing the king charged you and Abishai and Ittai, For my sake protect the young man Absalom. And if I had treacherously struck a fatal blow, you would have set yourself against me.'

'I cannot waste time here with you,' said Joab. And he took three darts in his hand and thrust them at Absalom's heart while he was still alive. And ten young men who were Joab's armour-bearers closed in and struck and killed him. Then Joab blew the trumpet and the host returned from pursuing Israel, for Joab ordered them back. They took Absalom and threw him into a great pit in the forest and raised over him a very great heap of stones. And the men of Israel fled to their homes . . .

[v. 24] Now David was sitting between the outer and inner gates, and the watchman went up on the roof of the gate to the wall's edge. He looked into the distance and suddenly he saw a lone runner, and he cried out and told the king. And the king said, 'If he is alone there are good tidings in his mouth.' And he came on fast, getting ever closer.

Then the watchman saw another man running and he cried down to the gate, 'See, another man running alone!' The watchman cried again, 'I think the running of the first man is like that of Ahima'az son of Zadok.' And the king said, 'He is a good man and comes with good tidings.'

And now Ahima'az called out to the king, '*Shalom!* All is well!' And he prostrated himself before the king with his face to the ground and said, 'Blessed be the Lord your God who has delivered up the men who lifted their hand against my lord the king!' And the king said, 'Is it well with the young man Absalom?' Ahima'az answered, 'When Joab sent the king's servant and me your servant, I could see a great tumult but I did not know what it was about.' And the king said, 'Turn aside and stand here.' And he turned aside and stood still.

And the Cushite [the Ethiopian] ran up and said, 'Good tidings for my lord the king, for the Lord has delivered you this day from the hand of those who rose up against you.' And the king asked the Cushite, 'Is it well with the young man Absalom?' And he answered, 'Like that young man be the enemies of my lord the king and all who rise against you to do you harm!'

And the king was deeply moved and went up to the room over the gate and wept and as he went he said, 'O my son Absalom, my son, oh that I had died instead of you, O Absalom, my son, my son!'

Passing from our previous extract relating the scandal of Uriah's murder, we find events in David's life traced in a breathtaking sequence. His eldest son Amnon, the likely heir, becomes ill with desire for his half-sister Tamar and violates her. Her full brother Absalom murders him in revenge, conveniently bringing himself nearer the succession. Absalom flees the country, but after three years contrives to return and loses no time in plotting to become king. When he judges the time ripe, he launches his rebellion and is backed by all the northern tribes. David has to flee from his capital across the Jordan with his faithful guards and foreign mercenaries, still a formidable force. There some further support rallies to him and he is ready to join battle with Absalom and the mustered host of Israel.

The fighting spreads widely and the thickly wooded areas claim more victims than the sword. The professional and veteran troops of David have the better of it, especially when Absalom himself meets his end in

the manner related in our extract. The elderly David, at the request of his
men, has remained seated by the town gates, and is eagerly waiting for
news from the field. The lone runners, he thinks, must bring good news
as they outstrip all others and strive to be first to arrive and earn the
reward. Yes, it must be good news, he says three times.

But the runners' good news of victory seems nothing to him. He only
asks if Absalom is safe. The news then for him is shattering. His heart
breaks for his beloved Absalom, and realistic, earthy Joab, commander in
the field, upbraids him with remarkable bluntness: would he sooner all
his loyal men were dead and Absalom still alive? If he doesn't stop crying
for Absalom and come out and congratulate his troops at once, not a man
will stay with him.

David's troubles are not over. Eventually the next son in succession
to the throne, Adonijah, makes a premature attempt at it, but is skilfully
thwarted by the prophet Nathan and Bathsheba. They work on the old
king, and Bathsheba's son Solomon secures the succession, becoming
coregent with David.

What a story of lust, ambition, plotting, action, war! It is told in a
natural, earthbound way, and yet there are glimpses of an underlying
divine judgement, of guidance and answered prayer. We should not
suppose that even the running of the royal mule under the great oak tree
happened by mere chance.

Ask What You Will: Solomon's Choice

1 Kings 3.5–15

It was in Gibeon that the Lord appeared to Solomon in a dream by night. 'Ask
for whatever you wish me to give you,' said God.

Solomon answered, 'You have shown much faithful love to your servant
David my father, as he walked before you in loyalty and justice and honesty
of heart towards you, and you have continued for him this faithful love in
giving him a son to follow him on the throne this day. And now, O Lord my
God, though you have made your servant king in place of David my father,
yet I am but a little child, not knowing how to go out or come in. And your
servant is in the midst of your people, a people you have chosen, so great that
they are too many to count or record. So give your servant a listening heart to
rule your people, able to discern between right and wrong, for who is able to
rule this great people of yours?'

Solomon's answer pleased the Lord in that he had asked for this one thing.
'Because you have asked for this and not asked long life for yourself or riches

or the life of your enemies, but have asked for yourself discernment to hear what is right, see, I have done as you have asked and given you a wise and listening heart, so that there shall not be any among the kings like you all your days. And if you will walk in my ways, keeping my rules and commandments as your father David did, then I will give you long life.'

Then Solomon woke to find it was a dream. And he came to Jerusalem and stood before the ark of the covenant of the Lord and offered up burnt sacrifices and peace offerings, giving a feast for all his servants.

David now 'sleeps with his ancestors' (1 Kings 2.10) and is buried in Jerusalem. Bathsheba's son Solomon is established as the new king and early in his reign goes to worship the Lord at the hill-shrine adjoining Gibeon, a town 6 miles north-west of Jerusalem. It is likely that he is sleeping in the sanctuary, seeking revelation, when the Lord appears to him in a dream, bringing a blessing to shape the new reign.

The Lord's question is testing, but Solomon passes the test. Of all he could have wanted, he requests a 'hearing heart'. Whether turned to God or some aspect of nature or some human situation, the heart must be attentive, humble and open to learn, freed from the grip of selfishness. This is a listening heart, open to receive the wisdom and discernment so necessary in the ruler of a great state, father of a vast population. He has asked in effect for a contemplative heart, the spring of just and effective action.

Abundance of Wisdom Given by God

1 Kings 4.29–34

And God gave Solomon an abundance of wisdom and understanding and a width of mind as broad as the sands on the seashore. And Solomon's wisdom excelled all the wisdom of the peoples of the east and all the wisdom of Egypt. His fame spread among all the nations round about. He spoke 3,000 proverbs and composed 1,005 songs. And he spoke of trees, from the cedar in Lebanon to the hyssop that springs out of the wall. He spoke also of animals and birds, creeping things and fishes. And from all nations they came to hear the wisdom of Solomon, and from all the kings of the earth they came when they heard of his wisdom.

Following Solomon's prayer for a 'hearing heart', God gives him vast wisdom (it is clear to the biblical people that wisdom is a gift from God). Products of his wisdom are the numerous 'proverbs', concentrated little poems of observation which he has composed and is ready to speak on fitting occasions. Many also are his compositions designed to be sung with the lyre, musical poems of love and nature's wonders. While plants and animals often feature in these proverbs and songs, he also discourses out of a wide knowledge of earth's flora and fauna.

A beauty of such utterances is that though they are grounded in deep awe of the Lord and love for all the grace and order proceeding from his hands, yet they are readily received and treasured by people of all faiths and races. It is truly ecumenical discourse, and all the peoples can sit together in awe of the Creator, and meditate on the divine work which gives dignity and beauty to every creature in his living world.

There is a link here to the time when he who is the wisdom and power of God (1 Corinthians 1.24), he in whom are hidden all the treasures of wisdom and knowledge (Colossians 2.3), comes for the salvation of all.

Solomon's Prayer for the Temple

1 Kings 8.22–61

Then Solomon stood at the altar of the Lord before the whole congregation of Israel. Spreading out his hands towards heaven he said, 'O Lord, God of Israel, there is no god like you in heaven above or on earth beneath, keeping covenant with faithful love for your servants who walk before you with all their heart . . . [v. 25] So now, O Lord, God of Israel, fulfil for your servant David what you promised him, saying, "You will never lack a man before me to sit upon the throne of Israel if only your descendants take heed to their way to walk before me as you have walked before me" . . . [v. 27] But will God indeed dwell on earth? For see, the heaven and heaven of heavens cannot contain you, and how much less this house that I have built. Yet you will be open to the prayer of your servant . . . May your eyes be watching this house night and day, this sanctuary of which you have said, "My name shall be there." So you will heed any prayer which your servant prays towards this place and hear the supplication of your servant and of your people Israel when they pray towards this place. Hear in heaven your dwelling place, and when you hear, forgive.

'And for foreign people too, those not of your people Israel but come from a far country for your name's sake – when they shall come and pray towards this house, hear in heaven your dwelling place and do according to all that these foreigners implore you, so that all the peoples of the earth may know your name and fear you, as do your people Israel.'

Developing his capital Jerusalem on to a higher hill on the north, Solomon has completed a key building there, the splendid 'house of the Lord'. Now he dedicates it as the people gather for the great festival at the autumn new year. The ark of the covenant is solemnly brought from its tent-shrine in the old city and installed in the inmost shrine of the temple building, and Solomon now stands before the altar in the open court to offer a prayer of prayers – a supplication which will sound for ever, beseeching the Lord to answer all prayers that ever will be made in or towards this holy place.

The temple is 'the house of the Lord', his dwelling. And yet this prayer guards against a rude literalism. The presence of God in the sanctuary is here understood as his 'name' which he has put there. Through this self-expression, this 'name', he is truly there, giving and revealing himself, meeting humble worshippers. But his being is beyond temples, beyond earth, even beyond heaven.

Solomon gives instances of prayer that will be made from great need – the plight of accused persons; of national defeat, drought, famine, plague, exile. He asks that forgiveness and relief may be granted to those who pray in or towards this temple. And devout foreigners are also covered by the prayer. Some of them will make pilgrimage to the temple – may they be the first fruits of all the nations, when all come to know and fear the Lord.

Such giving of the holy 'name' and presence foreshadows New Testament themes of the Father's coming to us in the Son. Jesus is the self-expression of God in love, the name by which God is present. And through this name will come the breakthrough to all nations, the light that goes out to the Gentiles. And the church will always be strengthened in prayer by the knowledge that Christ's intercession is raised for ever, mightily joining with every cry of the believing heart.

5.

Struggles for Faithfulness to the Lord of History

The Prophet, the Ravens and the Widow

1 Kings 17.1–16

Elijah the prophet from Tishbe in Gilead said to Ahab, 'As the Lord lives, the God of Israel before whom I stand, there shall be no dew or rain in these years except at my word.' And the word of the Lord came to him: 'Go from here and turn eastwards and hide yourself in the valley of Kerith facing the Jordan. You can drink from the stream, and I have commanded the ravens to feed you there.' So he went and did as the Lord had commanded, living in the valley of Kerith facing the Jordan. And the ravens used to bring him bread and meat in the morning and again in the evening, and he drank from the stream. But after a while the stream dried up for lack of rain in the land. So the word of the Lord came to him: 'Rise, go to Zarephath in the territory of Sidon and live there. See, I have commanded a widow there to feed you.' And he arose and went to Zarephath.

When he came to the entrance of the town, see, there was a widow gathering sticks. So he called to her and said, 'Bring me, I pray, a little water in a vessel.' As she was going to fetch it, he called, 'And bring me, pray, a piece of bread in your hand.' But she answered, 'As the Lord your God lives, I have nothing but a handful of flour in a jar and a little oil in a flask. See, I am gathering a few sticks to go back and prepare it for myself and my son to eat before we die.'

'Have no fear,' said Elijah. 'Go and do as you have said, but first make me a little cake from it and bring it out to me, and afterwards bake for yourself and your son. For thus says the Lord the God of Israel: The jar of flour shall not be used up and the flask of oil shall not fail until the day that the Lord sends rain on the land.'

And she went and did as Elijah had said, and for many days she and Elijah and her household had enough to eat. The jar of flour was not used up or the flask of oil emptied, just as the word of the Lord had promised through Elijah.

After the long reigns of David and Solomon the great kingdom has broken apart. The northern tribes, 'Israel', are ruled by a succession of short dynasties, while Judah and Jerusalem continue under the descendants of David. A powerful king in the north has been Omri, who built the fine capital Samaria. His son Ahab, who is to reign twenty-two years, is married to a Sidonian princess, Jezebel. Throughout his reign and the reigns of his sons, Jezebel will be a powerful force, especially in promoting her Phoenician religion, the worship of Baal.

A cycle of tales about the prophet Elijah depicts a fierce contest between the followers of Baal and those of the Lord, as they struggle for the nation's soul. For Baal the queen wields the advantage of royal power, while for the Lord the often lonely figure of Elijah bears the brunt of the battle.

Our extract begins with Elijah on the offensive as he warns the king he faces a drought only the Lord can break, and then goes into hiding. The ravens that feed him are faithful servants of the Lord. The widow, too, herself a Sidonian, responds in faith, giving to the Lord's representative the little that stands between her and death. (The incident will take a drastic turn when the child dies of another cause, but the Lord answers prayer and restores him through the prophet.)

The 'widow's cruse' has remained to our time a parable of the Lord's provision for those who depend only on him. The ravens too have their message, as also the rain which returns at the Lord's bidding. These are inspiring signs which can lead us deep into the mysteries of trust in God and the discovery of his grace.

The Still Small Voice

1 Kings 19.3–16

Elijah was afraid, and he rose and went for his life and came to Beersheba in Judah. There he left his servant and went on a day's journey himself into the wilderness. Coming to a juniper tree he sat down under it and prayed that he might die. 'It is enough now, O Lord,' he said. 'Take away my life for I am not better than my ancestors.' And he lay down and slept under the tree.

Then see, an angel touched him and said to him, 'Rise and eat.' He looked round and there at his hand was a loaf baked on hot stones and a jar of water. So he ate and drank and lay down again. And the angel of the Lord came a second time and touched him and said, 'Rise and eat, or else the journey will be too long for you.' So again he ate and drank, and with strength from that food he went on for forty days and forty nights to reach Horeb, the mountain of God. There he found a cave and took rest . . .

[v. 11] Suddenly the Lord was passing by, and a great and stormy wind ripped over the mountains and smashed the rocks before the Lord, but the Lord was not in the wind. And after the wind came an earthquake, but the Lord was not in the earthquake. And after the earthquake came fire, but the Lord was not in the fire. And after the fire came a sound that was but a whisper. And when Elijah heard it, he wrapped his face in his cloak and went out and stood at the entrance of the cave.

And now a voice came to him, saying, 'What are you doing here, Elijah?' And he answered, 'I have been full of zeal for the Lord, the God of hosts, for the Israelites have forsaken your covenant, torn down your altars and killed your prophets with the sword, and I alone am left and they seek to take away my life.' Then the Lord said to him, 'Go back and make your way through the wilderness to Damascus. When you arrive anoint Hazael to be king over Syria, and Jehu son of Nimshi to be king over Israel, and Elisha son of Shaphat to be prophet in your place.'

The story of conflict between the Lord and Baal, between Elijah and Jezebel, has come to a tremendous climax in a national gathering on Mount Carmel. There the unique power of the Lord has been shown as he strikes the sodden altar with fire, and soon after breaks the drought with torrential rain. The discredited prophets of Baal have been put to death.

But now Elijah faces the wrath of Jezebel. He receives a message that she has sworn to kill him 'by this time tomorrow' (19.2). In fear he flees to the southern wilderness, towards the traditional 'dwelling' of the Lord on Mount Horeb. On the holy mountain he is given a revelation which lifts from him his fear and despair and sends him back to the conflict to consecrate new leaders. They will be instruments of judgement on the Baal faction, and one of them, Elisha, will be Elijah's successor. It is not yet disclosed whether Elijah is simply to be dismissed. Could it be that the Lord has some new service for him, in another place, and in highest honour?

Remarkable is the manner of the Lord's revelation. The hurricane, earthquake and fire go before him like heralds and outriders. But the sound of his own coming, his holy presence, is so fine, so slight, that you might miss it. Yet the soul of the prophet recognizes it. He knows it at once and wraps his cloak about his head to avoid a fatal glimpse of the overwhelming glory.

The story here is very deep. There is a contrast between the blaze of
lightning on Mount Carmel and the forerunners of tempest, quake and
fire on the one hand and the still small voice or sound on the other. The
intimate encounter with God which brings his voice into the soul and
changes and recreates a life is something secret, close to silence. In hidden
depths the new creation is made. In deepest quietness the God beyond
imagining is passing by.

The Mantle of Elijah

2 Kings 2.1–15

> When the Lord was going to take up Elijah by a whirlwind into heaven,
> Elijah had set off with Elisha from Gilgal. And Elijah said to Elisha, 'Stay
> here now, for the Lord has directed me to go as far as Bethel.' But Elisha
> replied, 'As the Lord lives and your soul lives, I will not leave you.' So they
> went down to Bethel, and the community of prophets who lived in Bethel
> came out to Elisha and said to him, 'Do you know that the Lord will take
> away your master from over you today?' And he said, 'Yes, I know, but do
> not speak of it.'
>
> Then Elijah said to him, 'Stay here now, for the Lord has directed me to
> go to Jericho.' But he answered, 'As the Lord lives and your soul lives, I will
> not leave you.' So they came to Jericho. And the community of prophets who
> lived at Jericho came up to Elisha and said, 'Do you know that today the Lord
> will take away your master from over you?' And he answered, 'Yes, I know,
> but say nothing.'
>
> And Elijah said to him, 'Stay here now, for the Lord has directed me to go to
> the Jordan.' And he answered, 'As the Lord lives and your soul lives, I will not
> leave you.' So the two of them went on. And fifty men from the community of
> prophets went out and stood to watch them from a distance as the two stood
> together by the Jordan. Then Elijah took his mantle and rolled it up and struck
> the water, which parted this way and that, so that the two of them could cross
> over on dry ground. As they crossed, Elijah said to Elisha, 'What would you
> have me do for you before I am taken from you?' Elisha replied, 'I pray you,
> let a double portion of your spirit fall on me.'
>
> 'You have asked a hard thing,' said Elijah. 'Yet if you see me as I am taken
> up from you, it shall be so for you, but if not it shall not be so.' And as they
> went on and talked, suddenly there appeared chariots of fire and horses of fire
> which parted them from each other, and Elijah went up in a whirlwind into
> heaven. Elisha saw it and cried out, 'My father, my father! The chariots and
> horsemen of Israel!'

Then he saw him no more, and he seized his own garments and tore them in two. And he took up the mantle of Elijah that had fallen from him, and he went and stood on the bank of the Jordan. Then with Elijah's mantle he too struck the water and said, 'Where is my Lord, the God of Elijah?' And as he struck it, it parted this way and that and Elisha crossed over. When the prophets from Jericho who were watching saw this, they said, 'The spirit of Elijah has come to rest on Elisha.'

In this story the 'sons of the prophets' have quite a part. Such groups were like monastic communities and lived in companies near sacred places. They had a master who was held in awe, and they gathered and handed down stories about his great deeds of the spirit. There was a cycle of such tales about Elisha, and our passage is its introduction, showing how he became the successor of Elijah.

On this fateful day, Elisha is aware that the Lord is about to take his master Elijah from him. The prophetic communities that Elijah is guided to visit for the last time are also aware of it, but Elisha forbids them to speak of it. The coming event is already clothed in mystery and awe, as well as grief.

Elisha, faithful disciple, will not leave his master's side. His request for a double portion of Elijah's spirit, the double share inherited by a first-born son, would, if granted, confirm him as Elijah's heir and successor. But it is a hard thing to ask because the prophetic spirit is not inherited but freely given by God. If the Lord lets him see the marvel of Elijah's ascension, it will be a sign of God's grace and so of the granting of the request.

Suddenly an apparition of a chariot (or chariots) and horses of fire comes between them and sets Elijah on his own and he is snatched up and away by a whirlwind. Only Elisha sees it well and in the grief of separation exclaims, 'O my father, my father – the chariotry and horsemen of Israel!' The great defender of God's people has gone, he who was worth more than any earthly army.

The incident of the mantle is a sign that Elijah's spirit has indeed passed to Elisha, as the prophets recognize when they acknowledge him as the revered master. After our extract it is related how the men of this community thought Elijah might have been whirled away by the storm only to be dropped again somewhere in the wild. For three days they scoured the countryside, but no trace was found, and the belief that he had been taken into heaven was accepted.

At that time death was commonly thought of as a passing for ever into silence and darkness, the ultimate sleep, the opposite of life. The story of Elijah's end would stand out for the people of that era – the Lord as sovereign over heaven and earth and death, the faithful servant whom he chose to take away from earth to a higher life in his presence. This tradition about Elijah is one of several influences which will lead through certain Jewish circles to the great hope of eternal life in the New Testament.

When the Eyes of Faith Are Opened

2 Kings 6.8–17

> The king of Aram was warring against Israel, and he consulted with his servants and concluded, 'In such and such a place I shall camp.' But the man of God sent word to the king of Israel: 'Beware of passing through this place, for the Arameans are going down to it.' And the king of Israel sent scouts to the place which the man of God had warned him of and he avoided danger more than once or twice. And the heart of the king of Aram was much troubled over this matter. Calling his servants together, he said to them, 'Will you not show me which of us is helping the king of Israel?' One of his servants said, 'No, my lord the king. It is Elisha the prophet in Israel; he tells the king of Israel the words you speak in your bedroom.' The king replied, 'Then go and find out where he is, and I will send and capture him.'
>
> The report came back: 'Behold, he is in Dothan.' So he sent a large force with horses and chariots, and they came by night and surrounded the town. And when the man of God rose early and went out, there was the army with horses and chariots encircling the town. Elisha's servant said to him, 'Alas, my master, what are we to do?' And he answered, 'Do not fear, for those who are with us are more than those who are with them.' Then Elisha prayed, 'O Lord, I pray you, open his eyes and let him see!' So the Lord opened the eyes of the young man, and he saw, and there was the mountain covered with horses and chariots of fire all around Elisha!

The circle of traditions about Elisha continues, memories from the communities of prophets. We see how prophets were involved in politics and military operations – they were revered for their psychic 'second sight' and their prayers which might be answered with miracles. In their popular style the tales have a certain crudity, but also elements of spiritual depth.

Rising and leaving the house at dawn, Elisha and his disciples find the little town encircled by the hostile forces come to seize them. Aghast, the young man cries out, 'O master, what are we to do?' It is typical of so many situations – the shock of sudden adversity or danger, the sense of no way out, the helplessness. But the man of God is prepared and calm, confident in the superior power of the Lord encompassing them. He prays for the young man until he too is enabled to see the angelic host protecting all around.

It still remains for Elisha to act, and in the sequel to our extract we find him praying again. This time it is for the dimming of eyes – the enemy's eyes. In their confusion the enemies are captured. But the prophet cures them and has them treated well, and even feasted. This kindness results in a period of peace.

Another curious tale, but memorable especially for those anguished eyes which were opened to see the mountain covered with the fiery forces of God's salvation.

Judah, the Last Standard-Bearer

2 Kings 18.13–15; 19.10–36

In the fourteenth year of Hezekiah's reign, Sennacherib king of Assyria attacked all the walled towns of Judah and captured them. So Hezekiah king of Judah sent messengers to the king of Assyria at Lachish, saying, 'I have done wrong. Turn back from my country. Whatever imposition you lay on me I will accept.' The king of Assyria demanded of Hezekiah 300 talents of silver and 30 talents of gold. And Hezekiah gave him all the silver from the house of the Lord and from the treasuries in his palace . . .

[19.10b, Sennacherib now demands surrender and sends this message] 'Do not let your god in whom you trust deceive you, saying, Jerusalem shall not be given into the hand of the king of Assyria. You have surely heard what the kings of Assyria have done to all the countries around, utterly destroying them, and shall you be saved?' . . .

[v. 14] And Hezekiah took the letter from the hands of the messenger and read it. Then he went up to the house of the Lord and opened it before the Lord. And Hezekiah prayed before the Lord and said, 'O Lord, the God of Israel, enthroned above the cherubim, you alone are true God of all earth's kingdoms. You have made heaven and earth . . . [v. 19] So now, O Lord our God, save us, I beseech you, from his hand so that all the kingdoms of the earth may know that you, O Lord, alone are God.'

Then Isaiah son of Amoz sent word to Hezekiah, saying, 'Thus says the God of Israel, What you have prayed to me concerning Sennacherib king of Assyria I have heard . . . [v. 33] By the way that he came, by that same way shall he return. And he shall not come into this city, says the Lord. For I will defend this city and deliver it for my own sake and for the sake of my servant David.'

> That night the angel of the Lord went out and struck in the camp of the Assyrians 185,000 men . . . So Sennacherib departed and went and returned to his residence in Nineveh.

Assyria (present-day northern Iraq) was extending its empire westwards. The smaller states in its path could sometimes submit and become vassals, paying annual tribute to the Assyrian king. Often, however, they formed alliances to resist, only to suffer defeat and devastation. The kingdom of Israel (the northern tribes) with its capital Samaria became enmeshed in this process. It was finally brought to an end in 721 BC after a terrible three-year siege of Samaria. The country became a province governed by the Assyrians, and some of its skilled population was deported and replaced by settlers from other Assyrian territories. There was a continuing community holding the old Israelite faith – the Samaritans – and even surviving to our own day, but these were scorned by the Judeans as partly of mixed descent.

Our extract concerns the fate of the southern kingdom, Judah, and Jerusalem. Their turn soon came to be devastated by the Assyrians, but the kingdom just survived, its final doom being postponed for a little over a century.

The progress of Sennacherib's invasion of Judah is clear at first, with agreement between the biblical record and the Assyrian annals. Most of the towns were built compactly on hills and defended by strong, wide walls. But the Assyrians captured forty-six of them and had just overcome the city of Lachish to the south-west of Jerusalem when Hezekiah sent his message of submission.

Not so clear is the history of the long story that now follows in 2 Kings (18.17 – 19.37), going over the ground twice, while the whole is repeated in Isaiah 36 – 37. It seems that Sennacherib, with pressures from home and from the rival great power Egypt, has decided that he needs a complete surrender of Jerusalem and sends a threatening demand to this effect. But he has to withdraw from the country when his campaign-weary army is smitten by plague. It is cause for celebration indeed in Jerusalem.

Yet all these accounts of tragedies and mercies in the history of the Lord's chosen city, dynasty and people raise profound questions about the nature of his promises and protection. On this occasion a 'remnant' was saved, but there were catastrophes yet to come for city, kings and people. We must conclude that their peace was not to be 'as the world giveth' (John 14.27 AV), but some more wonderful gift of God yet to be revealed. The inspiring poetry of Isaiah will play its part, focused as he is on the destiny of the royal house and city. And Hezekiah's action, when he spread out the letter for the Lord to read, gives a memorable example of simple faith. Who knows what miraculous turns in wars of our own time may have come from such full-hearted prayer?

The Book That Caused a Storm

2 Kings 22.3–13

It was in the eighteenth year of his reign that Josiah sent Shaphan the scribe to the house of the Lord, saying, 'Go up to Hilkiah the chief priest that he may reckon up the money which has been brought into the house of the Lord and collected from the people by the guardians of the threshold, and let it be given into the hand of the foremen in the house of the Lord to give it to the craftsmen repairing the house – the carpenters, builders and masons – and for buying timber and hewn stone for the repairs. But there shall be no accounting required for the money given into their hand, for they deal faithfully.'

And Hilkiah the chief priest sent word to Shaphan the scribe: 'I have found a book of the law in the house of the Lord.' And he gave the book to Shaphan and he read it. Then he came and reported to the king and said, 'Your servants have emptied out the money that was in the house and given it into the hand of the foremen in the house of the Lord.' And he added, 'Hilkiah the priest has given me a book.' Shaphan now read it to the king, and when the king heard the words of the book of the law, he tore his clothes and he commanded Hilkiah the priest and Ahikam the son of Shaphan and Akbor the son of Micaiah and Shaphan the scribe and Asaiah the king's attendant, saying, 'Go and consult the Lord for me and for the people and for all Judah concerning the words of the book that has been found, for great is the wrath of the Lord that is kindled against us because our ancestors did not listen to the words of this book and do according to all that is written for us.'

Assyria continued to dominate the region for most of the seventh century BC. So Hezekiah's son Manasseh, who is said to have reigned fifty-five years, had to remain subservient, and it is not surprising that the national religion in Judah and Jerusalem grew less distinctive and more tolerant of non-Israelite beliefs and practices. Manasseh's grandson Josiah came to the throne as a child of eight. By the time he was old enough to shape policy, Assyria, following the death of its last powerful king, was in rapid decline and the pressure on Jerusalem eased off. So Josiah now emerges as a king who can assert strict principles in the national religion and also regain something of the old Davidic kingdom.

Our extract tells of a key moment. During repairs in the temple, a book (or scroll) comes to light, probably a work related to our book of

Deuteronomy, and it is adopted as the programme for reform, especially the purging of alien practices from the temple and from the provincial shrines ('high places'). Indeed these latter were abolished, to leave only strictly controlled public worship in Jerusalem.

Towards the end of the century, however, a new pressure arose on the house of David, for Babylonia (present-day southern Iraq) took up the mantle of Assyria. The sons and the grandson of Josiah had to face fresh invasions and a slide into utter catastrophe. Yet the great call to serve the Lord alone, which Josiah heard and answered, had not sounded in vain. That fresh stream of faithfulness to the Lord, loyalty to his covenant at all costs, flowed on through many centuries of hardship and tragedy – and still flows.

The Death of Royal Jerusalem

2 Kings 25.1–12

Then Zedekiah rebelled against the king of Babylon. And in the ninth year of his reign, in the tenth month and on the tenth day of the month, Nebuchadnezzar king of Babylon came with all his army against Jerusalem and laid siege to it, building an enclosure all round it. And the city was under siege until the eleventh year of King Zedekiah. By the ninth day of the fourth month the famine was so bad in the city that there was no food for the ordinary people. Then the defences were broken open and the king and all his soldiers fled in the night through the gate between the two walls near the king's garden, although the Babylonians were ringing the city. They made for the eastern wilderness. The army of the Babylonians pursued the king and overtook him in the plains near Jericho when all his forces were scattered from him. They captured him and brought him up to the king of Babylon at Riblah where he passed sentence on him. They killed Zedekiah's sons before his eyes and then put out his eyes and bound him in chains and took him to Babylon.

In the fifth month, on the seventh day of the month (it being the nineteenth year of Nebuchadnezzar's reign), there came to Jerusalem Nebuzaradan, captain of the guard and servant of the king of Babylon. And he set fire to the house of the Lord and the king's house and all the houses of Jerusalem. And all the Babylonian forces who were with the captain of the guard pulled down the walls round Jerusalem. And the remnant of the people in the city and those who had deserted to the king of Babylon and any remaining craftsmen Nebuzaradan the captain of the guard took into exile. But he left some of the poorest people to be vine dressers and land workers.

With the rapid decline in Assyrian power, other contestants were drawn into the area. King Josiah met his death challenging the northward march of an Egyptian army. His successor Jehoahaz was at once deported by the pharaoh, who installed Josiah's second son Jehoiakim as vassal king. But it was the Babylonians (from what is today southern Iraq) who soon began to dominate the region and Jehoiakim switched allegiance accordingly. He was not a loyal vassal and so provoked a Babylonian invasion. He had died and been succeeded by his son Jehoiachin, aged 18, when the Babylonians laid siege to Jerusalem. Surrender in the year 597 BC led to the deportation of the young king with many leading people (including Ezekiel) and skilled workers. The Babylonians gave the city another chance, installing another vassal king, Zedekiah (Jehoiachin's uncle, aged 25). His was a difficult task and the pressures for independence proved too strong for him and he rebelled. So the Babylonian army came again in 587, and the final tragedy narrated in our passage unfolded.

With this cruel end of Zedekiah, the last to occupy David's throne, we think also of the grief for him in the sorrowful worship that was later offered amid the temple ruins. For these mourners, Zedekiah, the Lord's anointed, had been their life, the very breath in their nostrils. Thus went their lament before the Lord:

> Our pursuers were swifter than eagles in the sky;
> they chased us over the mountains
> and laid wait for us in the wilderness.
> The breath of our nostrils, the Lord's anointed,
> was caught in their traps,
> he of whom we said,
> Under his shadow
> we shall live among the nations.
> (Lamentations 4.19–20)

Yes, a cruel and bitter end for the last reigning Lord's anointed, heir of David.

A Glimmer of Hope

2 Kings 25.27–29

Now in the thirty-seventh year of the exile of Jehoiachin, King of Judah, in the twelfth month, on the twenty-seventh day of the month, Ewil- Merodak King of Babylon, in the year that he began to reign, showed favour to

Jehoiachin. He released him from prison and spoke kindly to him and gave him a seat above the kings who were with him in Babylon. So Jehoiachin changed from his prison clothes and ate at the king's table regularly all the days of his life.

In Babylon the long reign of Nebuchadnezzar has ended, and his successor marks his accession with an act of clemency to the poor King Jehoiachin who has been in exile and in prison for thirty-seven years. In placing this episode at the end of their book of Kings, the authors seem to say that, despite the catastrophe, all is not lost. The divine purpose with the house of David is not dead.

King Jehoiachin is a significant figure. It is possible that this long-suffering king is the suppliant in the great Psalm 119, and also that he is in the mind of the prophet who portrayed the Suffering Servant in Isaiah 53. Certainly, Davidic hopes were to be kindled briefly around his grandson Zerubbabel, who would attain a position of authority in Judah.

Yet the end of the kingdom was final enough, and only a transformation of the Davidic hope could be meaningful in the eras to come.

A Great Day for Jerusalem

Nehemiah 8.1–9

Then all the people gathered with one accord in the square before the water gate. And word was given for Ezra the scribe to bring the book of the law of Moses which the Lord had commanded for Israel. So Ezra the priest brought the law before the assembly, both men and women and all who could hear with understanding, on the first day of the seventh month. Facing the square before the water gate, he read out the book from early morning until midday to the men and women and those who could understand. And the ears of all the people were attentive to the book of the law.

Ezra the scribe was standing on a wooden platform made for this purpose. And he opened the book in the sight of all the people, for he stood higher than all the people. And when he opened it all the people stood up. And Ezra blessed the Lord, the great God, and all the people answered, 'Amen Amen', with raising of hands. And they bowed and knelt before the Lord with their faces to the ground. The Levites explained the law to the people as they remained in their place. And Ezra read from the book, the law of God, clearly and gave the sense, so that they understood the reading.

Then Nehemiah the governor and Ezra the priest and scribe and the Levites who were teaching the people said to them all, 'This day is holy to the Lord

your God, so do not mourn or weep.' For all the people were weeping when
they heard the words of the law.

The hopes and prayers that persisted through the half-century of exile
in Babylonia were not in vain. A sun now rose further east – the rising
power of Persia (present-day Iran). Its king Cyrus swallowed up the
Babylonian empire in 539 BC, entering Babylon to a peaceful welcome. He
launched a new policy towards the subjugated peoples. Deportees were
free to return home as they wished and provision was made for the restoration of temples. In Jerusalem a native governor was established and the
new temple was built and dedicated by 515 BC.

It was to be a long time, however, before the ruinous province would be
truly revitalized. Our extract takes us to perhaps the latter half of the next
century, when much-needed efforts to revive Jerusalem were still being
made. The benign Persian authority has commissioned Jews from Babylonia to bring fresh help – Nehemiah to rebuild the city walls and replenish
its population, and Ezra the learned priest to publish and widely promote
a book of 'the law of Moses'. This law will have been drawn up from old
traditions by scribes and priests among the Babylonian Jews. We cannot
know its contents, but no doubt it was part of the materials that were yet
to develop into our Pentateuch (the first five books of our Old Testament).

Early one new-year's day, a great holy day in September-October, and
before a great gathering in a space south-east of the temple precinct as it
was then, Ezra mounted a high pulpit specially constructed and began to
read aloud this 'law of the Lord'. It comes as a revelation to the people.
Their tears of lamentation arise from fear, for so much in their past life
has not been in accordance with these commandments. But they are
urged not to weep, but to rejoice for the Lord's presence on his holy day.
It is a time for acknowledging his greatness and rededicating to him the
whole life of the community.

Nehemiah Defends the Sabbath and Racial Purity

Nehemiah 13.15–31

In those days I saw people in Judah treading winepresses on the Sabbath
and bringing in sacks of grain and loading them on donkeys, along with
wine, grapes, figs and all kinds of loads, bringing them into Jerusalem on
the Sabbath day. I warned them not to sell food on that day. There were also
people of Tyre, who lived in the city, bringing in fish and all kinds of goods on
the Sabbath for the people of Judah and Jerusalem . . .

[v. 1 9] And when the gateways of Jerusalem began to grow dark before the Sabbath, I gave orders that the doors should be shut and not opened again till after the Sabbath. I placed some of my servants at the gates to see that no load was brought in on the Sabbath day. Once or twice merchants and traders in all kinds of goods camped overnight just outside Jerusalem. I warned them, saying, 'Why do you camp near the wall? If you do so again I will lay hands on you.' From that time on they did not come again on the Sabbath. And I commanded the Levites that they should purify themselves and come and guard the gates to keep the Sabbath holy. Remember this also in my favour, O my God, and spare me according to the greatness of your mercy.

Also in those days I saw Jews who had married women of Ashdod, Ammon and Moab. Half their children spoke the language of Ashdod or the other peoples and could not speak Hebrew. I remonstrated with them and cursed them and beat some of them and I pulled out their hair and made them swear by God, saying, 'You shall not give your daughters to their sons or take their daughters for your sons or for yourselves' . . .

And one of the sons of Jehoiada, son of Eliashib the high priest, had married a daughter of Sanballat the Horonite. So I chased him out of my presence. Remember them, O my God, because they have defiled the priesthood and the covenant of the priests and the Levites.

Thus I purified them from everything foreign and regulated the duties of the priests and the Levites, each in his work, and I provided for the wood offering at their appointed times and for the first fruits. Remember me, O my God, for my good.

Sent from the Persian king on a mission to improve conditions in Jerusalem, Nehemiah strove valiantly against many difficulties. With the restoration of the city walls, he was able to foster a Jewish community distinctive in its religion and life.

It seems that he wrote a kind of memoir of his activities, a vivid personal account which is now embedded within the broader records of the time. In our chapter he relates how he left Jerusalem for a while to report to the king. On his return he finds things have been slipping. A large room in the temple has been cleared of its store of sacred vessels and offerings and given over to the use of one of his adversaries, Tobiah the Ammonite, a worshipper of the Lord, but a man of mixed race. So out on the street goes all Tobiah's furniture, and the room is quickly purified and returned to its former use.

Then, on a Sabbath day, Nehemiah sees great activity of trade, with donkey loads of produce being brought into the city. When he has the gates shut against the Sabbath traders, merchants from the coast, partly resident in Jerusalem, set up their stalls outside the walls and can readily have goods hoisted up in baskets. With his usual vigour he drives them away.

He is particularly distressed at the readiness to arrange marriages across the racial divide – even the high priest's family are involved. Loss of the Jewish language among the children signals weakening of distinctive culture and religion. He records his fiercely corrective actions and prays that God will reckon all that he has done to his credit.

It all illustrates the tension in a community trying to preserve a racial purity bound up with laws of daily living. The policies sometimes offend our conscience (for example, 13.1–3). But Nehemiah and the other reformers from Babylonia, faithful in their day, did succeed in putting a protective wall round the religious community. This temple-centred society endured for another five hundred years. By that time, as we see in the Acts of the Apostles, provision was developed for the great numbers of foreigners who worshipped the Lord and who made a vital link to the era of Christ's church of all nations.

6.

A Drama on the Mystery of Suffering

The Sufferer Who Wishes He Had Never Existed

Job 3.3–26

Perish the day when I was born
and the night that said, 'A boy is conceived.'
Let that day be darkness and God above not seek it,
nor any light shine on it.
Let darkness and the shadow of death claim it,
cloud settle upon it,
all that blots out daylight dismay it,
dense darkness seize it.
Let it not rejoice among the days of the year
nor come into the reckoning of the months.
And let that night be barren,
no cry of joy ring out in it.
Let it look for light and find none
and never see the eyelids of the dawn,
because it did not shut the doors of the womb against me
and hide trouble from my eyes.
Why did I not die from the womb,
and give up my breath when I came out from the belly,
and why did the knees receive me,
and the breasts so that I should suck?
For now should I be lying still,
asleep and ever at rest . . .
[v. 17] There the wicked cease from troubling,
there the weary are at rest.
The prisoners take their ease together,
untroubled by the shout of the taskmaster.
The small and great alike are there,

and the slave is free of his master.
Why is light given to one in misery,
life to the bitter in soul,
who long for death, but it will not come,
and dig for it more than for buried treasure,
and then rejoice exceedingly,
glad indeed to find the grave?
Why is light given to one who sees no way ahead,
for God has hedged him in? . . .
The thing I fear overtakes me,
all I dreaded now befalls me.
I have no peace, no time of quiet,
I cannot rest for constant troubling.

The great book of Job has the form of a drama. A prologue gives the scene and background, and at the end an epilogue sums up the whole outcome. In-between, the characters make long speeches, each responding in turn. There are three rounds of such speeches by Job and his three consolers and then, originally, the Lord himself comes and speaks at length and Job makes brief response. An extra character, the young and confident Elihu, suddenly speaking at enormous length just before the Lord's appearance, probably represents a later expansion of the drama, blurring it, making it less radical, but no doubt helping its acceptability and so its preservation.

If it was indeed intended for dramatic presentation, it might still have been recited by one gifted speaker, or otherwise by one actor for the prologue and epilogue, one for Job, three for the consolers and one (prophet-like) for the voice of the Lord. The speeches are in poetry of the highest quality and would be heard with enchantment by the audience. Though the prologue and epilogue are in prose, they are composed in a gripping folk-tale style and vividly convey all the events which such early drama could not otherwise aspire to present.

The author explains the mystery of innocent suffering and for his central character he imagines Job, a man declared by God himself to be the best person on earth. Job is wholly good and true, fearing God and shunning evil. He is consequently blessed in family and possessions, comfort and honour. That is, till the heavenly prosecutor, 'the Satan' (the opponent), the angel who searches out people's faults, suggests that Job is good and loves God because it pays him.

The challenge must be taken up. It must be shown that the best fellowship of God and human beings is not based on such a false motive. So Job, knowing nothing of all this, has to go out into the darkness, deprived of all his wealth and health, tormented and disgraced, as the champion of faith.

Three dignitaries from other tribes have come to console and counsel him. Seven days and nights they have sat with the stricken Job, speechless and in mourning. Then, with our extract, the poetic speeches begin. Job, for so long submissive, bursts out at last in a bitter wish never to have existed. As it is, he can only long for the repose of death. Sheol, the place of the dead, is (as generally in the Old Testament) imagined as a dark and silent land below the earth, attractive only to such an acute sufferer who is never at rest.

Already we see that Job will not mince words. He speaks the truth he knows. He causes great offence to the conventional friends, but, in the end, unlike them, will have the approval of God.

Friends Conclude Job Has Brought It on Himself

Job 4.12–19; 5.3–7

[The senior friend, Eliphaz, speaks]
A word from above came stealing to me,
and my ear caught the whisper of it.
In a tangle of fantasies of the night,
when the world lay deep in slumber,
Terror took hold of me and shuddering,
making my very bones tremble.
The hairs of my flesh stood up
as a spirit glides before my face.
It stood still, but no face could I discern;
only a shape was before my eyes.
I heard the whisper of its voice:
'Can a mortal human being be just in God's sight,
a creature be pure before its maker?
If God puts no trust in his own servants
and charges his angels with faults,
How much more those who dwell in clay houses
with foundations made of mud' . . .
[5.3] I have seen fools taking root,
then suddenly their dwellings fall in ruins.
Their children were cruelly oppressed in court
with no one to deliver them . . .
Such misfortune does not grow from dust;
trouble does not just sprout from the ground.
We creatures of earth beget our troubles
as sure as sparks fly upwards.

Goaded from their long vigil of silent sympathy by Job's bitter words, the delegation of friends venture their advice. Eliphaz leads the way, taking the line that will only harden as the turn of speeches goes round and round. Their line of argument is full of proverbial wisdom, admirable in its right place, but their reasoning here is most wounding to poor Job. Without any evidence, the counsellors assume that Job has secretly committed some sin, enough to bring heaven's wrath upon himself. If he will confess and repent, he will be restored.

The argument is eloquently put. Do not all sin? And Eliphaz recounts how the truth was revealed to him in the night by an apparition from heaven. Authoritative indeed! Only we already know from the prologue of the drama that this line of argument, applied to Job, is as misguided as could be. It is an additional wound for the stricken man. But he will valiantly resist the relentless argument of his friends, till he keeps all his remaining strength for appeals to God.

In this fine portrayal of the eloquent and confident counsellors, the dramatist shows the dangers of a dogmatism that explains what it does not understand. There is a reason for Job's ordeal, but in the drama it is known only in heaven and never disclosed on earth. More appropriate in the friends was that initial sympathy of silence, humility and kindness.

Job Speaks to God in Bitterness of Soul

Job 10.1–22

> [Job speaks]
> My soul is sick of my life,
> I will give free course to my complaining,
> speaking out in the bitterness of my soul.
> I will say to God, 'Do not condemn me;
> show me why you are set against me.
> Is it your pleasure to oppress,
> despising the work of your hands
> and approving the plan of the wicked?
> Do you have eyes of flesh,
> do you see as mortals see?
> Are your days like the days of mortals,
> your years as mortals' years, that you should go searching for fault in me
> and seeking for my sin,
> although you know I am not guilty
> and no one can deliver from your hand?

Your hands have shaped and made me,
and now would you turn and destroy me? . . .
[v. 10] Did you not pour me like milk
and curdle me like cheese?
You clothed me with skin and flesh,
and knitted me together with bones and sinews,
You gave me life and constant care
and your providence watched over my spirit.
Yet these things you had hidden in your heart,
I know you meant this fate for me all along . . .
[v. 20] Are not my days few? Cease then,
let me alone that I may have a moment's gladness
before I depart, never to return
from the land of darkness and the shadow of death.'

Casting aside all caution. Job speaks freely to God and tries to make sense of his terrible fate. He has known God's love, evident especially in the intimate manner of his creation and the years of peaceful care. So what now is this terrible assault, the ruin of all his happiness, the constant pain? If only God would come and tell him what is happening! Or otherwise leave off the assaults, leave him a last interval of peace!

We see that for Job dialogue with the self-assured counsellors is losing importance. His heart and soul centre more and more on his relation with God. God is all to him, and there in the end he will find his peace.

Can Death Really Be the End?

Job 19.19–27

[Job speaks]
All my close friends abhor me
and those I love have turned against me . . .
Have pity on me, have pity on me, you my friends . . .
must you pursue me as God does?
When will you have enough of slandering me?
Oh that my defence could be written,
cut deep in an inscription,
with iron tool and filling of lead
engraved in the rock for ever!
Yet I know that my champion lives
and afterwards he will stand up on the dust.

And though my skin be consumed,
my flesh gone, yet I shall see God.
Yes, I myself shall see him on my side,
My own eyes shall see him estranged from me no more;
my heart within me faints for longing.

The speeches of the counselling friends have been ever more grieving to Job, as they openly suppose God has found him out in some wickedness and his only course is to repent. He grieves even more at God's apparent hostility, bringing on him so much unjustified suffering. But Job can never quite let go of his fundamental faith in the goodness of God, and here and there in his bitter laments this faith surges up.

So it is in our present extract. He has just lamented that God is acting like a fierce enemy, leading Job's dearest companions to abhor him. He appeals to the friends at least for pity. Must they join in the hostility of God? He anticipates that death will soon claim him and wishes that his protest of innocence could be preserved for ever like the lead-filled inscriptions cut in rock. And that wishful thought leads him to express a great conviction which suddenly rises like a vision in his soul. There must be, yes, there must be a 'redeemer', the champion who will stand up for him when he is dead, clear his name and secure the triumph of right and truth.

But who could do this against the weight of hostility from earth and heaven? Job now sees his champion more clearly: 'I shall see God.' It is God himself, revealed as no alien foe but as siding with Job. The visionary glimpse is enough to melt Job's heart with longing and love.

God Comes and Speaks to Job

Job 38.1–18

Then the Lord answered Job out of a whirlwind and said:
'Who is this that darkens counsel
by words without knowledge?
Gird up your loins like a man,
and I will ask you and you shall inform me.
Where were you when I founded the earth?
Tell of it if you have understanding.
Who decided its measurements – surely you know?
Or who stretched the line over it?
On what were its bases sunk,

or who laid its cornerstone,
When the stars of morning sang together
and the heavenly host all shouted praise?
Who shut up the sea with doors
when it burst out from the womb,
When I wrapped it in a garment of cloud
and in a swaddling band of fog,
When I made my boundary around it
and set up its bars and doors,
saying, "Thus far you shall come but no further,
and here shall your proud waves be halted" . . .
Have you come to the springs of the sea,
or walked in the recesses of the deep?
Have the gates of death been revealed to you,
have you seen the gates of the shadow of death?
Have you comprehended the expanses of the earth?
Tell me if you know all this.'

The counselling friends have failed to help, and Job has become wholly concerned to appeal to God. Through chapters 29 – 31 he has built up his final plea. Recollecting the happiness of his former days and his position of great respect in the community, he has shown up the appalling contrast now that all has turned against him. In the months of old, he says, God guarded and held a lamp over his head to guide him through every darkness. But now all his happiness and honour have vanished like a cloud before the wind. 'I have cried to you for help but you do not answer,' he says to God. 'You have changed and become cruel to me' (30.20–21b). And although his end seems near, he will still stretch out his hand and cry for rescue.

His final words are an oath of innocence. He swears that he is innocent of such crimes as people might suppose have brought on his troubles. Going through them one by one, he pronounces a solemn curse on himself if he is guilty of any of them (chapter 31). He is confident that no servant, no needy person, not even the ground he has farmed, will have a complaint against him. So his appeal stands: 'Oh that I had one to hear me! Behold my signature. Let the Almighty answer me!' (31.35)

As mentioned above, the block of chapters 32 – 37 is best regarded as an insertion by a later writer. Originally, then, Job's appeal was followed by that long-awaited event, yearned for so desperately: God's coming and speaking to Job. Our extract gives the beginning of that surprising and wonderful speech sounding out from the whirlwind. Surprising, because it does not engage with the foregoing arguments and protests.

The ironical questions and the theme of the marvels and mysteries of God's creation are not an answer or indeed an argument of any kind. Rather, they convey an experience of the Holy One, God beyond all our thoughts and imaginings and reasonings. Power, wisdom and, not least, beauty are revealed to such a degree that Job can only bow in worship.

Revelation through the Animals

Job 38.39 – 39.10

> Will you fetch food for the lioness
> and satisfy the young lions' hunger, as they crouch in the lair
> and lie in wait in their covert?
> Who provides the raven with its portion
> when its young ones cry out to God
> and wander in need of food?
> Do you know the birth time of the mountain goats
> or attend the wild does in their labour?
> Do you count the months they must fulfil
> and know the time for them to give birth?
> They crouch and bring forth their young ones
> and set free their offspring.
> Their little ones strengthen and grow,
> they go forth and do not return to them.
> And who has let the wild ass run free,
> and loosed the bonds of the swift ass,
> To whom I have given a home in the wilds,
> its dwelling in the salt lands?
> It scorns the tumult of the city,
> it hears no driver's shouts.
> The range of the mountains is its pasture
> and there it seeks out every green thing.
> Is the wild ox willing to serve you,
> will it spend the night by your crib?
> Can you bind the wild ox with rope in a furrow
> or will it harrow the valleys after you?

Speaking to Job from the whirlwind, the Lord has brought glimpses of his original creation, then of the care of all the immense elements as they function continually to this day, and now of the animals, especially those in the wild where he alone provides and cares for them. In the description there is appreciation of their beauty and amazing abilities. It is Hebrew poetry at its finest. But how does it answer Job?

The apparent irrelevance, disconnectedness, is part of the answer. The divine is not so accessible, so understandable as to be easily handled and packaged by masterful humans. But from Job's own reaction, which we shall come to next, the great speech has evidently brought him what he wanted most: a vivid revelation of God. Through contemplation of the creation, the wisdom and beauty of it all, there has been a deep meeting with the divine mystery. In an unexpected way, but with all his heart, the Holy One has come to his faithful servant.

Job Responds Awed and at Peace

Job 42.1–6

> Then Job answered the Lord and said,
> 'I know that you can do all things
> and no purpose is too hard for you to accomplish.
> Who is this that darkens counsel without knowledge?
> But I spoke of things I did not understand,
> things too wonderful beyond my knowing.
> Hear now, and I will speak and you shall inform me.
> I had heard of you by the hearing of the ear,
> but now my own eye has seen you.
> So now on the dust and ashes I melt away,
> and my heart is changed.'

Job's response to the Lord is notably short. It is not a moment for many words. In profound humility he expresses his utter inadequacy to speak of the ways of God. Those words of God still echo in his mind, prolonging the moment of confrontation, that transforming experience of knowing God so directly. Amazingly, the man whom God had pronounced as his best servant on earth can now say that his earlier knowledge of God was only indirect, like hearsay. But now he is immediately before the Holy One, his own eye seeing him. He melts away in self-abasement, deeply knowing the 'otherness', the marvellous mystery of the divine. Still on the ash heap, still so poor, he 'repents', not in the friends' sense of being penitent for secret sins, but as coming to a new mind. His heart is changed – we might say he is born again. And not because his sufferings have gone (as yet, they have not), but because he has known the Lord come to him and speak to him. His own eye sees him. In this directness all is changed and he finds peace.

God Openly Sides with Job

Job 42.7–17

> After the Lord had spoken these words to Job, the Lord said to Eliphaz the Temanite, 'My wrath is kindled against you and your two friends, for you have not spoken of me what is right as my servant Job has. Now, therefore, take seven bulls and seven rams and go to my servant Job and offer for yourselves a whole offering, and my servant Job shall pray for you, for to him I will show favour and grant his prayer that I should not deal with you according to your folly, for you have not spoken of me what is right as my servant Job has.' So Eliphaz the Temanite, Bildad the Shuhite and Zophar the Naamathite went and did as the Lord commanded them. And the Lord showed favour to Job and granted his prayer. And the Lord restored the life of Job when he had prayed for his friends and gave him twice as much as he had before . . .
> [v. 16] And after this Job lived 140 years and saw his children and his children's children to four generations. So Job died, old and full of days.

The interplay of speeches in poetry has been completed and now the author skilfully rounds off his drama with an epilogue in prose. Like his prologue, it is in folk-tale style, simple, charming and effective. Very decisively, it is told how the Lord pronounces Job in the right and the friends so wrong that to escape God's fury they must offer sacrifice for their misdeeds and beg Job to intercede for them.

The reason for Job's sufferings as given in the prologue is not disclosed to the protagonists on earth or even alluded to here. But the Lord's approval of Job is shown to the whole community by the granting of many more years of prosperous and happy life. In the framework of thought in that period, this was the clearest way for the story to show God's delight in Job.

The deeper perspective of our previous passage remains: in the vision of God, Creator and Saviour, Job has all. Not yet a belief in the afterlife. But Job, through all his pain, has held on to his conviction of God's ultimate fidelity. And that, in the end, is enough.

7.

Music of Prayer, Praise and Vision

The Son of God: Victor and Saviour

Psalm 2

> Why are the nations in tumult,
> and the peoples muttering folly,
> the kings of the earth rising up
> and the rulers conspiring together
> against the Lord and his anointed?
> 'Let us break their bonds,' they say,
> 'and throw off their cords from us.'
> He who is enthroned in heaven laughs,
> the Lord of all derides them.
> Then he speaks to them in his wrath,
> dismaying them in his anger:
> 'Enough that I have anointed my king
> on Zion, my holy mountain!'
> I will quote from the Lord's decree:
> he says to me, 'You are my son,
> this day have I begotten you.
> Ask of me and I will give you the nations as your heritage,
> the ends of the earth as your possession.
> You shall break them with a rod of iron,
> and shatter them like a potter's vessel.'
> So now be wise, O kings,
> Be prudent, you rulers of the earth.
> Serve the Lord with fear,
> rejoice before him with trembling.
> Pay homage sincerely, lest he be angry

and you perish from the way.
For his anger can blaze in an instant,
but happy are all who shelter in him.

Psalms were at the heart of ancient worship, not least at the Jerusalem temple, from which stems this collection of 150 psalms. They were musical and poetic chants of prayer and praise, but sometimes also of teaching and words that express the meaning of the ceremonies. Psalm 2 is one of those that served the Israelites in the ceremonies when a new king was installed. The ceremonies and chants gave a glimpse of God's action, as he anointed and empowered the king, thereby asserting the power of his own kingdom against evil in the world. The kings of the house of David, of course, were far from perfect, but such inaugural ceremony set forth the ideal and pressed towards it. When the monarchy was no more, such psalms were valued as visions of what would be when the perfect ruler, the Messiah (= 'anointed', 'Christ'), brought in the fullness of the kingdom of God.

In Psalm 2 the Lord's anointed one is imagined as remonstrating with rebellious rulers and peoples. They should reflect on the power of the Lord who means to crush the evil that spoils his world. Already, he warns, God has installed him as his royal Son and given him power to defeat evil and take possession of all the world for God. He quotes from a divine decree to this effect, a scroll of God's authorization given him at his enthronement. And he ends by exhorting the rebellious ones to be wise and return to God while there is time. That way there is happiness, the joy that all will have who put their trust in the Lord.

The psalm is taken in the New Testament as a prophecy of Christ, portraying the enmity against him, the resurrection that confirmed him as Son of God, and the certainty of his final victory (Acts 4.25–26; 13.33). And the message of this certainty is still heard from the psalm in worship today, along with the counsel to nations to turn from foolish ways and trust in the Lord.

Not Forsaken in the Land of Death

Psalm 16

Keep me, O God,
for I take shelter in you.
I say, 'Lord, you are my Lord,
I have no good apart from you . . .

The Lord is my portion and my cup;
it is you that hold my lot.'
My share has fallen in pleasant land,
my heritage shines fair upon me.
I will bless the Lord that he counsels me
and in the depths of night instructs my heart.
I will set the Lord always before me,
with him at my right hand, I shall not be overthrown.
Therefore my heart shall rejoice and my glory be glad,
and my flesh shall abide in safety.
For you will not abandon my soul to the land of death,
you will not hand over your faithful one to see the abyss.
You will cause me to know the path of life,
Fullness of joys before your face,
and pleasures in your right hand for ever.

In a time of danger a king might spend the night at the temple, as it were to shelter under the divine wings. In prayer and contemplation he would put his need before the Lord, and express his trust and his delight in the beauty of God's presence. His hope was that in the depth of the night, perhaps by vision or dream, the Lord would draw near and give him counsel and blessing, enabling him to go out in the morning to face the danger with confidence.

Psalm 16 seems to come from such a situation. The short prayer ('Keep me, God') is unfolded in statements of trust and wholehearted devotion. In the Lord alone he has hope, and from him alone he lives. As the priestly tribe owned no land but lived on a share of the temple offerings, so he counted God as his only true source of life and sustenance. The Lord himself is his lot and portion and heritage.

He expresses confidence that the Lord will come in the night to counsel and bless him. Bound in the faithfulness of God, he will not be abandoned to death. He will come through this crisis. Moreover, being close to the Lord as his chosen and anointed one, he will in some sense remain with him for ever.

The meditation of an ancient king was treasured centuries later as casting a prophetic light on the fate of Christ, the true Anointed, the Faithful One. It seemed to shine with the message of Christ's resurrection (Acts 2.25ff.; 13.35). God has not forsaken his Faithful One in the land of death, but caused him to ascend the path of life and fullness of eternal joy.

And still today Christians, led by Christ, pray on the lines of the psalm, 'Keep me, O God. I have no help but you, the very source of my life. In my darkness, come and counsel me and bless me. Bring me also up from the abyss, to walk with you the path of life for ever.'

A Mystery of Suffering and Salvation

Psalm 22

My God, my God, why have you forsaken me,
and are so far from my salvation
and from the words of my crying?
My God, I call you by day and you do not answer,
by night, and still I find no rest.
And you sit enthroned as the Holy One,
you that are the glory of Israel.
In you our ancestors trusted,
they trusted and you delivered them.
To you they cried and were rescued,
in you they trusted and were not put to shame.
But I am a worm, not a human being,
the scorn of all, despised by people.
All that see me mock me,
they curl their lips and wag their hands.
'He relied on the Lord,' they say, 'that he would deliver him;
let him save him, since he delights in him!'
But you were the one who drew me from the womb,
and laid me on my mother's breast.
On you I was cast at birth,
from my mother's womb you have been my God . . .
[v. 18] My garments they divide among them,
and cast lots for my clothing.
But you, Lord, do not stay far away,
O my help, come quickly to my aid.
Deliver my soul from the sword,
my poor life from the grip of the dog.
Save me from the lion's mouth,
from the horns of the wild oxen
you will surely answer me.
I will tell of your name to those who worship with me,
in the festal assembly I will praise you.
You that fear the Lord, praise him,
all you seed of Jacob, glorify him,

stand in awe of him, all you seed of Israel.
For he has not despised or abhorred the sufferer's pain,
he did not hide his face from him,
but heard when he cried to him . . .
[v. 27] Let all the ends of the earth remember and return to the Lord
and all the families of the nations worship before you.
For the kingdom is the Lord's,
and he is the ruler over the nations.
All the living shall eat together and worship,
and all gone down to death's dust shall bow before him,
for he has made my soul live again to him.
My soul shall serve him,
witness shall be borne to the Lord for ever.
They shall come and declare his saving work,
telling a people yet to be born all that he has done.

In the first half of the psalm the royal figure cries out from extremes of suffering. He is sinking into the land of death. In the second half we see him at the centre of a great assembly praising God for his salvation. Did some historical event give rise to the psalm, or was it part of a symbolic enactment in worship? The psalm at any rate rings out with prophetic force, penetrating far into the sphere of agony and the victory that lies beyond.

The opening puts sharply the point that this sufferer has been in closest bond with God, 'my God' (three times), on whom he placed his reliance and who had been there as a father ever since he was born. This chosen one, instead of reigning in glory on behalf of the heavenly King, is like a worm, despised, rejected. His body fails and death threatens in the shape of animal monsters – weird dogs, giant wild oxen, lions. God, he says, has already laid him in the dust of death. God the Helper, the Friend and Saviour, seems far away, forsaking his royal Son.

And yet this is all addressed to God. So the sufferer has not given up all hope, and his cry comes with a gleam of light – 'you will surely answer me.'

The second half of the psalm is set in a great service of thanksgiving in the temple. Praise and testimony resound, for the Lord has answered the sufferer's cry. And such a tremendous work of God is this, such a miracle of immense meaning, that it will summon all nations in generations to come to remember and return to the Lord. Through it the kingdom of God will shine forth, and its force of life will touch even the realm of the dead.

The psalm has first voiced the tragedy of Godforsakenness, sharpest when promises and hopes are high. Yet it has held on to prayer, held on to faith. And then it lets the light flood in, as God proves true to his promise. The New Testament will draw on it to portray the crucifixion, the mockery, the sharing of the garments, the sufferer's great cry, and then (Hebrews 2.12) the miracle of salvation. The psalm's anticipation of a witness that will sound for ever, a life-giving call to all the world, becomes a prophecy of the gospel of Christ crucified and risen.

God Lets Holy Jerusalem Be Destroyed

Psalm 74

Why, O God, have you so utterly rejected us,
why does your anger burn against the flock of your pasture?
Remember your congregation which you purchased long ago
and redeemed as the tribe for your own possession;
remember the hill of Zion where you dwelt.
Lift your steps to the utter ruins,
to all that the enemy has done in the holy place.
Your foes roared in the place for your worship,
instead of its signs they set up their standards.
They were like warriors with axes,
swinging them on high in a thicket of trees . . .
[v. 10] How long, O God, shall the adversary taunt,
and the enemy utterly revile your name?
Why have you withdrawn your hand,
and held back your right hand in your bosom?
O God, my King of ancient time,
who did deeds of salvation in the midst of the earth,
It was you that cleft the sea by your power,
you that broke the dragons' heads on the waters.
You alone crushed the heads of Leviathan,
you gave him as food for the creatures of the desert.
It was you that cleft fountain and river,
you that dried up ever-flowing rivers.
From you came day, from you the night,
you established the sun and all the lights of heaven.
It was you that set up all the edges of the earth,
you that fashioned both summer and winter.
Remember, Lord, how the enemy derides,
how a foolish people scorns your name.
Do not give to wild beasts the soul of your turtledove,

or forget the life of your suffering ones for ever.
Look upon your covenant,
for the dark places of earth are filled,
filled with victims are the fields of violence.
May the oppressed not return ashamed,
but let the poor and needy praise your name.
Arise, O God, take up your own cause,
remember how fools revile you all day long.
Do not forget the voice of your enemies,
the din of your foes that sounds continually.

The end of the books of Kings showed us the tragedy of the destruction of Jerusalem by the Babylonians. Lamenting worship continued on the ruined site of the temple and no doubt included this passionate psalm. It urges upon God that it is his own house, his own name and presence that have been violated, and he is implored to come in his power against the enemy. That power, says the psalm, was shown in creation when (as ancient poetry related) he conquered the chaos that took the form of raging sea and sea monsters. By his might those waters were mastered and made to serve the purpose of life, the heavens also made and the seasons established in their fruitfulness. Will not that mighty hand act now against the present evil of chaos? Will not God save his beloved, his turtledove, from these savage ones?

The Lord's apparent tolerance of cruelties and blasphemies has remained an agony for his people. But related to the cross of Jesus such outrages can be brought towards a gleam of hope. The New Testament will tell how God's 'name' will again be violated – through his giving of his very self, his holy presence in his Son. The mighty hand again will not intervene. The soul of his turtledove is to be left to the cruel ones. The eye of contemplation will see all the world's tragedies as gathered there, and it foresees that the hidden victory of the cross will in the end be disclosed upon them all.

Jerusalem to Be Mother City of All Nations

Psalm 87

On the holy mountains is the city he founded.
The Lord loves the gates of Zion
above all the dwellings of Jacob.
Weighty things are spoken for you, O city of God:

'I enrol Egypt and Babylon as those who know me,
Philistia and Tyre with Ethiopia, each was born there.'
Yes, of Zion it shall be said, 'Each one was born in her
whom the Most High has established.'
The Lord shall record, as he writes up the peoples,
each one was born there.
And as they dance, they shall sing,
'All my fresh springs are in you.'

As the central place for the worship of the Lord, Zion (Jerusalem) appeared to the eye of faith as the gate of heaven, the dwelling place of God corresponding to his dwelling in heaven. Such a vision of Zion shines through this psalm, which has also a weighty word of God to announce to the city, promising an amazing destiny.

The singer, with the inspiration of a prophet, sees God writing up a register of peoples, and hears him declare that all, including great enemies of the past, are to be registered as knowing him and as natives of Zion. It is like a second birth for them, all becoming united as one family, loving and praising the Lord together with joyful dance and witnessing to the fresh springs of life that they drink in this transfigured Zion.

It is a wonderful vision, given with all the weight of God's own word. It will live afresh in the New Testament, where already nations come together in Christ, knowing a citizenship that is of heaven (Philippians 3.20) and belonging to a Jerusalem that is above, the mother of many children (Galatians 4.26).

One Who Dwells in the Shadow of God

Psalm 91

You that sit in the shelter of the Most High,
and rest in the shadow of the Almighty,
saying to the Lord, 'My refuge and my strength,
My God, in whom I put my trust',
he shall deliver you from the fowler's trap
and from the word that would destroy.
He will cover you with his pinions,
and you will shelter under his wings,
his faithfulness will be your shield and rampart.
You shall not fear the terror of the night
nor the arrow that flies in the daytime,

the pestilence that walks in the darkness
nor the plague that destroys at noon . . .
Since you have made the Lord your refuge,
and God most high your stronghold,
no evil may befall you,
no plague come near your tent.
But he will command for you his angels,
to keep you in all your ways.
They will carry you on the palms of their hands
lest your foot should strike a stone.
You shall trample on dragon and cobra,
on lion and sea lion you shall tread.
'Because he loves me I will deliver him.
I will set him on high because he knows my name.
When he calls to me I will answer him
and be with him in danger.
I will deliver and glorify him.
With days unending I will satisfy him
And fill him with my salvation.'

The ancient ideal of the king, the Lord's anointed, his chosen, his Son, saw him as dwelling close to the heavenly King and Father as an eaglet nestling under the parent's wing. The psalm expresses this closeness beautifully, and in response to the king's trust and love spells out the marvellous care and protection which God will give him.

By the time of Jesus these promises would be related to the expected Saviour-King, the Messiah. In this sense it will be quoted in the story of his temptation (Matthew 4.6). If he threw himself from the pinnacle of the temple, the angels would bear him up, and his messiahship would be proved to all!

Christ will reject the glib suggestion, knowing that the Father's love works at a deeper level. For Christ, and then for all who follow him, the promises will often be hidden in an agonizing mystery. Trust is tried to the uttermost on a way that leads to fullness of life only through suffering and death.

The Stone the Builders Rejected

Psalm 118

[v. 5] From the grip of distress I called to the Lord,
the Lord answered and set me in a wide place . . .

All nations surrounded me,
with the name of the Lord I drove them back.
They surrounded me like bees,
they blazed like fire among thorns;
with the name of the Lord I drove them back . . .
I did not die but found new life,
that I might recount the deeds of the Lord.
The Lord sorely chastened me,
but he did not give me over to death.
Open to me the gates of salvation,
I will enter to give thanks to the Lord.
This is the gate of the Lord,
only the just may enter by it.
I will give you thanks because you answered me,
and you became my salvation.
The stone which the builders rejected
has become the head of the corner.
This has come from the Lord,
it is marvellous in our eyes.
This is the day that the Lord has made,
we will rejoice and be glad in it.
Come, Lord, give salvation,
Come, Lord, give prosperity.
Blessed be he that comes in the name of the Lord,
we bless you all from the house of the Lord.
The Lord is God and has given us light;
with green boughs link the dance
up to the horns of the altar.
You are my Lord and I will thank you,
my God, and I will lift high your praise.
Give thanks to the Lord for he is good,
his faithfulness is for ever.

An individual, probably the king, passes up the temple hill and through the gates to the great altar in the open court. He is part of a grand procession in the autumn festival, and with all his people he gives thanks for deliverance. Describing what seems to have been a symbolic ceremony of ordeal, he pictures how all nations attacked him, like angry bees or fierce flames. He was near to death, but when he invoked the power of the name of the Lord, he was saved. Chastened indeed and conscious of his own powerlessness, but exultant now in the faithfulness of the Lord, who with a mighty hand has raised him up. Such a blessed day, specially made by the hand of the Lord! With joyful calls and responses the procession moves about the altar. The branches of palm, myrtle and willow held by the worshippers link them all together and touch the four horns or spikes that rise at the corners of the altar, all symbolic of God's gift of new life.

'Blessed be he who comes in the name of the Lord' – so Christians would also echo the psalm in their own great 'thanksgiving', their Eucharist. For its drama would prove prophetic of Christ's humiliation and exaltation. Found just and true, he too will ascend through the gates of salvation, taking his people with him, rejoicing in God's day of light and life.

The Signs of the Kingdom of God

Psalm 146

Alleluia!
Praise the Lord, O my soul,
let me praise the Lord as long as I live,
make music to my God all my life long.
Put no trust in princes, nor in any human being,
for there is no salvation from them.
When their breath is gone they return to the earth,
on that same day their thoughts will perish.
Happy those whose help is the God of Jacob,
who set their hope on the Lord their God.
For he is the maker of heaven and earth
and sea, and all that lives in them,
keeping faith for evermore,
doing justice for the oppressed,
giving bread to the hungry,
the Lord who sets the prisoners free,
the Lord who gives sight to those that are blind,
the Lord who raises those who are bowed down,
the Lord who loves the faithful,
the Lord who watches over the strangers,
who upholds the fatherless and widow,
but overturns the way of the wicked.
The Lord shall reign for ever and ever,
your God, O Zion, throughout all generations.
Alleluia!

After so many prayers from the depths, the collection of psalms ends with a joyful series where the key note is 'Alleluia' ('Praise the Lord'). The worshippers shift the focus from themselves to him, trusting and testifying, for a while living only for him.

Psalm 146 combines praise of God's kingly power with teaching for the assembly of pilgrims. That God is King means first that he is the Creator, and then that he upholds and rules the world with his justice. Then he protects the vulnerable against oppression, feeds the hungry and heals the sick. Such enthusiastic praise tends to present the ideal of God's kingship, almost a vision of what will be when all is made right.

The gospels will show Jesus proclaiming the coming of God's kingdom, and it is this hope of the fulfilment which comes to the fore. And already in the present a wonderful anticipation can be experienced. As a sign of this, Jesus will not only preach, but also heal, comfort and set free. In his ministry the finger of God the King is already at work, bringing the royal salvation to the lonely and suffering ones.

8.

Wisdom in Nature and Society

Wisdom as Knowledge of God

Proverbs 2.1–5,10

> My child, if you will receive my words,
> and treasure in yourself my directions,
> inclining your ear to wisdom,
> and turning your heart to understanding,
> if you cry out for insight
> and call out for understanding,
> if you seek for her as silver,
> and dig for her as hidden treasures,
> then you will discern the fear of the Lord
> and find the knowledge of God . . .
> for wisdom will enter your heart,
> and knowledge will be pleasant to your soul.

'My child' or 'my son' – in Proverbs it is usually an individual student or disciple who is addressed by the teacher or sage. A kind of schooling is offered, particularly useful for princes and future administrators. There is indeed a lot of practical advice – on self-discipline, attentiveness humility, and so on – but underlying it all is a view of wisdom as from God the Creator. The world exists and functions through his wisdom, a wonderful right order. A wise person is essentially one who can live in harmony with this right order, this cosmic truth.

The wise person 'knows' and 'fears' the Lord, as is made evident in our extract. Characteristic, however, is the need for the disciple to be eager for this wisdom, to cry out for her (wisdom is often imagined as a female person, a confidante of God). The disciple diligently seeks her, studying and learning, growing in the way of reverence for the Creator and all his work, taking the knowledge and wisdom deep into heart and soul.

Wisdom as Faithful Love and Trust

Proverbs 3.1–8

> My child, do not forget my teaching,
> let your heart guard my commandments,
> for length of days and years of life,
> peace also they shall add to you.
> Never let faithful love and truth forsake you,
> but bind them around your neck,
> write them on the tablet of your heart.
> So shall you find favour and good understanding
> in the eyes of God and others.
> Trust in the Lord with all your heart
> and lean not on your own understanding.
> Know him in all your ways,
> and he will make plain your paths.
> That will be healing for your body,
> Medicine for your bones.

The sage's way calls for earnest commitment. The heart must guard and treasure the teachings. Kindness and faithfulness must become an inseparable part of you, bound about your neck, written on the heart as on a writing tablet. Above all you must stay close to the Lord, trusting him, looking for his guidance rather than depending on your own judgement; in every moment of life, be conscious of his decisive reality, 'knowing' or 'fearing' him.

The rewards are great: fullness of life, the approval of God and respect in the community, God's clearing of the path ahead, healing and peace in one's whole being. There is deep truth here, but a glib, superficial application could go far astray, as we have seen illustrated by the friends in the book of Job.

Wisdom as the Creator's Thought

Proverbs 8.22–31

> The Lord begot me in the beginning of his way,
> before any of his works, at the outset.
> In the dawn of time I was woven for birth,
> in the beginning before earth existed.

There were no oceans when I was brought to birth,
No springs heavy with water.
Before the mountain bases were sunk,
before the hills I was born.
Not yet had he made earth and fields,
nor the rims of the dry land.
When he fixed the heavens, I was already there,
when he drew a circle on the face of the deep,
when he set the skies above,
when he established the springs of the ocean,
when he appointed the sea its law
and the waters, not to pass the limit he had spoken,
when he marked out the foundations of the earth,
then I was at his side, his darling child,
and I was his delight day by day,
playing before him continually,
dancing through the good land of the earth,
and delighting in the human race.

The Creator's wisdom, imagined as a person, calls out to the throngs in the city gateway as they go about their getting and spending. She calls them from folly to wiser ways and sets the practical things of life – government, economics, morals – in the light of the cosmic order, the truth, right and beauty which God has given to uphold all things. When there is just rule, kindness, humility, quiet consideration of the good of the world, there is a blessing of harmony with the order of creation.

This lovely 'Wisdom' embodies that good order, and she stresses the authority and absolute priority of her message by recounting how she was already with God before anything was created.

She was already there, his 'darling child' (another reading has 'a skilled artist/architect'). Ever close to the Creator as he makes the universe, she is pictured dancing, playing, delighting in the emerging world and in the human race. Here we see that the creation is a matter of joy. Here is the spirit of beauty, fragility, tenderness, love. And she is the prior one, the meaning from the heart of God that must be heeded and must change our priorities. Through the clamour of the city's greed and strife her voice rings, so sweet and yet so strong.

When we come to the New Testament's message of the Word made flesh in Jesus, we shall see a close connection with this passage. For 'Word' (Greek *logos*) also means 'right order', 'meaning'. This Word represents God's thought and mind in every act of creation. So 'Word' and 'Wisdom' are virtually one, and to our passage we shall be especially grateful for the poetry and imagination that it brings to the conception.

Happy with a Little

Proverbs 15.16–17; 16.8; 17.24; 30.7–9

> Better is a little with fear of the Lord
> than great store and all the trouble with it.
> Better a meal of vegetables and love with it
> than a fatted ox and strife with it . . .
> Better is a little with right
> than great income without justice . . .
> The face of the discerning is turned towards wisdom,
> but the eyes of a fool are on the ends of the earth . . .
> Two things I ask of you, Lord,
> do not deny me them before I die.
> Put far from me falsehood and lies
> and give me neither poverty nor riches.
> Feed me just with the food necessary for me,
> lest I be well filled and deny you, saying, 'Who is the Lord?'
> or lest I be poor and steal,
> profaning the name of my God.

The short poetic proverbs were easy to memorize or copy. But they were each to be the focus of much reflection. They were gleams of truth gladly received from a mysterious world. The sage did not aspire to a masterful understanding of the world on a grand scale but humbly accepted such gleams as were given to light up a fruitful path of life. So the little sayings teach values such as discipline, restraint of appetites, attentiveness, humility, kindness, silence, work, trust and knowledge of God, and we shall sample some of these.

The present extracts advocate contentment with a little. Space is then left for the true values of life, such as love, and the knowledge of God. The roaming eye and the rushing far and wide of the greedy, superficial person are deprecated; better to be still and deeply satisfied with wisdom.

But the wise person does not seek utter poverty. The sage prays for neither poverty nor wealth, but just what is necessary to keep one's heart attentive to God.

Humility – Awareness of God

Proverbs 15.33; 26.12; 29.23

> The fear of the Lord is the discipline leading to wisdom
> And before glory comes humility . . .
> Do you see someone wise in their own eyes?
> there is more hope for fools than for them . . .
> The high pride of human beings brings them low,
> but one lowly in spirit shall have glory.

The first saying shows the close connection between the fear of the Lord and humility. One who is ever aware of the reality of God has the foundation of humility. The sage shrinks at the thought of those who have a high opinion of their own wisdom. They have made themselves unteachable and have quite mistaken the nature of wisdom.

Haughtiness only debases a person; lowliness is the true glory. For the humble person is close to the Lord and has a blessing that the arrogant have denied themselves.

In all such teaching, we may say, the sage sees all the virtues in the way of wisdom as arising from 'the fear of the Lord', that constant sensitivity to the presence and reality of almighty God.

Appointed Times of Sorrow and Joy

Ecclesiastes 3.1–8,11,15

> For everything there is an appointed moment,
> a time for every business under heaven,
> a time for birth and a time for death,
> a time to plant and a time to uproot what was planted,
> a time of killing and a time of healing,
> a time of breaking down and a time of rebuilding,
> a time to weep and a time to laugh,
> a time to mourn and a time to dance . . .
> a time of war and a time of peace . . .
> He has made everything beautiful in its time. Moreover he has put eternity in people's hearts, yet still they cannot find out what God has done from the beginning to the end . . .
> That which is has been already, and that which is to be has likewise already been. And God seeks again what has been driven away.

A surprising work to find in the Bible! Ecclesiastes is fascinating despite its pessimism. It is from about the third century BC but draws on ancient wisdom. The author presents a meditation in the person of King Solomon seven centuries earlier. It is a good choice, since the king was famed for wisdom and also for having all this world could offer. We read that over all human endeavours and achievements hangs the verdict of 'vanity', futility. But because this honest author faces life's tragedy without illusion, it is all the more poignant when we discern the light, sweet light, in the midst of the darkness, and the book has been greatly treasured by Christian teachers of the way to contemplation of God.

In the present extract the typical events of human life are set out in pairs of opposites. Each has its proper time – appointed by God. So we must recognize the limits of our initiatives. We must expect good times and bad, joy and sorrow, and in the one not forget the other.

God has made everything right for its time. Though he has given us a sense of distant past and future, we cannot comprehend his eternal work, and so we had best live in a sober humility.

Is there anything new? It seems as if the ages turn and return like the seasons. But here we realize our inability to view God's eternal work, and can only rest in the thought of his watching over it all and ensuring that the fading beauty should not be irretrievably lost.

Remember Your Creator While You Can

Ecclesiastes 12.1–7

> Remember also your Creator in the days of your youth, until the troublous days come and the years draw nigh when you will say, 'I have no pleasure in them', before the sun and the light and the moon and the stars grow dark and the clouds return after the rain, in the day when the keepers of the house shall tremble and the strong men stoop, and the women that grind give up because they are few, and those that look out through the windows are dimmed, and the doors to the street are shut, and the sound of the mill is faint and one gets up at the sound of a bird, and all the songbirds are silent, when steep places cause alarm and the way is full of terrors, and the almond tree shall blossom, and heavily goes the grasshopper, and the caper berry shall fail.
>
> For men and women go to their eternal home, and the mourners go about the streets, until the silver cord is snapped and the golden bowl is broken, and the pitcher smashed at the fountain, and the wheel broken at the cistern, and the dust returns to the earth as it was, and the breath returns to God who gave it.

Seeing the beauty of what we can achieve, our sage insists on full use of worthwhile opportunities – the satisfaction of simple toil, the enjoyment of sweet light and sunshine, and so on. Above all, we are to be mindful of our Creator while we have the freshness and vigour of life. Too soon ageing and death will come, and of these the author gives a haunting poetic description, its sad beauty reinforcing the message to use life well. Too soon the eyes will dim and the sweet light darken. The bright spells which in Palestine follow days of winter rain will not be seen.

Then images are taken from the decline of a great house. So the members of the body fail – hands, legs, teeth and eyes. It is the time of the tooth-less mouth, restless nights and deafness. The head is white as almond in blossom, the limbs bent and stiff, and the caper berry no remedy for the extinction of desire.

The professional mourners anticipate some earnings before the life has gone. That precious life is symbolized first by light – an oil lamp with precious bowl and cord – and then by water drawn from a fountain or hoisted from a rock-cut cistern. The cord breaks and the lamp falls, and likewise the water at well and cistern is lost from the broken vessel. But the spirit-breath returns to God, its source.

Is anything good really lost? Our sage indeed sees the vanity of human aspirations, but at the beginning and end is God, he who appointed our times and ever seeks and finds what is driven away. In him we may be content.

When the Winter of Death Is Over

Song of Solomon 2.8–13

> The voice of my beloved!
> Behold, he comes leaping over the mountains,
> skipping over the hills.
> My beloved is like a roe or a young hart,
> behold, he stands behind our wall.
> He looks in at the windows,
> peeping through the lattice.
> My beloved spoke and said to me,
> Rise up, my love, my fair one and come away.
> For lo, the winter is past,
> the rain is over and gone.
> The flowers appear on the earth,
> The time of the singing of birds is come,

and the voice of the turtledove
is heard in our land.
The fig tree puts forth her green figs,
and the vines in blossom are fragrant.
Rise up, my love, my fair one,
and come away.

The love poetry of the Song of Solomon (otherwise known as the Song of Songs – 'the Supreme Song'), was received by Jewish rabbis and later by Christians as expressive of divine love – the love between God and his people or (for Christians) between Christ and his church or individual believers. And if in the end there is only one Love, as there is only one Truth and one Beauty, then we understand how this poetry of young love came to be so treasured by the lovers of God.

In this passage the young woman imagines her lover leaping over the hills like a gazelle, so eager is he to find her. He peeps in at windows and calls her to come away with him into the spring-blessed land. Winter rain is over and has bequeathed a carpet of new grass and bright wild flowers over the hills. Birds sing among the blossoming trees. The whole world is touched by the Creator's love.

We are minded of Wisdom, his first-born Thought, his darling who danced and played and delighted in the freshness of the first dawn (Prov. 8). Yes, the way of the mystics is a good way. For all the teachings and revelations of God and all the life of service find their fulfilment in love.

9.

A Great Prophet and His Disciples

Isaiah Sees the Lord

Isaiah 6.1–10

> In the year that King Uzziah died, I saw the Lord sitting on a throne, high
> and exalted, and his train filled the temple. Seraphim attended him, and
> were calling one to another, saying, 'Holy, holy, holy is the Lord of Hosts. The
> whole earth is full of his glory.' And at each call the threshold shook to its
> foundations, and the house was filled with smoke.
>
> And I said, 'Ah me, I am lost, for I am a man of unclean lips and dwell
> amid a people of unclean lips, and my eyes have seen the King, the Lord of
> Hosts.' Then one of the seraphim flew to me, carrying a burning coal in his
> hand which he had taken with the tongs from the altar of incense. He touched
> my mouth with it and said, 'See, this has touched your lips and your guilt is
> taken away and your sin purged.'
>
> I heard the voice of the Lord saying, 'Whom shall I send and who will
> go for us?' Then I said, 'Here am I, send me.' And he said, 'Go then and tell
> this people: Hear indeed but understand nothing. See indeed, but perceive
> nothing. Coarsen the heart of this people, make their ears dull and close their
> eyes, in case they see with their eyes, and hear with their ears, and understand
> with their hearts, and turn again and be healed.'

In 642 BC a reign of forty years in Jerusalem has ended with the death
of King Uzziah. Now the people are gathered for the new-year festival,
when the Lord is manifest as King of all and destinies may be revealed.
The prophet Isaiah's vision brings him overwhelming awareness of
the reality symbolized in worship. Boldly he can relate that he saw
the enthroned Lord with the heavenly beings – fiery, multi-winged,
serpent-like creatures – in attendance. The symbolic identity of temple
and heavenly palace becomes real to him. He hears the tremendous cries
of praise, feels the quaking of the foundations, sees the temple filled

with the train of the Lord's robes and with the smoke of the incense of adoration.

Frail human, he can only survive by the purging of his sins, and then he is bold enough to offer himself as the Lord's messenger. To the assembled people he will bring their eagerly awaited new-year message. Alas, it is a heavy one. Ruinous invasions are foreseen, for the nation as a whole will continue to be insensitive to the Lord's will, refusing to turn about and so be saved.

No doubt Isaiah's work will not be wholly in vain. Some good seed will be sown. But the general prospect expressed here with a bitter irony is dark indeed. It will be a long, hard journey to find the fulfilment of Isaiah's name, which means 'The Lord saves'.

The Birth of Immanuel

Isaiah 7.10–17

Again Isaiah spoke to Ahaz and said, 'Ask for a sign from the Lord your God, be it from the depths below or from the heights above.' But Ahaz said, 'I will not ask and put the Lord to the test.' So Isaiah said, 'Hear then, O house of David. Is it not enough for you to weary others that you must weary my God also? Therefore the Lord will himself give you a sign. Behold, the damsel conceives and bears a son, and she will name him Immanu-el ['God is with us']. By the time he can reject evil and choose good he will eat curds and honey. For already the land of the two kings you abhor will be derelict. On you and your people and your father's house the Lord shall bring such days as have not come since the day the people of Ephraim broke away from Judah.'

The kings of (northern) Israel and Syria conspire to attack Judah to replace King Ahaz and have it join their alliance against Assyria. Fear grips Jerusalem, but Isaiah confronts Ahaz: if the king will trust in the Lord, the threat will melt away. Isaiah offers him a 'sign', a marvel of his own choosing to confirm the message. Ahaz declines it, wanting to distance himself from Isaiah's counsel and try a plan of his own.

Isaiah announces a sign all the same. He refers perhaps to the young queen. Within the time span of her pregnancy, help will have come against the foe, and accordingly she will name her son at birth 'Immanuel' (God is with us). As this child grows, within a few years, marvellous days could come for his people. Relief did come, but the king's lack of trust stores up future trouble.

The wording of the prophecy of Immanuel resembles poetry preserved on clay tablets in northern Syria at least a thousand years older. The prophet echoes this ancient poetry as he hints at divine marvel in the salvation which God will give through the house of David. Much later, about 200 BC, the learned Jewish scholars who translated the Hebrew Scriptures into Greek were sensitive to the layers of meaning in the prophecy. Instead of putting the plain 'young woman' for the Hebrew word *alma*, they rendered, 'Behold, the virgin will conceive and will bear a son . . .' This translation, quoted in Matthew 1.23, will have helped Christians accept the marvel of Mary's destiny.

The Birth That Brings Light

Isaiah 9.2–7

> The people that walked in darkness have seen a great light. Those who dwelt in the land of the shadow of death, on them the light has shone. You have increased the nation and filled them with joy. They rejoice before you as in a time of harvest or in the sharing of spoil.
>
> For the burdensome yoke and the staff at their shoulder, the rod of their oppressor you have broken as when Midian perished. And every boot of the trampling, storming soldiers and every garment rolled in blood shall be for burning, for fuel in the fire.
>
> For unto us a child is born, unto us a son is given. And the government shall be upon his shoulder. And his name shall be called Wonderful Counsellor, Mighty God, Everlasting Father, Prince of Peace. Of the increase of his dominion and of peace there shall be no end, on the throne of David and over his kingdom to establish it and uphold it with justice and right, from now and for evermore.
>
> The zeal of the Lord of Hosts shall accomplish this.

Around Isaiah's foreboding of ruin for the nation winds a thread of hope. He never ceases to offer hope to those who trust in the Lord. And somehow he always holds on to a deep belief that God will bring a marvellous salvation through the royal house or lineage of David. The present passage may be a prophecy given when a newborn prince was invested as heir to the throne. The prophet gives thanks that the nation that has walked in the deathly darkness of foreign oppression is now blessed with a light of salvation. The names or titles given to the royal heir in the ceremonies express the ideal. May he be a ruler wise in policies, brave and successful in war, father to his people, establisher of peace and prosperity.

It is all far from the present experience of troubled times, but the Lord in his 'zeal', his determined purpose, will accomplish it. The manner and the time – the rolling of the world's ages – all are known only to God. But the prophet is certain that the Lord is preparing such salvation, and that nothing is too hard for him.

When Wolf and Lamb Dwell Together

Isaiah 11.1–9

> Then a shoot will grow from the stump of Jesse,
> from his roots a branch will blossom.
> On him the Spirit of the Lord shall rest,
> a spirit of wisdom and understanding,
> a spirit of counsel and might,
> a spirit of knowledge and fear of the Lord,
> and in the fear of the Lord he shall delight.
> And he will not judge by a glance of his eyes
> or decide by what comes to his ears,
> but with justice shall he judge for the poor,
> and with fairness decide for the humble folk.
> He will smite the cruel with the rod of his mouth,
> and slay the wicked with the breath of his lips.
> Honesty shall be bound about his waist,
> faithfulness a girdle about him.
> And the wolf will dwell with the lamb
> and the leopard lie down with the kid.
> The calf and the lion will grow up together,
> with a little child to lead them.
> The cow and the bear will be friends,
> and their young will lie down together.
> The lion shall eat straw like the cattle,
> and the baby will play by the cobra's hole,
> and over the nest of the viper
> the young child will skip and clap.
> In all my holy mountain
> they will not kill or destroy
> For the earth shall be full of the knowledge of the Lord
> as the waters cover the sea.

Isaiah's vision of God's perfect kingdom is so far and yet so near. Far indeed from the current situation of his people, with its Davidic dynasty (Jesse being David's father) cut down from its treelike beauty and strength to a mere stump. But near all the same – near as God is near. In his sense of God's kingly power and the world ever in his mighty hand, Isaiah knew how swiftly the good kingdom could come. From the sad stump a new shoot would spring and blossom, a new David, possessed by the Holy Spirit.

Ruling with the Spirit's gifts, especially communion with the Lord, he will mediate God's peace to all the species. The ideal of Genesis (1.29–30), where all feed only on fruit and herbs, will be realized. No harming now. Everywhere love and peace, because everywhere the knowledge of the Lord.

Good Tidings for the Exiles

Isaiah 40

> Comfort my people, comfort them,
> says your God.
> Speak to Jerusalem's heart
> and proclaim to her
> that her bondage is served
> and her iniquity atoned,
> for she has received from the Lord's hand
> ample for all her sins.
> A voice proclaims,
> In the wilderness clear the way of the Lord,
> make straight in the desert a highway for our God . . .
> [v. 5] And the glory of the Lord shall be revealed
> and all flesh shall see it together,
> for the mouth of the Lord has spoken it . . .
> [v. 9] Go up on a high mountain,
> women with good tidings for Zion.
> Lift up your voice with strength,
> you with good tidings for Jerusalem.
> Lift it up without fear
> and say to the towns of Judah,
> See, your God! See, the Lord God!
> He comes as victor, his arm is ruler now.
> See, his spoils are with him,

his gains are before him.
Like a shepherd he tends his flock
and takes up the lambs on his arm
and carries them in his bosom
and leads the mothers to water.
Who measured the waters in the hollow of his hand
and marked out the heavens with a span,
enclosed in a measure the soil for the earth
and weighed the mountains in scales? . . .
[v. 28] The Lord is the everlasting God,
Creator of the ends of the earth.
He does not faint or grow weary,
his wisdom is past searching out.
He is ever giving power to the weary,
to the exhausted ample strength.
When the young tire and faint
and the young men fall exhausted,
those who wait on the Lord will find new strength.
They shall rise on wings like eagles,
they shall run and not be weary
– they shall walk and not faint.

With this passage begins a sequence of flowing, song-like prophecies (chapters 40 – 55) which presuppose a historical situation some century and a half after Isaiah's death. It seems that among the exiles in Babylonia about 540 BC was a circle of prophets continuing the line of Isaiah's disciples, guardians and continuers of his work. Sensitive to God's hand among the nations, as Babylon is about to succumb to the rising power of Persia, they believe he will bring a new era of liberation and restoration for his captive people.

When the exiles meet at the time of the old festivals and lament their forsakenness, these prophets bring a word of the Lord vibrant with hope. They see the coming of the Lord as victorious Saviour, leading his exiled people back to their homeland.

They dwell also on his power as Creator, for over the years the faith of the exiles, surrounded by the foreign temples and worship, has contracted. So the prophecies affirm his power over all, and not least to renew those who from long adversity are spiritually exhausted. As the great birds of the wilderness sweep over vast spaces by yielding themselves to the wind, so those who trust in the Lord rest on the power of his Spirit and are borne over every mountain and rugged way.

The Lord's Anointed Dies for Sinners

Isaiah 52.13 – 53.12

Opening oracle: The anointed will triumph
Behold, my Servant shall be triumphant,
he shall be very high, exalted, supreme.
Though many were appalled at him,
I have anointed his face above others,
his form above humankind.
So he shall purify many nations,
while kings shut their mouths before him,
for things never told they see,
and things unheard of they contemplate.

Choral unfolding of the mystery
Who has believed our revelation,
to whom has the working of the Lord been disclosed?
For he grew up like a shoot before him,
like a slip from arid ground.
He had no beauty, no majesty
that we should look and admire him,
no features that we should desire him.
He was scorned and avoided by people,
a man of sorrows, familiar with sickness.
Like one from whom all hide their face,
he was scorned and we disdained him.
But the ailments he bore were ours,
ours the torments he carried.
We were thinking him plagued,
smitten by God and punished,
but it was for our sins he was pierced,
for our wrongdoing he was crushed.
On him came the punishment for our well-being,
and through his wounds came healing for us.
We had all strayed like a flock,
we had all gone our own way,
but the Lord laid on him
the fault of us all.
He was ill-treated and afflicted,
but he did not open his mouth.
He was led like a lamb to the slaughter,

and like a sheep silent before its shearers
he did not open his mouth.
Of power and rule he was deprived,
and who gave heed to his rank?
He was cut off from the land of the living,
for the sin of my people he was stricken.
He was given his grave with the wrongdoers,
his burial mound with the outcast,
though he had done no harm,
and there was no wrong in his mouth.
But the Lord had willed to crush him with suffering,
truly his soul made an offering for sin.

Concluding oracle: new life and victory
He shall see his descendants, long life shall he live,
by his work the will of the Lord shall prosper.
The outcome of his soul's pain
he shall see and be satisfied.
By his knowledge the Righteous One makes right,
yes, he rights the multitudes,
for it is he who bore their guilt.
Therefore I give him the multitudes as his share,
and the masses he may take as his spoil,
as reward for exposing his soul to death
and being numbered with sinners,
though truly he bore the sin of the multitudes
and for sinners interposed himself.

Echoing the poetry of Jerusalem's old festivals, the Isaiah prophets have proclaimed that 'the Lord is King' (52.7) – he comes to his holy city as conqueror and deliverer. In their imagination the old ceremonies of procession live anew.

In those new-year festivals the theme of God's kingship involved presentation of the role of his Anointed, his royal Servant, the ideal of the one who would carry out God's wishes on earth. With roots in ancient tradition, this ideal seems to have involved an element of suffering – the king who gives himself in sacrifice for his people, 'the many', and who, like the innocent scapegoat, bears away their sin. At all events, this is the royal portrait the Isaiah prophets now present as part of their message of salvation. The Lord's Anointed One is here deprived of his outer glory, suffers to the death and is assumed to have been stricken by God for some sin. But the prophets reveal that it was for others he suffered, giving himself to make them right with God and whole. And the Lord will give him new life and joy in reward for his sacrifice.

The prophets do not give a name or a time to this royal figure. He remains hidden as though waiting for God's moment. It will not be surprising, however, when the apostle Philip preaches Jesus to the great man from Ethiopia 'beginning from this scripture' (Acts 8.35).

But is our passage offending the logic of justice? How should God want the righteous person to suffer in the sinner's place? Should not sinners suffer for their own guilt (Ezek. 14.20; 18.20)? But in the fuller unfolding we see the Father in the Son. God is not standing apart, supervising a legal system. In love he himself suffers to redeem.

An Invitation and an Assurance

Isaiah 55.1–11

Ho, thirsty ones! Come for water.
You without money, come buy and eat.
Yes, come, buy wine and milk
without money or price.
Why spend money on what is not bread,
your earnings on what cannot satisfy?
Listen to me and feed on what is true,
and your soul will delight in goodness.
Turn your ear and come to me,
hear, and your soul shall live.
For I will renew for you the everlasting covenant,
the sure promises I have given to David.
As I made him a witness to the peoples,
A leader and commander for the nations,
so you shall call to a nation you do not know,
and the nation you do not know shall run to you
because of the Lord your God,
the Holy One of Israel who has glorified you.
Seek the Lord while he may be found,
call upon him while he is near.
Let the wicked give up their ways,
the wrongdoers their thoughts,
and let them return to the Lord that he may have pity on them,
to our God for he will generously pardon.
'For my thoughts are not your thoughts,

nor my ways your ways,' says the Lord.
'But as the heavens are higher than the earth,
so are my ways higher than your ways
and my thoughts than your thoughts.
As truly as the rain and snow come down from heaven,
and do not return till they have watered the earth,
making it bring forth and bud,
giving seed for sowing and bread to eat,
so shall my word be that goes forth from my mouth.
It shall not return to me fruitless,
but will accomplish my will,
and achieve the task I gave it.'

With metal jugs and cups fastened about his person, the traditional seller of soft drinks could still be seen in the streets of old Jerusalem in our lifetime. With many a picturesque phrase he invites customers, 'O thirsty one, free water! I have brought it from the mosque of the Prophet. God is generous', and so on.

In the Bible the figure of Wisdom sometimes invites in this style, and in the present passage the Lord himself invites to a feast like that of the sacred meals in the old festivals. For the exiles in Babylonia the feast must still be in the imagination, but still it stands for a spiritual reality. The Lord offers his people renewal of life and all the blessings of his ancient bond with 'David', his covenant with the royal house.

The passage sets the seal on the stirring prophetic messages of chapters 40 – 55. The kingly power of the Lord is very near. And through the sacrifice of his Anointed, the era of forgiveness is near to dawning. Let all be ready to come to God's feast of good things, the life with him that alone can satisfy. Let them seek and find the Lord in the day of opportunity.

His ways and purposes are indeed beyond our understanding and remain hidden in mystery. But his word has gone out and will certainly achieve its mission of redemption.

A Garland for Ashes

Isaiah 61.1–3

The Spirit of the Lord God is upon me
for the Lord has anointed me.
He has sent me to bring good tidings to the poor,

to bind up the broken in heart,
to proclaim liberty to the captives,
and the opening of prison to those in chains,
to proclaim the year of the Lord's favour
and the day of requital for our God,
to comfort all who mourn,
to appoint for those who mourn in Zion
A garland instead of ashes,
oil of joy instead of mourning,
a garment of praise instead of a weary spirit.
And they shall be called oaks of salvation,
planted by the Lord for his glory.

Passing to Isaiah 56 – 66, we find these chapters reflect the situation in Jerusalem in the early decades of the Persian empire, when the Jews were at liberty to return from exile and encouraged to rebuild city and temple. Prophets of the Isaiah tradition seem to have been among those who have returned from exile, and they continue their work in the difficult conditions of the resettling and rebuilding.

They still have thrilling promises to give, but also criticisms of the leading classes, intercession for the struggling community, words of guidance, and visions of judgement. They remind the temple-restorers that the Lord is free and high above all earthly buildings (57.15; 63.15; 66.1–2). And they declare that the Lord will warmly welcome into his house devout Gentiles and others traditionally forbidden access (56.3–8; 66.18–21).

Once again, the present extract reflects scenes and thoughts from the new-year festival. The emphasis on mourning before God, lamenting the ruin of Zion, has continued from the tragic years of exile. But the message is that the Lord will give cause for the mourning rags and ashes to be replaced with the clothing of joy and thanksgiving. The one who carries the message speaks in the person of the Lord's Anointed, the royal Son sent to save the humble sufferers. It seems that the prophet is dramatically carrying the voice of the Saviour who is yet to appear. The divine kingdom itself is so near. The prophets have seen it and still see it in their visions. Times of God's favour, his relieving grace, are already known. But the fulfilment of these prophecies is not yet given. Centuries later, one Sabbath morning in Nazareth, Jesus will read out this passage in the synagogue and declare it fulfilled (Luke 4.16–22).

10.

Messages of Doom and of Love

Reluctant Jeremiah

Jeremiah 1.4–10

> There came to me this word of the Lord: 'Before I formed you in the womb, I chose you, and before you came out of the womb I consecrated you. I appointed you prophet to the nations.'
>
> And I said, 'Ah, Lord God, I do not know how to speak for I am but a lad.' And the Lord said to me, 'Do not say I am but a lad, for to whomever I send you shall you go and whatever I command you shall speak. Do not be afraid of them, for I am with you to deliver you' – so said the Lord. Then he reached out his hand and touched my mouth, and he said to me, 'See, I have put my words into your mouth, and I have this day set you over the nations and over the kingdoms, to uproot and to break down, to destroy and to overthrow, to build and to plant.'

It is about the time of the death of the last great king of the Assyrian empire (627 BC). The world order is on the verge of great changes. Jeremiah, no doubt sensitive to the omens of change, receives his call at this very time to be God's instrument among the nations.

God chose him (literally 'knew' him) even before he created him – the strongest expression of his destiny. The shy, reluctant, sensitive young man cannot elude such a calling, arguing his unsuitability. God will give him all he needs for the work.

How close and personal is Jeremiah's relation to the Lord! The touch of God's own hand upon his mouth gives him words of power. His prophecies will have force to bring down kingdoms, but also to build and plant for the time of salvation.

The chapter continues with examples of how Jeremiah receives inspiration. He sees and meditates on a blossoming branch of almond – the Hebrew name *shaqed* means 'watchful', and he knows that God watches over his word to fulfil it. He sees a cooking pot on the boil, the steam and flame driven by a north wind, and he knows that the smoke and flame of invasions will blow down over the land from the north.

That strand in the large book which is most directly from Jeremiah's mouth is poetic and passionate. He watches over his people through years of tragedy, suffers to the extreme, but holds on to hope, to faith in the good purpose of God.

Forsaking the Lord to Embrace Futility

Jeremiah 2.10–13

> Cross over to the isles of the west and see,
> and send to Kedar in the east and study well,
> and see if there has ever been anything like this.
> Has a nation ever changed its gods,
> though they were no gods?
> Yet my people have exchanged their Glory
> for what does not profit.
> Be appalled, O heavens, at this
> and tremble with horror, says the Lord.
> For my people have committed two evils:
> they have forsaken me,
> fountain of living water,
> and hewed for themselves cisterns,
> broken cisterns at that,
> which cannot hold water.

The young Jeremiah attacks the people's fickleness, as they lose trust in their Lord who has always been their Saviour, and turn to other gods. In its youth the nation was like a young bride, devoted to her husband. But now Israel restlessly follows every desire like a camel in heat.

Here is a people of extraordinary folly, for they abandon a fountain of fresh, life-giving water and prefer to trust in a faulty cistern they have made for themselves, where the water grows stale and leaks away. What will be the end of it all? Even the skies, the earth and the creatures must suffer for this folly. And the prophet foresees a silent, wasted world as the day of reckoning comes (4.23–26).

Darkness Closes in on the Prophet

Jeremiah 20.7–18

> O Lord, you deceived me, I was indeed deceived,
> you are the stronger and overcame me.
> I have become a laughing-stock all the day,
> everyone mocks me.
> For whenever I speak and cry out,
> I proclaim violence and ruin.
> Yes, the word of the Lord gets me only reproaches,
> derision all the day long,
> And if I resolve not to mention you
> or speak any more in your name
> there is in me a blazing fire
> shut up in my bones,
> till I have no strength left
> to hold it in.
> On every side is terror.
> 'Denounce, let us denounce him,'
> say those who were my friends, watching for my fall.
> 'Perhaps he can be lured and we can catch him,
> and take our revenge upon him.'
> But the Lord is with me,
> fearsome and mighty . . .
> I shall see you requite them,
> for I have entrusted my cause to you . . .
> [v. 14] Cursed be the day on which I was born.
> the day my mother bore me be never blessed!
> Cursed be the man who brought my father tidings,
> saying, 'A boy has been born to you',
> filling him with joy . . .
> Why did I come from the womb to see trouble and sorrow,
> and spend my days in shame?

In some half-dozen passages we hear Jeremiah in intimate dialogue with the Lord. He speaks frankly of the burden of his ministry and sometimes hears from God words of encouragement. His chief torment is the fear that his message warning of doom may be wrong and those who oppose him and mock him may be right. Has God, for some hidden purpose, misled him – deceived him even? This passage is the last of these dialogues, the sharpest and in the end the darkest. In public he has appeared confident enough. He has just been facing bravely the public's fury by prophesying the destruction of Jerusalem, even miming it symbolically by shattering a jar. They have beaten him and fastened him in the stocks, but he has held to his message. But how agonized now is his complaint to the Lord who has led him into this predicament, and given him a word that burns within his bones if he tries to restrain it.

There have been influential friends protecting him, but now he fears they too are out to trap him and secure his downfall. For a while in the prayer, confidence seems to return as Jeremiah follows ancient patterns of intercession. He foresees God's retribution on his adversaries. But the end is even more bitter than the outburst of the suffering Job. Oh that he had never been born! Curse on that day and on the messenger that gladdened his father with the news!

Here the Lord is not named or addressed directly. It is the bottom of the abyss. But we know that Jeremiah has yet more years of ministry to fulfil. He does so faithfully, and even finds great words of hope for his broken people. His cry from the depths was evidently not in vain.

Promise of the New Covenant

Jeremiah 31.31–34

> 'See, the days are coming,' says the Lord, 'when I will make a new covenant with the house of Israel and the house of Judah. It will not be like the covenant that I made with their ancestors on the day when I took them by the hand to bring them out of the land of Egypt, a covenant which they broke, although I was a husband to them,' says the Lord.
>
> 'But this is the covenant that I will make with the house of David in those coming days,' says the Lord. 'I will put my teaching within them and write it on their hearts, and I will be their God and they shall be my people. They shall no longer teach their neighbours and relatives to know the Lord, for they shall all know me, from the least to the greatest of them, says the Lord. For I will forgive their wrongdoing and no more remember their sins.'

Among a collection of hopeful prophecies comes this little oracle where the Lord speaks and promises a new covenant, a new relationship with his people, essentially different from the old. The ancient formula still applies, a mutual devotion – 'I will be their God; they shall be my people.' But the people will no longer just be exhorted to keep the law of the Lord. He will write it on their hearts, transforming their character to a new sympathy and harmony with him. All will instinctively 'know the Lord', responsive to him, eager to do his will. The barrier of former sin will have been swept away by his forgiveness, and the people will be in close communion with their God.

The oracle reaches beyond any time yet known, in that the work of teaching the faith has never yet become redundant. But the followers of Christ will experience a new birth and a life with God made possible by his Spirit rather than by elaborate efforts to observe a multitude of laws.

You Shall Live Again

Ezekiel 37.1–14

> The hand of the Lord was on me, and he carried me out in the Spirit of the Lord and set me down in the midst of a valley, which was full of bones. Then he caused me to float over them, round and round. There were masses of them lying on the surface of the valley, and they were very dry.
>
> And he said to me, 'Son of man, can these bones live again?' I answered, 'O Lord God, you alone know.' And he said to me, 'Prophesy over these bones and say to them, O dry bones, hear the word of the Lord. See, I will bring breath-wind into you and you will live again. Sinew, flesh and skin I will lay on you, breath I will put in you, and you will live again and know that I am the Lord.'
>
> So I prophesied as I was commanded, and as I prophesied there came a rattling and the bones drew together, each bone to its bone. And as I looked, sinews appeared on them, flesh came up, and skin covered them over. But there was no breath in them. Then he said to me, 'Prophesy to the breath-wind, son of man, and say to it: Thus says the Lord God, "From the four quarters of heaven come, O breath-wind, and blow into these slain ones that they may come to life."' So I prophesied as he commanded me, and the breath came into them, and they lived and stood up on their feet, a vast host.
>
> Then he said to me, 'Son of man, these bones are the whole house of Israel. They are saying, "Dried up are our bones, perished our hope, our life cut off." Therefore prophesy and say to them. "Behold, I will open up your sepulchres and bring you out of them . . . And I will put my Spirit within you, and you shall live again, and I will place you in your own land, and you shall know that I the Lord have spoken it and done it, says the Lord."'

The priest-prophet Ezekiel was one of those taken into exile from Jerusalem to Babylonia early in the sixth century BC. In spite of the pedantic, lawyer-like style of his book, it is remarkable for its visionary character. He often fell into prophetic trances as, in his words, the hand of the Lord or the Spirit of the Lord came upon him. He ministered long and faithfully to sustain his fellow exiles in trust in the Lord and hope in his good purposes.

They would assemble at the old holy seasons on the riverbank and put their sorrows before God and appeal for his mercy. On this occasion their lament through the night has depicted their plight as a kind of death, and the cantor sings, 'Dried up our bones, perished our hope, our life cut off.' Will the Lord hear and respond, perhaps as dawn appears?

As Ezekiel sits among them he falls into a trance. He feels he is carried up and away by the Spirit-wind of God to a valley, the scene of some ancient battle. It is strewn with the bones of the fallen and long dead, bones as far from life as could be. He calls to them as God directs and they are reconstructed and become a vast, living host.

It is a kind of parable, with a message for the exiles. However bad the plight of the people now, so far from true life, the Lord can bring them home and will renew their life. So it is a message for a community and about life on this earth.

But through it shines the conviction that God is faithful and that he is the Lord of life. He has the power and will to redeem his own from the most extreme suffering, yes, from the lowest depths of death.

How Can I Give You Up?

Hosea 11.1–9

> When Israel was a child I loved him,
> and from Egypt I called my son . . .
> It was I who taught Ephraim to walk,
> and held them in my arms,
> but they did not know that I healed them.
> With children's reins I drew them,
> with cords of love.
> I was to them as one who lifts a child to his cheek,
> and gently I led him . . .
> How can I give you up, Ephraim,
> how can I hand you over, Israel?
> How can I destroy you like Adma,
> how devastate you like Zeboim?
> My heart is overturned within me
> and all my compassion grows warm.
> I will not effect my burning anger,

I will not turn to destroy Ephraim.
For I am God, not a human being,
the Holy One in the midst of you,
and I will not come to destroy.

The kingdom of the northern tribes, centred at Samaria and known as 'Israel' or 'Ephraim', was eliminated by the Assyrians in 721 BC after some years of instability, damaging invasions and a three-year siege of Samaria. Throughout this period, their prophet Hosea urged them to turn again to the Lord, showed them meaning in it all and kept hope alive. Not surprisingly, his words are not well preserved, but they still contain some lines of the greatest poetic prophecy.

Sometimes he pictures the nation's relation to God as a marriage bond – the unfaithful wife and her persevering husband. He lived out a parallel in his own marriage, but the circumstances remain obscure. In our present passage he pictures the bond rather as that between parent and child. The grown son does not remember all the love and tenderness the parent has shown from the first. But the grieved and angry parent draws back from casting off the son – 'How can I give you up . . . my heart is overturned . . . my compassion grows warm.'

In the divine heart the rejected love will not give up. Wounded indeed, it still perseveres and means to triumph.

The Spirit Poured Out On Young and Old

Joel 2.28–32

After this I shall pour out my Spirit on all flesh,
and your sons and daughters shall prophesy,
your old men shall dream dreams,
your young men shall see visions,
and also upon the male servants and maids
in those days I will pour out my Spirit.
And I will show wonders in the heavens and on earth,
blood and fire and pillars of smoke.
The sun will be turned into darkness
and the moon into blood
before the coming of the day of the Lord,
so great and terrible.
But everyone who calls on the name of the Lord
shall be saved . . .

Through a particular crisis – a plague of locusts – the prophet sees through to the ultimate crisis: the coming of the Lord to judge the world. The greater realities are never far away, and especially this is sensed in gatherings for worship. So Joel speaks to his people of repentance ('Turn to me with all your heart . . . rend your heart and not your garments', 2.12) and gives them a wonderful perspective on the fragility of this age, the constant imminence of the world's end, and what it means to be face to face with the Lord, our Judge and Saviour.

He speaks of marvellous events which herald the ultimate crisis, including the pouring out of God's Spirit on his creatures. The young and old, the high and low, will have that special sensitivity to God which characterizes prophets. They will hear his voice, see and read his signs, and so be close to his will.

The prophecy will come to mind centuries later at Pentecost, when Christ's community, the church, will be brought by the Spirit into this life of ready hearing and following the guidance of God, and of bearing inspired witness.

A Chance amid the Ruin of an Unjust State

Amos 5.2–24

> She has fallen, no more to rise,
> The maiden Israel.
> Prostrate she lies on her land,
> And none can raise her . . .
> [v. 4] Thus says the Lord to the house of Israel,
> Seek me and live, but seek not Bethel
> nor enter Gilgal, nor pass to Beersheba.
> For Gilgal shall go into exile,
> And Bethel become a ruin . . .
> Seek him who made the Pleiades and Orion
> And turns the shadow of death into morning
> and day he darkens into night,
> who calls for the waters of the sea
> and pours them on the face of the earth,
> the Lord is his name . . .
> [v. 21] I hate, I spurn your festivals,
> I take no delight in your sacred assemblies.
> Though you bring me sacrifices and offerings,
> I will not accept them or look at your peace offerings.

Take from me the sound of your songs,
for I will not hear the music of your harps,
But let justice roll down like waters,
and compassion as an ever-flowing stream.

Preaching between 760 and 750 BC, Amos is the earliest of the prophets from whose work a book has resulted and survived. Yet his prophecies are among the most eloquent and poetic, as he denounces a prosperity founded on injustice, which no amount of religious celebrations can disguise. Coming himself from the south of the kingdom of Judah, he targets especially the more northerly kingdom of Israel, and indeed is found preaching there in the great sanctuary of Bethel (7.10–13).

Our passage begins like a funeral dirge, as Amos foresees the kingdom destroyed. The chance still to 'live' (be saved) is there for the repentant, but the doom of the state seems certain. The rich who have climbed by treading down the poor are prominent in the great religious festivals at such temples as flourished at Bethel, Gilgal and Beersheba. They even look forward to the joy of these occasions, the 'light' that would shine on them from the Lord. No, says Amos, that great festival day of the Lord will prove to be darkness for you. Worship concealing cruelty and injustice is abhorrent to the Lord, however rich the offerings, however beautiful the music of praise. Rather let the thunderous music of great waters sound out, the copious and ever-flowing river of justice and compassion for God's little ones.

11.

Reaching Out to a New Era

The Wonder of God's Mercy

Jonah 3.3 – 4.1; 4.10–11

So Jonah rose and went to Nineveh, in obedience to the word of the Lord. Now Nineveh was a huge city, three days' walk across. He began to cross it, going a day's journey. And he proclaimed, 'Yet forty days and Nineveh shall be overturned.' And the people of Nineveh believed God, ordered a fast, and all put on sackcloth, from the greatest of them to the least. When the news reached the king of Nineveh he rose from his throne, laid aside his robe and put on sackcloth, and sat in ashes. Then he made proclamation in Nineveh: 'By the decree of the king and his peoples, let neither humans nor animals, herd nor flock, taste anything. Let them not take food or drink water. But let them be covered with sackcloth and cry mightily to God. Let them all turn from their evil ways and from the violence of their hands. Who knows whether God will not turn about, yes, turn from his fierce anger, so that we do not perish?'

When God saw what they did, turning from their evil ways, he took back what he had said he would do to them, and did it not. This greatly displeased Jonah and made him really angry . . . {4.10–11} And the Lord said, 'You are sorry for the gourd which cost you no labour; of its own it came up in a night and perished in a night. And should I not take pity on Nineveh, that huge city with 120,000 persons who do not know their right hand from their left, and also many animals?'

The prophet Jonah is mentioned in 2 Kings 14.25 as having proclaimed, in the eighth century BC, that the king of Israel would regain some lost territory. What we have now, however, is a picturesque tale written some four hundred years later, as shown by its language. Rather like Jesus in several parables, the author uses ironic humour and exaggeration to wrest people's hearts from entrenched prejudice.

Jonah (whose name means 'Dove') is given a message to the people of Nineveh (in present-day northern Iraq) which may save them from destruction. He set off at once – in the opposite direction, so much does he want Nineveh, the capital of the Assyrian oppressors, to be destroyed. Indeed he boards a ship bound for Spain.

But God is able to turn to more faithful servants from among the elements of creation and from animals. The storm obediently gets Jonah overboard, and a great fish obediently swallows him and coughs him up safely three days later on a beach. Jonah now obeys, preaches warning to the people of Nineveh and then goes out into the desert to watch the result.

The greatest miracle has happened. The people have believed, and respond perfectly. God has accordingly spared them. Jonah smoulders with indignation. But the Lord works on him still. He makes him a shelter from the fierce wind and heat – a gourd or cucumber plant that has obediently grown up over Jonah in a night. Then God ordains a worm to eat and wither it, much to Jonah's further vexation.

God's final words ironically ignore the selfish reason for Jonah's concern about the plant. And the story ends with a question. Has the resentful heart been changed? Only the listeners, searching their own hearts, can answer.

Out of Bethlehem the Second David

Micah 5.1b–5

> With a rod they strike the ruler of Israel on the cheek.
> But you, Bethlehem in Ephrata, small as you are
> to be among the clans of Judah,
> from you shall come forth for me
> one to be ruler in Israel
> whose rising is from the Beginning,
> from the days of eternity.
> Then he shall leave them
> for the time a woman takes to bear a child.
> And the rest of his brothers and sisters shall return
> to the children of Israel.
> He shall stand and feed his flock in the strength of the Lord,
> in the majesty of the name of the Lord his God,

and they shall dwell in safety,
for he shall be great to the bounds of the earth
and a man of peace shall he be.

The book of Micah, like the contemporary utterances of Isaiah, contains fierce denunciation of the upper classes combined with colourful hopes for the future, when the Lord will give salvation through the house of David and the temple-city of Jerusalem. The present city has built its wealth with 'blood and iniquity' (3.10). Judgements can be bought from the rulers and rulings from the priests for a large fee. Supernatural knowledge can be purchased from the prophets. For all this greed and corruption, the holy city will become a ruin, merely a ploughed field.

But in a new age, the Jerusalem that focuses the world's worship and knowledge of God will become a reality. Swords will be beaten into ploughshares and no one trained for war.

Our passage tells of the Saviour from David's line. A time of siege for Jerusalem and cruel assault on her leader will give way to wonderful peace. The 'David' who comes from the eternal world will appear from the Davidic town of Bethlehem. The scattered people will be gathered home. He will rule in God's name – in the majesty of the one who expresses and effects the divine mind and purpose.

What God Requires

Micah 6.1–8

Hear now what the Lord says!
'Arise and plead your case before the mountains,
and let the hills hear your voice.'
You mountains, hear the Lord's contention,
hear, you enduring foundations of the earth,
for the Lord has a contention against his people,
and he will argue his case with Israel.
'O my people, what have I done to you,
how have I wearied you? Testify against me.
For I brought you up out of the land of Egypt
and redeemed you from the house of bondage' . . .
With what shall I come before the Lord
and bow low before God on high?
Shall I come before him with burnt offerings,
with calves that are one year old?

Will the Lord be pleased with thousands of rams
or with ten thousand rivers of oil?
Shall I give my first-born for my wrongdoing,
the fruit of my body for the sin of my soul?
He has shown you, humankind, what is good,
and what does the Lord require of you,
but to act justly and love kindness,
and to walk humbly with your God?

In ancient covenants there would be provision for airing complaints
and disputes between the parties. At the chief festival also, where the
covenanted people met their Lord, the prophets might also speak of
complaints between the two parties, disputes between God and people.

In the present passage the prophet Micah, writing in the later eighth
century BC, voices a contention that the Lord has with his people. They
are ready enough to bring offerings to the temple, even on a lavish scale.
They even treat him as one of the terrible gods that might demand the
sacrifice of children. But the Lord's requirement is simple, though alas
often avoided. It is for the doing of justice, a justice that saves the little
people from exploitation, and bound to this, devotion to enduring kindness, and then the fount of all, a quiet walking with the Lord, daily going
his way, conversing with him, rejoicing to be with him. Seldom has the
Lord's will for every person and for society been so well expressed.

The Rising of the Healing Sun

Malachi 4

For behold the day comes, glowing like a furnace, and all the arrogant and
the evil-doers will be as stubble. But for you who fear my name the sun of
salvation shall rise with healing in its wings . . .
Remember the law of Moses my servant which I commanded him on Mount
Horeb. Behold, I will send you again the prophet Elijah before the great and
terrible day of the Lord comes, and he will turn the heart of parents to their
children and the heart of children to their parents, lest I come and smite the
earth with a curse.

The last of the prophetic books is ascribed to 'Malachi' ('My messenger')
who seems to have worked in Jerusalem about 480 BC. He speaks out
boldly against the irreverence of priests in the sanctuary and, remarkably,
states that worship among the Gentiles across the world (he is thinking

of the worship of 'the God of heaven' promoted by the Persian rulers) is more acceptable to the Lord than the worship at his Jerusalem temple.

Malachi has urgent words about the approach of the Day of the Lord. For centuries prophets had spoken of this awesome day, of which the festal days were a foreshadowing. It was the time when God would judge the earth and rectify wrongs. Our extract uses two striking images. For the wicked the day will be like a fiery furnace that consumes stubble. But for those who revere the Lord, heeding him at every point in life, the great day will be like the rising of a sun in blessing, salvation and healing. The Persians had taken up an ancient use of the image where the sun's rays are portrayed as wings signifying the healing divine order spread by their rule. The Jews themselves had already used it on jar handles and coins. Now from Malachi it conveys a message of restoration, of healing for society and for individuals.

Two little messages end the book, messages added perhaps by final collectors keen to emphasis the concerns of their day. First comes warning to be mindful of the law given through Moses. This ancient teaching has only recently, in the fifth century, begun to take on the dominant role which we still see in the time of Jesus.

Second and last comes allusion to the other mighty prophet associated with Mount Horeb (also called Mount Sinai). Elijah was said never to have died but to have been caught up into heaven. Now it is promised that he will return, making ready for the Lord's own coming by reconciling parents and children. The strains of the resettled community have been so strong that the very fabric of family life has been torn. This has also been injurious to the land itself.

It will seem to New Testament writers that with the coming of John the Baptist and of Jesus the prophecy finds its goal. The great reconciliation is begun, and the earth itself begins to be freed from the curse of ruin.

One Like a Son of Man Made King for Ever

Daniel 7.9–14

As I watched, thrones were set in place, and one who was venerable in years took his seat. His robe was white as snow, and the hair of his head like purest wool. His throne was of fiery flames and its wheels of burning fire. A torrent of fire streamed out before him. Thousands of thousands served him and ten thousand times ten thousand waited before him. The court sat in judgement and the books were opened. And I watched until the beast was slain and its body destroyed and given over to be burned with fire. As for the rest of the beasts, their dominion was taken away but their lives were prolonged for a time and a season.

Still I watched in visions of the night, and see with the clouds of heaven came one like a son of man. He approached the Ancient in years and was presented to him. And he was given dominion and glory and the kingdom, that all peoples and nations of every language should serve him. His dominion is an everlasting dominion which shall not pass away, and his kingdom is one that shall never be destroyed.

Among the encouragements given to the persecuted in the book of Daniel are visions of the future. These show the present tyrannies destroyed and the good kingdom of God triumphant. Daniel sees an ocean stirred up by raging winds. Four beasts emerge, chaos figures representing the succession of world empires. The fourth is the most fearsome, its several horns representing its particular kings. The worst king is the current ruler, Antiochus IV. But the court of the Most High, God Almighty, 'the Ancient in years', condemns and destroys his tyranny. Who now will rule the world?

In contrast to the chaos-beasts, Daniel now sees a figure in human form, 'one like a son of man', coming with the clouds of heaven before the Most High God. In the image of God, he comes from heaven, in contrast to the wicked figures from the chaos waters. Before the Most High he is installed as ruler, entrusted with the execution of the will of God for ever. He appears as both an individual and as representative of the suffering people of God, now victorious in the everlasting era of the kingdom of God.

Preserved not in Hebrew but in Aramaic, our passage will be an important influence on the Gospels, with their imagination of the dawning of the kingdom of God and the royal figure of the Son of Man.

Awakening of Sleepers in the Land of Death

Daniel 12.1–3

And then shall Michael arise, the great prince who watches over your people. And there shall be a time of trouble such as never has been since there was a nation. But at that time your people shall be delivered, every one found written in the book. And many of those who sleep in the dust of the earth shall awake, some to everlasting life and some to shame and everlasting disgrace.

And those who triumph shall shine like the brightness of the heavens, and those who bring many to righteousness like the stars for ever and ever.

Persecution has raged for several years from 167 BC. For the people as a whole the promise is that their guardian angel, the archangel Michael, will lead the heavenly hosts to save them and defeat their oppressors.

But many have already died for their faith, and the encouraging prophecies of Daniel now include a clear promise that these will awake from the sleep of death. The noble martyrs will shine in their victory over evil, for like the Suffering Servant (Isaiah 53) they have atoned for the sins of many by their sacrificial deaths. They have 'made right' multitudes. But the cruel will be awakened to answer for their crimes against God's faithful ones.

Such a statement of an awakening from the dead is very rare in the Old Testament. The severity of the crisis and the courage of the martyrs have brought a new perspective, accepted by many but not by all the faithful. It will not be long before the followers of Christ will add their testimony to this growing belief in a resurrection.

12.

What Manner of Man? Perspectives on the Nature of Jesus

The Image of the Unseen God

Colossians 1.15–20a

He is the image of the unseen God, the first-born of all creation. For in him were created all things in the heavens and on the earth, things seen and unseen, thrones, dominions, rulers, powers . . . all things have been created in him and for him. Before all things he is, and in him all things hold together.

And he is the head of the body, the church. He is the beginning, the first-born from the dead, that among all he should be the foremost. For God in all his fullness chose to dwell in him and through him to reconcile all things to himself, having made peace through the blood of the cross . . . yes, through him, all things on the earth and in the heavens.

In his letter to the church in Colossae (present-day inland, western Turkey) Paul writes of his prayer for all its members. May they be given increasing knowledge of God, patience and joy. And may they ever thank the Father who has brought them out of darkness into the kingdom of 'the Son of his love' (1.13), his beloved Son in whom we have our redemption and forgiveness of our sins. This thanksgiving becomes all the richer as we contemplate who it is that has come to us as our Lord Jesus Christ. God the Father is invisible, beyond our knowledge, but he is manifest and known in his Son. The Son is God's showing forth, his 'image'. As 'first-born' he has authority over all his creation, he is pre-eminent; but he is also representative of all. In the cross and resurrection is enacted the death of all and new life for all.

Being the manifestation of God, his role is utterly comprehensive. His work of creating, sustaining and reconciling is for all visible creatures, not just humankind, and also for all unseen spiritual forces. Nothing, no being, no identity, lies outside his work of creation and redemption. In creation, in the life of the church, in victory over death, he is ruler and representative, supreme Lord and Saviour. The *pleroma*, the fullness of the Godhead, dwells in him, so that his work is fully God's work, making peace through the sacrificial death on the cross, the outpouring of the divine life.

What a thankfulness to live in, what a song to sing! What faith-knowledge to grow in! Here everything in our life is brought under Jesus. Nothing is kept from him. For him alone is all our worship. This is to live already in the realm of light, to be translated, carried across to the kingdom of God's beloved Son.

The Son through Whom God Has Fully Spoken

Hebrews 1.1–4

> In time past God spoke to our ancestors through the prophets in fragmentary and various ways. Now, at the end of these days, he has spoken to us in the person of his Son, whom he made heir of all things and through whom he made the worlds. He is the outshining of God's glory and the impress of his very being, and he upholds all things by the word of his power.
>
> When he had made purification of sins, he sat down at the right hand of the majesty on high, as far above the angels as the name he inherited is superior to theirs.

Again the Son is seen as the manifestation of the invisible God, the effulgence of God's power and wisdom, indeed of his very being, to create, sustain and reveal. As the 'impress' of God's being, he conveys a faithful image and the divine authority.

Along with this cosmic work goes historical revelation. This Son, disclosing God's being, thought and power, is also the fulfilment of the utterances, visions and signs given through the prophets. Come among us as Jesus and put to death on the cross, he has made the true sacrifice, overcoming the barrier of sin.

This letter of unknown origin may have been sent to the Jewish Christians in the region of Rome to assure them of the fulfilling reality of the gospel, their former religious practice having been but a shadow. So the letter unfolds its rich interpretation of Jesus as Son of God – expression of God from before all worlds, fulfilment both of prophecy and of the symbolism of priestly service, ascending from his sacrificial to his eternal place in the majesty of God.

The Word Come to Dwell on Earth

John 1.1–5,14

> In the beginning was the Word, and the Word was with God, and the Word was God. He was in the beginning with God. All things came to be through him, and without him came nothing to be that has come to be. In him was life, and the life was the light of humankind. And the light shines in the darkness, and the darkness has not overcome it . . . And the Word became flesh and dwelt among us, and we beheld his glory, glory as of the Only Begotten from the Father, full of grace and truth.

The simple but inexhaustible words sound a music of the deepest solemnity. The 'beginning' here evokes a time before time began, before the creation. Only God existed, his Word being as it were his thought, that expression of his being through which he would cause to be all that was to exist. The Word would effect the divine creative power to give the meaning, order and beauty that we call 'life'. Such life, blessed and holy, is to the human race as a light, an experience of the joy and goodness radiating from the Creator. The true light is indeed the Word himself, and he has shone in a world darkened by sin. Great was that darkness, but it could not put out the light.

In Jesus the Word became flesh, incarnate, fully human on this earth. For a while he 'tabernacled' among us (v. 14), as the glory of God had dwelt in a fragile tent in the wilderness journey. The disciples looked on with wonder, for he had a glory from God, being the beloved Son of the Father. They beheld him full of grace and truth, a fullness not of power but of the divine humility.

John's gospel invites us likewise to contemplate Jesus with awe. These solemn opening verses are meant to place us at the viewpoint from which we too can see Jesus in the unfolding story with wonder and discernment.

The Word of Life, Made Visible and Tangible

1 John 1.1–4

> That which was from the beginning, that which we have heard, seen with our own eyes, contemplated, touched and held with our own hands – the Word of life, this is our theme. The life was made visible and we saw it. So we testify and declare to you the life eternal which was with the Father and was made

visible to us. We declare to you what we have seen and heard so that you also may have fellowship with us, a fellowship that we have with the Father and his Son Jesus Christ. We write these things so that our joy may be complete.

This letter lays great stress on the truth of the Word made flesh – the Son indeed from before all worlds, yet known so concretely, so humanly, in Jesus. From the Father came this Word who is the essence of life and giver of life to all creation; he came as Jesus who was seen and heard and touched and held. This is the testimony of apostles who experienced for themselves this amazing reality. And we today, receiving the testimony, entering in and proving it, we have fellowship with the church and with the Father and the Word, his Son Jesus Christ. This fellowship and communing is joy indeed.

The Lord Jesus Christ, Son of David and Son of God

Romans 1.1–6

Paul, servant of Christ Jesus, called to be an apostle, set apart for the gospel of God which he promised through his prophets in the holy Scriptures. This is the gospel concerning his Son, born a descendant of David in human terms and designated Son of God with power in terms of the Holy Spirit through resurrection from the dead – even Jesus Christ our Lord. Through him we received grace and the commission for the sake of his name to gain obedience of faith among all nations – among them yourselves, called to belong to Jesus Christ.

Paul is writing to the Christians in Rome about AD 57. His letter will be a lengthy statement of his gospel to prepare the way for a hoped-for first visit. He thinks to develop his mission from Rome westwards to Spain and will look for their support in unity of faith. In these opening lines he speaks of his calling and of his Lord.

He shows a strong sense of the divine work in history. God's gospel, he says, was already announced beforehand through the prophets and handed down in the Scriptures. It was the promise of the coming of the 'Christ', the Messiah, the Lord's Anointed. On the level of the natural order, Jesus as this Messiah was of King David's line. He was the promised royal one who was to reign through God's will and power to bring salvation to the world. But in the deepest perspective, in the mystery of the Holy Spirit, he is Son of God in power, as signalled and revealed by his rising from the dead.

So he is 'our Lord' (v. 5): his bond with us, his love for us, is wholly one with God the Father's claim upon us. We belong to Jesus, and in him to the Father.

The Spirit Descends on Jesus, Messiah and Son of God

Mark 1.1,9–11

> The beginning of the gospel [good tidings] of Jesus Christ, the Son of God . . . Now it happened in those days that Jesus came from Nazareth in Galilee and was baptized by John in the River Jordan. And at once, coming up out of the water, he saw the heavens torn apart and the Spirit, like a dove, descending on him. And a voice came from the heavens: 'You are my beloved Son; my delight is in you.'

The swift and vivid story of the coming of Jesus that will be told by Mark, echoing the preaching of Peter, rests on a profound understanding of the person and work of Jesus. The book is to recount a 'gospel' – good tidings such as runners might bring from a decisive victory. Here the bearer of the glad tidings announces the salvation won by the Son of God, Jesus the 'Christ', that is, the Messiah. Thus Jesus is known as the one who comes from the bosom of God to do the work of God. He is the one promised through the prophets to bring in a new age, a new world. 'Prepare the way of the Lord,' they had said, and indeed Mark recognizes in the coming of Jesus that coming of the Lord himself.

John 'the Baptizer' is the promised forerunner who has been calling the people to a new openness to God, a readiness for him, as they pass under the cleansing water. Jesus affirms John's work as he humbly undergoes the dipping. But God makes the occasion the inauguration of the royal mission. Jesus sees the Holy Spirit in the form of a dove descend from heaven to rest on him, while the Father speaks over him the solemn affirmation. This is his Beloved, his Chosen One, the Son who is to do God's work, bringing in the Creator's new reign, the new world.

Mary Conceives Jesus by the Holy Spirit

Matthew 1.1,20b

The genealogy of Jesus Christ, son of David, son of Abraham . . .
   An angel of the Lord appeared to Joseph in a dream, saying, 'Joseph, son of David, do not fear to take to you Mary your wife, for the child conceived in her is from the Holy Spirit.'

Matthew begins his gospel with a table of descent. Its symmetrical arrangement is symbolic and emphasizes the divine purpose in bringing Jesus the Messiah as successor of and fulfilment for Abraham and David. He will be the Promised One who embodies the kingdom of God and the blessing for all nations.

Then we have quoted one verse from the story of the birth. The man so careful to follow the Mosaic law is guided beyond it by an angel. Mary his betrothed is with child, but the angel reveals that she has conceived through the action of the Holy Spirit, and Joseph is to take her fearlessly into his home as his wife.

The vast truth of the Son of God come to earth, the Word become flesh, is here concentrated into tense moments of individual lives. Everything is traced from the ancient purpose of God, now fulfilled.

The wondrous conception is related also by Luke (see below). Does Paul allude to it when he writes in Galatians (4.4), 'When the fullness of time came, God sent forth his Son, born of a woman'? More definitely we can catch an allusion in John (1.13), the new birth of Christians being linked with the marvel of Christ's birth: 'not of blood, nor of the will of the flesh, nor of human will, but of God.'

Jesus the Living One Holds Death's Keys

Revelation 1.16b–18

And his face was as the sun shining in full strength. And when I saw him, I fell at his feet as though dead. And he laid his right hand upon me, saying, 'Fear not. I am the First and the Last and the Living One. I *was* dead, and behold, I live for evermore, and I have the keys of Death and its country.'

A Christian brother called John is suffering for his faith in what is probably a penal settlement on the island of Patmos. One 'Lord's day' he was 'in the Spirit' and was given this vision of the risen Christ.

Jesus appears to him in a form symbolic of both the Son of Man and God the Ancient of Days in Daniel 7. We may say that the Father is in the Son. From Father and Son alike the words can be heard, 'I am the Alpha and the Omega' (1.8), 'the First and the Last'. The Messiah Jesus is the revelation of Almighty God. As 'first-born of the dead' (1.5) he is the one who will lead them to life beyond death. He has the keys of Hades and is able to unlock the gates and bring the dead up to be with him, the risen Lord, the Living One.

Mary's Vocation and Willing Response

Luke 1.26–38

> Now in the sixth month the angel Gabriel was sent from God to a town in Galilee called Nazareth, to a girl betrothed to a man named Joseph, of the house of David, and the girl's name was Mary. And he came to her and said, 'Hail, O highly favoured one, the Lord is with you.'
>
> But she was troubled at these words, wondering what this greeting could mean. And the angel said to her, 'Fear not, Mary, for you have found favour with God. And behold, you will conceive in your womb and bear a son, and you shall call his name Jesus. He will be great and will be called the Son of the Most High. And the Lord God will give him the throne of his father David. He will be king over the house of Jacob for ever, and of his reign there will be no end.'
>
> And Mary said to the angel, 'How can this be, for I am a virgin?' The angel answered and said to her, 'The Holy Spirit will come upon you and the power of the Most High will overshadow you, and so the holy one that will be born will be called the Son of God. And behold, your kinswoman Elizabeth also has conceived a son, though she is old. This is the sixth month with her that was called barren – for no word of God will fail.'
>
> And Mary said, 'Here I am, the Lord's servant. Let it be to me as you have said.' Then the angel departed from her.

From our selection of verses that have glimpsed the nature of Jesus as Son of God, we pass on to narratives of his birth and childhood. The account of the angel's visit to Mary is simple in style, but it calls for the awakening of our spirits to a world where simplicity goes with depth, beauty is truth, and the way of wonder and worship leads to knowledge of God.

Gabriel, one of the greatest angels according to Jewish belief, comes to a little town which earns no mention in other records of that time. His mission is to a girl simply called Mary. She is single still but engaged to Joseph, who is of Davidic descent. Gabriel tells her that she is to conceive a child not through a husband, but as she is embraced by the Spirit and power of God. So the eternal Word and Son of God will become a human, born of a woman.

In the profoundest meaning of the promises to David, the messianic hope will be fulfilled: in Jesus God will reign in wholeness of peace without end. The link with Elizabeth's child, the future John the Baptist, not only shows again the marvel of God's working, but also that it is for the coming of the Lord himself that all is being made ready.

Mary Visits Elizabeth before the Birth of John

Luke 1.39–45,56–7,80

Not long afterwards, Mary set out and hurried to a town in the hills of Judah. There she entered the house of Zechariah and greeted Elizabeth. When Elizabeth heard Mary's greeting, the child leapt in her womb. Elizabeth was filled with the Holy Spirit and exclaimed with a loud cry, 'Blessed are you above all women, and blessed is the fruit of your womb! Why should I be so favoured that the mother of my Lord comes to me? For indeed, when I heard your greeting, the babe in my womb jumped for joy. Blessed is she who believed that the Lord's promise to her would be fulfilled!' . . .

Mary stayed with her about three months before returning to her home. And now the time came for Elizabeth to have her child and she gave birth to a son. When her neighbours and kinsfolk heard how the Lord had shown her such great kindness, they rejoiced with her . . . The child grew well and became strong in spirit. He was in the deserts till the day when he appeared openly to Israel.

Mary knows now that Elizabeth is bound to her not only in a family tie, but also in the mighty work of God that is dawning over them. Eagerly then, she hurries through the hills to visit her. The child in Elizabeth's womb, the future John the Baptist, is already chosen to be a great prophet. Already he points to God's coming in Jesus, for at the sound of Mary's voice he 'leaps' or 'skips' for joy. Elizabeth understands the sign. Prophesying herself by the Holy Spirit, she acknowledges the supreme blessedness of Mary and reveres Mary's promised child as her 'Lord'.

The birth of John occasions more than the customary joy, since it has shown God's work of wondrous grace and kindness. The growing child grows strong also in spirit, his soul open to God and devoted to him.

For his unique mission he must prepare in the solitude and poverty of the wilderness. So it is from a special intimacy with God that he will come openly before his people, to prepare them also for the coming of the Lord.

The Infant Messiah is Revealed to the Shepherds

Luke 2.1–21

> Now in those days a decree went out from Caesar Augustus that all the world should be registered. This was the first census, made when Quirinius was governor of Syria. So all went to register, everyone to their town. Joseph also went up from Nazareth in Galilee into Judea, to the city of David called Bethlehem, for he was of the house and family of David. He went to register himself with Mary his betrothed who was expecting her child.
>
> While they were there, her days to give birth were completed and she bore her first-born son. She wrapped him in swaddling clothes and laid him in a manger, because there was no room for them in the inn. Now in that region there were shepherds dwelling in the open country, keeping watch over their flock all through the night. And an angel of the Lord stood before them and glory of the Lord shone round about them, and they were greatly afraid. But the angel said to them, 'Fear not, for behold, I bring you tidings of great joy which shall be for all the people. For there is born to you this day in the city of David a Saviour who is Christ the Lord. And this shall be the sign for you: you will find a babe wrapped in swaddling clothes and lying in a manger.' And suddenly there was with the angel a multitude of the heavenly host, praising God and saying, 'Glory to God in the highest, and on earth peace, good will among people.'
>
> When the angels went from them into heaven, the shepherds said one to another, 'Let us go now to Bethlehem and see for ourselves what the Lord has made known to us.' So they came with haste and found Mary and Joseph with the babe lying in the manger. And when they saw him, they related all they had been told about him. And all who heard were astonished at the things told them by the shepherds. But Mary kept all these sayings, pondering them in her heart. And the shepherds returned, glorifying and praising God for all that they had heard and seen, just as had been foretold to them.

The Roman Empire seemed to its citizens to embrace virtually the whole of civilization. Luke's reference to Emperor Augustus and his plans for taxation sets the story of the birth of Jesus, for all its enchanting poetry, in the heart of history. The Davidic descent of Joseph, father of the household, and the role of David's home town Bethlehem indicate that the child will be the fulfilment of the promises to David – he will be the greater David, the hoped-for Messiah.

At the outset of the journey Mary is still identified as Joseph's 'betrothed', marking continuity with the angel's visit to the maiden Mary. Some ancient texts, however, have instead 'his wife' and others again 'his betrothed wife', and no doubt these express Luke's intention. As her 'first-born', the child was thought of as specially belonging to God, having special dignity and vocation irrespective of whether other children might follow.

The 'inn' was where travellers, having unfastened and seen to their animals, would repose in a large common room. As it was already crowded, Mary and Joseph could only find space with the stabled animals. An early Christian tradition was to tell of the birth as happening in the shelter of a cave. In the chill of the night Mary is careful to swathe her child in the customary swaddling bands and to place him in the warmth of hay and straw in a feeding trough.

The story brings home the marvel of the divine humility. He came to those who had no room for him. The animals in their simplicity were his best friends. And now the angels appear, not to the grand folk, but to the shepherds out in the wild, watching through all the watches of the night, guarding the flock, perhaps tending the ewes in lambing. The glory that shone about them was a sign of God's own nearness. The angel's message points the contrast: born is the Saviour, the Messiah, the divine Lord – see, the babe lies bound in the feeding trough. Heaven rings with the joyful song of praise, while here on earth, unrecognized, is the bearer of God's peace and good will.

But the simple shepherds saw and believed, and so earth was not without its song of praise. Mary shared the thankfulness and the adoration, but it is her treasuring and pondering in the depth of her heart which Luke mentions. Already she divines that her little one is in a hostile world. Born in the night, he will continue to be a light shining in the darkness.

Eastern Sages Come to the Newborn Child

Matthew 2.1–12

Now when Jesus was born in Bethlehem of Judea in the days of King Herod, there came wise men from the east to Jerusalem, saying, 'Where is the one born king of the Jews? For we saw his star at its rising and have come to worship him.' When King Herod heard this he was troubled, and all Jerusalem with him. He gathered all the chief priests and scribes of the nation and inquired of them where the Messiah was to be born. They told him, 'In Bethlehem of Judea, for thus it is written by the prophet: O Bethlehem . . . out of you will come a governor who will be shepherd of my people Israel.'

Then Herod privately called the wise men and learned from them carefully what time the star appeared. Then he sent them on to Bethlehem, saying, 'Go and search out carefully concerning the child, and when you have found him, bring me word, that I too may come and worship him.'

They listened to the king and went on their way. And there before them went the star they had seen at its rising, till it came and stood over where the young child was. And when they saw the star, they rejoiced with very great joy. And entering the place, they saw the child with Mary his mother. They fell down and worshipped him, and opening their treasures, they presented to him gifts of gold, frankincense and myrrh. Then, being warned in a dream not to return to Herod, they left for their own country by another way.

These wise men or 'magi', perhaps from Persia or Babylonia (present-day Iraq), were learned men, knowledgeable about stars and their connections with events on earth. They have observed the rise of a brilliant star and interpreted it to correspond with the birth of a saviour-king of the Jews. Having perhaps already some sympathy with the Jewish faith, they appreciate the significance of the messianic hope. So they have travelled far through hardships and dangers to worship the divine child. They are the first representatives of the nations who will come to his light and rejoice in the brightness of his rising.

King Herod, now near the end of his long reign, has constantly suffered from fear of treachery, and in spite of some merits, he is notorious for ruthless executions and massacres. The news of the omen in the stars therefore arouses his worst fears and he forms his plan accordingly.

The wise men, being directed onwards to Bethlehem, rejoice greatly at the confirmation given by the fresh sight of the star, which draws them to David's town and then appears to stand above a particular property (the word 'house' here could be used very broadly of any site or dwelling.) Their worship of the child and their gifts acknowledge the divine royal one. They have been given the wisdom to see, through the poverty, the one who comes from God to rule in the name and power of God.

Herod Seeks to Kill the Child Messiah

Matthew 2.13–23

When the wise men had departed, an angel of the Lord appeared to Joseph in a dream and said, 'Rise, take the young child and his mother and flee to Egypt, and stay there until I bring you word. For Herod is going to search for the child to kill him.' So he rose and took the child and his mother by night and went away into Egypt. And there he remained until the death of Herod, fulfilling what was spoken by the Lord through the prophet: 'Out of Egypt did I call my Son.'

Now when Herod had seen that the wise men had got the better of him, he was enraged. He sent his soldiers and killed all the male children in and around Bethlehem from 2 years old and under that were born at the season he had ascertained from the wise men. Then was fulfilled the word spoken through Jeremiah the prophet: 'A voice was heard in Ramah, weeping and great mourning, Rachel weeping for children and refusing to be comforted, for they were gone.'

But once Herod was dead, there again was the angel of the Lord, appearing to Joseph in a dream and saying, 'Rise and take the young child and his mother and go into the land of Israel, for those who sought the child's life are dead.' So he rose and took the young child and his mother and came into the land of Israel. But when he heard that Archelaus was reigning over Judea in place of his father Herod, he was afraid to go there. Being warned in a dream, he withdrew to the region of Galilee and came and dwelt in the town called Nazareth. Thus was fulfilled the word spoken through the prophets: 'He shall be called a Nazarene.'

The wise men departed. They had come far to worship the child from heaven. Responsive to the movements of a universe knit together in God, they had acknowledged the holy one in humility and awe. Their good deed turned out to be a cause of peril to the child and of death to other children. The good ever stirs up the forces of jealousy, fear and hatred. The honour given to those children in later Christian worship guides us not to despair, but to trust and rejoice in the sure triumph of the good.

Matthew sees a deep connection with the words of the poet-prophet Jeremiah who heard the weeping that sounded through the centuries. He heard the ancestral mother Rachel bewailing the mass deportation of her descendants. For that ancient mother he had a word of God: 'Weep no more . . . for they shall return from the land of the enemy' (Jeremiah 31.16). For those exiled masses, for the Holy Innocents of Bethlehem, and for all God's sufferers the word still stands and in his way and time will not fail.

With the death of Herod, the refugees were guided to return.

Just One Episode from the Boyhood of Jesus

Luke 2.40–52

> The child grew and became strong and was filled with wisdom, and the grace of God was upon him. Year by year his parents would go up to Jerusalem for the Festival of Passover. When he was 12 years old, they went up together as was the custom. But when the days of the festival were completed and they began the journey home, the boy Jesus stayed behind in Jerusalem without his parents realizing it. They supposed him to be somewhere in the company and had gone a day's journey before they began to look for him among their kinsfolk and friends. When they did not find him, they returned to search for him in Jerusalem.
>
> After three days they found him in the temple, sitting in the midst of the teachers, listening to them and asking them questions, and all who heard him were wondering at his understanding and answers. When they saw him there, they were astonished. His mother said to him, 'My child, how could you treat us so? Your father and I have been searching for you, and so worried.' But he said to them, 'Why were you searching for me? Did you not know I would be somewhere in my Father's house?' They did not understand what he said to them.
>
> Then he travelled with them and came to Nazareth and was obedient to them. As for his mother, she kept all these things in her heart. And Jesus grew in wisdom and stature, delighting God and the people around him.

How happy are parents to watch their children growing and becoming ever more capable! And sometimes they notice added gifts of the Spirit – a wisdom to hear and see with humility and understanding, a grace of kindness that reflects a light from God. In such wisdom and grace Jesus grew.

Just one episode is recounted from these growing years. At the age of 12, entering into maturity in the traditional piety, he could now accompany his parents on the annual pilgrimage up to Jerusalem for the Festival of Passover. Their party of kinsfolk and friends helped to swell the immense throngs that gathered from all parts of the land and indeed from abroad. The holy week in Jerusalem being completed, the party from Nazareth set off again for home. Only after a day's journey was Jesus missed. He was not after all with others in the company. All the way back went Mary and Joseph with growing anxiety.

Only after three days did they find him. Under the porticos of the temple courts rabbis and disciples studied and debated the Scriptures, and there in the midst of the teachers sat young Jesus eagerly listening, inquiring and answering and causing some amazement. Mary's emotions and words are natural. But the child is caught up rather in the claim of his heavenly Father, kindled in his soul by the spiritual force of the festival, the dedicated scholars, and the holy place expressive of the presence of God. There will always be a tension between the natural ties of home and such a sense of the divine call. More signs of it will emerge in later years. But for now, the earthly parents must have their rightful due and the boy continues in acceptance of their authority.

Only one story of the boyhood preserved – but it is revealing. Through a natural family life there runs an extraordinary thread, an awareness of the heavenly Father ('my Father') and his claim. Where would it lead? Twenty years would pass. Again the Passover in Jerusalem, then Jesus, for his Father's sake, no longer with them. Grieving, searching – and on the third day he is found again in joy.

13.

Jesus Announces a New Era

John's Warning: Repent before the Mighty One Comes

Luke 3.3–20

John came into all the region around the River Jordan preaching a baptism of repentance for the forgiveness of sins, as it is written in the book of the words of the prophet Isaiah, 'The voice of one crying in the wilderness: Make ready the way of the Lord, make his paths straight. Every gully shall be filled and every mountain and hill made low. The crooked ways shall be made straight and the rough places plain. And all creatures will see the salvation of God.'

To the crowds that came out to be baptized by him John said, 'Brood of vipers, who has warned you to flee from the wrath to come? Produce fruit that shows true repentance. Do not begin to say, "We have Abraham for our father", for I tell you that God is able to raise up children of Abraham from these stones. See, the axe is already laid at the root of the trees. Every tree that does not produce good fruit is chopped down and thrown on the fire.'

'What must we do?' the crowds asked him. He told them, 'Anyone with two coats should give to someone who has none. Everyone who has food should do the same.' When the tax-collectors also came to be baptized and asked him, 'Master, what must we do?' he replied, 'Exact no more than is due to you.' Soldiers also asked him, 'What about us – what must we do?' To them he said, 'Do not terrorize people, extorting money by threats, but let your pay be enough for you.'

Expectation ran through the people and all the talk was whether John himself might be the Messiah. But John answered them all, 'I am baptizing you with water, but someone mightier is coming – I am not worthy to loose the thongs of his sandals – and he will baptize you with the Holy Spirit and with fire. His winnowing shovel is already in his hand to clear his threshing floor and gather the grain into his store, while the chaff he will burn in a raging fire.'

With many such exhortations did John announce the good tidings to the people. But Herod, the ruler of that province, had been rebuked by him over the affair of Herodias his brother's wife and for other wrongdoings. So now Herod added yet another crime to all the rest by shutting John up in prison.

From solitude in the wilderness came John with power, preaching and baptizing multitudes in the River Jordan. His mission evokes the prophecy of Isaiah 40 announcing the coming of the Lord and imagining the way being cleared, levelled and straightened for his procession of salvation through the wilderness and up to Jerusalem.

These good tidings, however, were dominated by John's emphasis on the urgent need to be ready for the Lord's judgement. The people, he said, needed to 'repent' – to come to a new heart and mind, having turned away from sinful ways. There was no room for complacent pride in being born children of Abraham. The rite of immersion in the river was an expression of such repentance in preparation for the Lord. And John gave practical examples of the required change of life.

Such a compelling figure is this austere prophet from the wilderness that people wonder if he may himself be the Messiah, the bringer of God's kingdom. But John declares he is only the forerunner, unworthy to do the lowliest service to the great one who is coming and who will baptize in the fiery power of the Holy Spirit and, in terrible judgement, sift the good from the bad. For his fearless honesty John will soon fall foul of the ruler, Herod Antipas, who through divorces had managed to marry Herodias, his half-brother's wife. John will first be imprisoned, then beheaded.

In all the gospels John is presented as the great precursor of Jesus. He was not one who sought to draw people with pleasing words. A change of heart and behaviour in daily life was needed. As they were plunged under the flowing waters by this gaunt man so strong in the Spirit, they put off the old life and joined a people made ready for the coming Lord.

The Dove and the Voice at Jesus' Baptism

Matthew 3.13–17

Then Jesus came from Galilee to the Jordan to be baptized by John. But John tried to dissuade him, saying, 'I need to be baptized by you, and do you come to me?' Jesus replied, 'Let it be so now, for in this way we shall fulfil all that is rightful.' So John consented. And when Jesus was baptized and came up from the water, at once the heavens were opened and he saw the Spirit of God descending like a dove and resting on him. And there came a voice out of the heavens, saying, 'This is my Son, my Beloved, in whom I delight.'

'Then Jesus came' – the day has dawned for Jesus to leave his home life. Not for him to decry John's work or consider himself above a ceremony which expressed a new turning to God. He comes in humility, showing solidarity with the humble rather than with those apparently needing no repentance. And he comes in faith that with this movement God's kingdom is drawing near. Coming himself for baptism, he endorses John's prophetic work to prepare a people for that kingdom.

But John demurs, seeming to know Jesus already as the one who will baptize with the Holy Spirit. For the present, says Jesus, it will accord with God's purpose for him to receive John's baptism. The immersion takes on at once a special meaning, sensed by John and others, but fully revealed to Jesus alone. The Father affirms the royal and divine destiny of Jesus as his Son whom he wills to represent him and to carry out his purposes. The divine Spirit rests on Jesus in token of the strength and wisdom of God that will enable and guide him, and of the bond with the Father that nothing will break.

A Contest with the Devil

Matthew 4.1–11

Then Jesus was led up into the wilderness by the Spirit to be put to the test by the Devil. When he had fasted forty days and forty nights he suffered from hunger, and then the Tempter came and said to him, 'If you are the Son of God, command that these stones become loaves of bread.' But he answered and said, 'It is written: Human beings shall not live by bread alone, but by every word that comes from the mouth of God.'

Then the Devil took him into the holy city and set him on the pinnacle of the temple and said to him, 'If you are the Son of God, throw yourself down, for it is written: He will command his angels concerning you and on their hands they shall bear you up, lest you dash your foot against a stone.' Jesus said to him, 'But it is also written: You shall not test the Lord your God.'

Yet again, the Devil took him to a very high mountain and showed him all the kingdoms of the world and their glory. And he said to Jesus, 'All these things I will give you if you fall down and worship me.' Then Jesus said, 'Go from me, Adversary, for it is written: You shall worship the Lord your God and him only shall you serve.' At this the Devil left him, and now angels came and cared for him.

Straight from the uplifting revelation at the baptism to stern time of trial! The 'Devil' represents the experience of temptation or testing which often comes at critical moments and which is not outside the purpose of God – it is his Spirit that has taken Jesus up from the Jordan into the harsh desert hills. It is the Father's will that he should at the outset confront and rebuff the false ways of exercising his calling which so readily present themselves.

Would not the Son of God, God's King, have power to provide for himself ample comfort? The Tempter suggests this self-concerned use of miraculous power at a time of sharp need. His opening 'If' implies that not to follow this prompting would be to doubt the divine sonship. But Jesus gains support from the scriptural story of God's people in the wilderness (Deuteronomy). In that story bodily appetites were to be kept in check. True life after all was given by the breath of God and through obedience to his gracious words.

The powers of the Son of God, then, are not for personal advantage but how will they shape his work? To demonstrate his messiahship and sway the nation, should he not give a spectacular sign such as they all demand? A leap from the heights of the temple? Again the Devil's 'If you are . . .' But again guidance comes from Scripture's story of wilderness days: do not test out God but wait for him in genuine trust.

The third temptation is one that comes to all who have a special talent or power. Success seems likely to be advanced by just a little compromise with – well, what is not quite right. For the Messiah the temptation took a grand scale. Power to own and rule the world! But to possess the whole world in its present glories of wealth and greedy pleasure would entail a fatal compromise, the shift from all-out belonging to God to a worship of the Devil. That story in Deuteronomy, above all the people's wanderings in the wilderness, sounds out the mighty theme: the Lord is our God, the Lord alone, and him only will we worship, with all our heart and soul and strength.

So Jesus, strained but illuminated by fasting and the rigours of the desert, stood firm in the knowledge of the humble way he must take to do the Father's will. Mark tells us of the animals that stayed with him in his trials. And now we hear of angels that came to comfort and refresh him, as still in many forms they come to us in our weakness with the refreshment of kindness and grace.

John Points to the Lamb of God

John 1.28–42

All this [John's response to a delegation from Jerusalem] took place on the far bank of the Jordan where John was baptizing. The next day he saw Jesus coming towards him and said, 'See, the Lamb of God that takes away the sins of the world. This is the one I spoke of when I said, "A man who comes after me has come before me, for he was before me." I did not know him, but it was to reveal him to Israel that I came baptizing with water.'

And John bore witness, 'I saw the Spirit descending as a dove out of heaven and it remained on him. I did not know him, but the one who sent me to baptize with water said to me, "He on whom you see the Spirit descend and remain, he is the one who baptizes with the Holy Spirit." And I have seen and borne witness that this is the Son of God.'

The next day again John was standing with two of his disciples. And he looked at Jesus walking by and said, 'See the Lamb of God.' The two disciples heard him speak and they followed Jesus. Jesus turned and saw them following and said, 'What are you seeking?' They replied, 'Rabbi [which means Teacher], where are you dwelling?' He said to them, 'Come and see.' So they came and saw where he dwelt and remained with him the rest of that day, for it was about four in the afternoon.

One of the two who heard John speak and followed Jesus was Andrew, the brother of Simon Peter. The first thing he did was to find his brother Simon, and he said to him, 'We have found the Messiah' [meaning the Anointed One, in Greek, Christ]. And he brought him to Jesus. Jesus looked at him and said, 'You are Simon, son of John, but you shall be called Cephas [that is, Peter, meaning 'A rock'].'

When a priestly delegation came down from Jerusalem to ask John if he was the Messiah or similar expected messenger of God, he described himself as the foretold voice crying in the wilderness to prepare the way of the Lord. He baptized, he said, only with water, but a far greater figure was already standing unrecognized in their midst.

And now, the following day, John sees Jesus approach and bears witness that this is that greater one, whose significance was revealed to him only when the Spirit descended at the baptism. This testimony begins with the remarkable words, 'See, the Lamb of God that takes away the sins of the world.' There are echoes here of the Day of Atonement, the annual ceremony when the sins of the people were symbolically loaded on to the head of the chosen goat, the scapegoat, which then carried them far away into the wilderness. Echoes also of Passover, and the lamb whose blood gave safety. Echoes, too, of the prophecy of Isaiah 53 which depicted the Lord's royal Servant led like a lamb to the slaughter and bearing the sin of the multitudes.

But as often in this gospel we have words simple yet reverberating, plain statements that are revelation and endless source of meditation. And John speaks the words to us: Behold this Jesus, the Lamb of God who bears and takes away the sin of the whole world!

The words also prompt action, and the two disciples of John show us the way. Hearing John's testimony, they at once follow Jesus. Inquiring where he is living, they show a desire to sit at his feet and receive his teaching. He welcomes them and soon they know they have found the one all were hoping for, the royal one of God, the Messiah. One by one the community of faith grows. Andrew fetches his brother, and Jesus, with his penetrating knowledge of people, names him 'Rock'. Impulsive, even unreliable, Simon may be, but the strength of God will work through his weakness. So the light shines in the darkness and does its work, though the darkness does not comprehend it.

Jesus with the Gospel of God in Galilee

Mark 1.14–39

After John had been imprisoned, Jesus came into Galilee preaching the gospel of God and saying, 'The time is fulfilled and the kingdom of God has drawn near. Repent and believe in the gospel.'

As he passed along by the Lake of Galilee, he saw Simon and his brother Andrew throwing a net in the lake, for they were fishermen. Jesus said to them, 'Come after me and I will make you fishers of people.' At once they left the nets and followed him.

Going on a little further he saw James son of Zebedee and his brother John who likewise were in their boat mending nets. At once he called them and they left their father Zebedee in the boat with men that he employed and went after him.

Then they went on to Capernaum. Directly on the Sabbath he went into the synagogue and taught. And they were astonished at his teaching, for he taught them as one who has authority in himself, unlike the scribes. Suddenly there appeared in their synagogue a man possessed by an evil spirit. He shrieked out, 'What do you want with us, Jesus of Nazareth? Have you come to destroy us? I know who you are – the Holy One of God.' Then Jesus rebuked the spirit, saying, 'Be silent and come out of him.' And the evil spirit convulsed the man, and with a loud cry left him. They were all amazed and were asking each other, 'What is this? New teaching, and with authority! He commands even the unclean spirits and they obey him.' So his fame spread quickly throughout the whole region of Galilee.

When they left the synagogue they went directly to the house of Simon and Andrew with James and John. Now Simon's mother-in-law lay sick with a fever. At once they told Jesus about her, and he came and took her by the hand and raised her up. The fever left her and she began to see to their needs.

In the evening when the sun had set, they brought to him all who were sick or possessed by demons; indeed the whole town crowded at the door. He healed many who were sick with various diseases and drove out many demons. He did not allow the demons to speak, for they knew who he was.

Next morning, still a great while before daybreak, he rose and went away to a remote place, and there he prayed. But Simon and his companions went in search of him. When they found him they said, 'Everyone is looking for you.' He replied, 'Then let us go away into the next towns that I may preach there also, for that is why I came out.' So he went throughout all Galilee, preaching in their synagogues, and driving out demons.

One door is closed and another opened. The shutting of John in the dungeon was the sign for Jesus to launch his mission in Galilee. The few words that summarize his message are rich in meaning. Jesus proclaims that the divine work foretold by the prophets has arrived. The age of reparation is completed and now the time of God's manifest rule is dawning, a new world of peace and goodness. As his judgement and salvation hasten in, his people must repent and believe the good news. For with a new mind and spirit they can become part of the kingdom.

Around him Jesus begins to form the community of believers, those open to the kingdom. He calls disciples to join him in his mission. They respond immediately and wholeheartedly. On the north-west shore of the lake lay the town of Capernaum and the home of Peter and Andrew. The impressive ruins of the synagogue which we can still visit today belong to a later century, but no doubt preserve the site of the building where Jesus spoke to a Sabbath gathering. People were astonished at the authority of his teaching. He did not cite opinions of former teachers and their schools or grope through a forest of scriptural quotations. From Jesus himself rose a fountain of divine wisdom.

And when he heals a man of disordered mind he does not, like other healers, resort to elaborate procedures. His authoritative word is suffi-cient. This story of healing, like so many others in the gospels and Acts, is formed in the thought-pattern general at the time – maladies caused by mischievous or malevolent spirits, demons that move into a person and take up residence as though occupying a house. Modern people usually do not so personalize the harmful forces or factors. But what comes across still in such stories is the authority of the Lord Jesus. The healings act out the same message as that which he preached – the kingdom of God is even now coming upon you. Jesus, the bearer of the kingdom, is banishing the long dominion of dark forces. They recognize this Holy One, Son of God and Messiah, and they flee away.

Mark's gospel is said to embody Peter's recollections, and certainly this account of a day's ministry in Capernaum conveys the excitement of someone who experienced it – from the synagogue back to the house, Peter's mother-in-law healed and able to serve the meal, and then, as Sabbath restrictions end with sundown, the multitudes crowding at the door with their invalids for Jesus to heal. Some hours of sleep, but long before the new day has broken, Jesus rises and goes away to a desert place to pray, only to be followed by the disciples with their report that 'everyone is looking for you'. And so on to the neighbouring towns, 'preaching and driving out demons', all in sign of the kingdom.

Jesus Cures Those Who Know Their Need

Mark 2.13–17

> Then he went out again beside the lake, and a great crowd came to him and he taught them. Passing on further, he saw Levi, the son of Alphaeus, at his seat in the customs house, and he said to him, 'Follow me.' And he rose and followed him.
>
> Now when Jesus was sitting in Levi's house, many tax-collectors and others who were similarly deemed sinners sat down with Jesus and his disciples, for there were many such people among his followers. When the scribes of the Pharisees saw that he was eating with the sinners and tax-collectors, they said to his disciples, 'How can he eat with tax-collectors and sinners?' When Jesus heard it he said, 'Not those who are well need the doctor but those who are ill. I did not come to call the righteous but to call sinners.'

The zeal of the Pharisees for the law of Moses led them to develop a strict and detailed system of observances. They came to abhor association with the ordinary folk who lived outside these rules. Prominent among those they despised as 'sinners' were the tax-collectors. These were agents of the government, ultimately the Roman Empire, and so were regarded as serving an unclean, evil power, not to mention their own reputation for corruption.

From the regions of Damascus and the Decapolis a rich trade flowed down towards the Mediterranean ports, passing near the north shore of the lake and entering there the territory ruled by Herod Antipas. In the customs house beside this road the revenue men would be busy. Seated there at his counter was Levi, a senior figure and later, it seems, given the name Matthew and made one of the twelve disciples. If he already knew Jesus, we are not told of it. The bare account suggests only the force of the Lord's presence, his eyes, his voice, his understanding of the moment and the man: 'Follow me?'

So Levi left his work and soon we find him celebrating his new life by giving a meal in his house for Jesus and many friends. But some leading Pharisees, learned in their laws and practices, found fault with Jesus for having table fellowship with such undesirables. What a contamination!

Yet for Jesus it was the essence of his mission. He had come to reach out. He could work fruitfully with those who knew their need. The effect of his friendship was profound. Here was a great teacher, far more than a teacher, who did not despise them. What that must have meant to them! He remained himself, but from his goodness, love and constant witness to the Father, many found the way to repent, to begin anew with God. Alas for these superior persons, zealous in their way and experts, who yet could not discern the divine grace that he brought them – 'I came not to call the righteous, but sinners.'

The theme echoes throughout all the gospel stories and has never lost its power. When we know our failure and need, he does not despise us. Through the wonderful friendship of Jesus we find the desire and then the strength to turn to God anew. With such a friend, we will live only to please him.

The New That Bursts from the Old

Mark 2.21–22

> You never sew a piece of unshrunk cloth on to an old coat. Instead of filling it up, it would only take from it, the new from the old, leaving you with a worse hole. And you wouldn't put new wine into old wineskins. The wine would burst the skins, and you would lose both the wine and the skins. No, new wine needs new wineskins.

In those days there was a great respect for the past. Greatly revered were the customs and beliefs handed down from the ancestors. Teaching carried weight if it could be linked to a sage of old time. But hardly had Jesus come on the scene when they were saying, 'What is this? New teaching, with authority!'

The behaviour of Jesus and his disciples also caused surprise. They did not observe frequent fasts as other groups did. When questioned about this, Jesus compared the happy scenes at a wedding – you would not expect the guests to be fasting in the company of the bridegroom. What a glimpse this gives of the effect of the presence of Jesus! Through him the light of the kingdom was shining about them and its music delighting them in these days of his companionship, the 'days of the Son of Man' (Luke 17.22), when he healed and led and talked of God as no one ever had.

Yes, here was a new era, prepared by the old but necessarily breaking from it. Jesus was not here to patch up the old garment. New cloth patched on old would only pull away and make a bigger rent. New wine, still vigorously fermenting, would only burst a tired old leather bottle. It must rather be put in strong new wineskins.

Yes, with Jesus comes a new light and a new power. And for all the challenge that his presence represents, it brings a new joy. In his presence his followers breathe the air of the new creation.

A Sign of His Glory

John 2.1–11

On the third day there was a wedding in Cana in Galilee. The mother of Jesus was there, and Jesus also was invited to the wedding along with his disciples. When the wine ran out the mother of Jesus said to him, 'They have no wine.' Jesus said to her, 'Mother, there is no need to worry. My hour has not yet come.' His mother said to the servants, 'Whatever he tells you, do it.'

Now six stone water-pots were standing there for the Jewish customs of purification. Each could hold 20 or 30 gallons, Jesus said to them, 'Fill the pots with water', and they filled them to the brim. Then he said to them, 'Now draw some out and take it to the president of the feast.' So they carried it to him, and he tasted the water now become wine, not knowing where it had come from [though the servants who had drawn the water knew]. Then the president of the feast called the bridegroom and said to him, 'Everyone serves the best wine first, and when they have drunk well, the poorer sort, but you have saved the best wine till now.'

So in Cana of Galilee Jesus did this, the first of his signs, and disclosed his glory, and his disciples believed in him.

'Mother of Jesus' – the phrase seems to be used as a name, a custom still common in Palestine, of naming mother or father from the first son. She would be helping to care for the guests and noticed the wine give out, and she was anxious for the bridegroom's sake. How confident she is that Jesus will know what to do!

But he holds himself away from the anxiety, waiting for the moment – a travail of waiting for the guidance and creative strength sought from his Father. To some of those present there will be a disclosure of his 'glory', his nature as Son of God.

It is described as the first of the 'signs', deeds which revealed something of that mystery. It spoke of transformation and the joy of a new life in God which Jesus brings to those who receive him. Water itself is infinitely precious and in other stories of Jesus itself represents God's gift of true life. But in the present story it is the wine which stands for a higher joy and the abundance of God's grace, as the wedding celebration is a thrilling time lifted above careworn days.

So the story is full of significance as the first of the seven signs set out in the Gospel of John. Jesus is revealed as the one come forth from the Father. To those who believe in him comes a profound change. They receive a new strength and a new joy. Of all they have known, this is the best. They begin to share in the very life of heaven. Yet although this first of the signs is indeed a disclosure to his disciples, it is but a glimpse of the reality they will possess on 'the third day' yet to come.

Coming to Jesus in the Night

John 3.1–19

There was a man named Nicodemus who was a Pharisee and a ruler of the Jews. He came to Jesus by night and said to him, 'Master, we know you are a teacher come from God, for no one would do these signs that you do if God was not with him.' Jesus answered, 'Truly, truly I say to you: unless you are born from above you, you cannot see the kingdom of God.'

Nicodemus said to him, 'How can anyone be born when already old? Can he enter a second time into his mother's womb and be born?' Jesus replied, 'Truly, truly I say to you: if you are not born from water and the Spirit, you cannot enter into the kingdom of God. What is born of the flesh is flesh, and what is born of the Spirit is spirit. Do not wonder that I say to you, you must be born from above. The wind blows where it wills and you hear the sound of it, but do not know where it comes from or where it is going. It is the same with everyone who is born from the Spirit.'

Nicodemus answered, 'How can these things be?' Jesus replied, 'Are you the teacher of Israel, yet not understanding these things? Truly, truly I say to you: we speak what we know and bear witness to what we have seen, and yet you do not receive our witness.' [A wider audience is now addressed.] 'I have told you earthly things and you do not believe. How will you believe if I tell you things of heaven? For no one has gone up into heaven except the one who came down out of heaven, even the Son of Man who belongs to heaven. And as Moses lifted up the serpent in the wilderness, so must the Son of Man be lifted up, so that whoever believes in him may have eternal life.'

In Nicodemus we see a man learned in the traditional religion, a recognized teacher or doctor of the sacred law and apparently a member of the ruling body, the Sanhedrin. He is drawn to Jesus, being convinced by his deeds of power that he has come from God. But Nicodemus has come to converse with him cautiously, under cover of the darkness, and we wonder if from the darkness of his spiritual understanding he will be able to recognize the light that is Jesus.

Quickly Jesus comes to the point: to see the kingdom of God and so to enter it, you must be born 'from above'. Such a rebirth into the things of heaven, into the true life, is by way of water and the Holy Spirit, the way of repentance, forgiveness and regeneration – we might say resurrection – which came to be embodied in Christian baptism.

But this master of the law, rigorous in his observations of prayer times, Bible reading, fasting, almsgiving and ablutions, is perplexed at this teaching of rebirth. Jesus only challenges him further with his parable of the wind (Greek *pneuma*). As the wind comes with power and we cannot see it or know its source or destination, so the Spirit (also *pneuma*) comes to do the divine work and we cannot explain or master it. In marvel and mystery God effects for us the new begetting or birth from above.

Jesus here is anticipating the work of salvation as it will be known in the community of faith that will result from his death and resurrection. In the ancient story (Num. 21), Moses had at God's command lifted high a bronze serpent on a standard, and when wounded people looked at it they were healed. The mission of Jesus, already bringing the call to faith and healing, will come to its climax when he, the Son of Man, is lifted up on the cross. Then indeed those who look upon him with faith – trusting in him and accepting him as the bearer of God's forgiveness and healing – will find true life, joyful and eternal life in God.

The suffering of Jesus and of God who 'gave' and 'sent' him was all for love's sake – God's love and good purpose for the whole world. And God so acted not to condemn but to save. Yet those who reject Jesus reject the light and so judge themselves, preferring darkness. Not that he will ever give up to seek and redeem them, but still the warning here is dire. To despise the light of God is to take oneself upon a long and bitter road.

Jesus and the Woman at the Well

John 4.4–28,39–42

Now Jesus had to pass through Samaria, and he arrived at a town in Samaria called Sychar, quite near to the piece of land which Jacob gave to his son Joseph, and Jacob's well was there. Jesus was tired from his journey and at once sat down by the well. It was about midday.

Then a woman of Samaria came to draw water. Jesus said to her, 'Give me a drink' – his disciples having gone to the town to buy food. The Samaritan woman said to him, 'How is it that you, a Jewish man, ask a drink from me, a Samaritan woman?' [For Jews do not share vessels with Samaritans.] Jesus replied, 'If you knew the gift of God and who it is who says to you, Give me a drink, you would have asked him and he would have given you living water.'

The woman said to him, 'Sir, you have nothing to draw water with and the well is deep. Where could you get that living water? Are you greater than our ancestor Jacob who gave us the well and drank of it himself, his sons and daughters also, and his cattle?' Jesus replied, 'Everyone who drinks this water will thirst again. But whoever drinks the water that I shall give them will never thirst again, for the water that I give them will become in them a well of water springing up to give eternal life.'

The woman said to him, 'Sir, give me this water so that I never thirst or have to come all this way to draw water.' Jesus said to her, 'Go, call your husband and come back again.' She answered, 'I have no husband.' Jesus said, 'You are right to say you have no husband, for you have had five husbands, and the man you now have is not your husband. You spoke the truth.'

'Sir,' said the woman, 'I can tell you are a prophet. Our ancestors worshipped on this mountain, while you say that Jerusalem is the right place to worship.' Jesus answered, 'Woman, believe me, the hour comes when you will worship the Father neither on this mountain nor in Jerusalem. You worship you do not know what, but we worship what we know, for salvation is from the Jews. The hour comes, and indeed is here, when the true worshippers will worship the Father in spirit and truth. For the Father seeks such people to be his worshippers. God is Spirit, and those who worship him must worship in spirit and in truth.' The woman said to him, 'I know that Messiah comes' [that is Christ] 'and when he comes he will make everything clear to us.' Jesus said to her, 'I am he, I who speak to you.'

Just then his disciples arrived. They were surprised that he was speaking to a woman, but no one asked him, 'What do you need? Why are you speaking to her?' So the woman left her water-pot and went back to the town . . . [v. 39] And many of the Samaritans from that town believed in him because of the woman's word when she testified, 'He told me all I ever did.'

And when the Samaritans came to him, they begged him to stay with them, and he did so for two days. And many more believed because of what he himself said to them. They told the woman, 'Now we believe not just because of what you told us. Now we have heard for ourselves and know that he is indeed the Saviour of the world.'

The province of Samaria lay in the central mountains between Judea and Galilee, and it was the natural route between the two. Like Judea, it was under direct Roman rule through the procurator Pontius Pilate. But there had long been deep animosity between the Jews, whose worship centred exclusively on the temple in Jerusalem, and the Samaritans who worshipped on Mount Gerizim, the more ancient centre of the old Israel. Both communities possessed and revered the law of Moses in the first five books of Scripture. Yet Jews holding to strict views of racial and ritual purity would avoid the Samaritans, especially their women and their drinking vessels.

But Jesus here crosses the boundaries with sovereign freedom, and after staying two days with the Samaritan townsfolk is recognized by them as Saviour, not just of Jews and Samaritans alike, but of the world. As in many other stories, he has reached out readily to the despised, to the fallen, and to women. The conversation he has at length with the woman at the well is itself of great depth, marking the wonderful gift of salvation that comes through faith in Jesus.

'If you knew the gift of God and what it is' – the gift is Jesus himself. He is there before us, yet we do not recognize him. He leads our understanding. 'Give me a drink' – there is a need for us to meet, a kindness to perform. It is a beginning, and we may be on the way to knowing how in love he reaches to *our* need, unworthy as we are. 'Living water' is such as wells up fresh from a spring and so represents here the fountain of God's grace that gives eternal life, the true life of communion with God.

Jesus affirms that 'salvation is from the Jews' – from them, after long preparation, the Messiah comes, but he also foresees the destruction that will befall the holy centres of Jerusalem and Samaria, and he speaks of the coming new era of worship led by the Spirit. It is as though the old order of worship was but a shadow now to be replaced by its reality, its 'truth', which is to be known through the gift of the Holy Spirit. In experience of this Spirit and Truth, the worshippers will have a marvellous freedom of communion with the Father.

But how to enter this new age? The revolutionary change is drastic, almost beyond imagination. The Samaritan woman rightly thinks of the Messiah, the Lord's Anointed (in Greek 'Christ'), and she is led from a hope of his coming to knowledge that he is present before her.

The disciples arrive with food they have bought, and the woman hurries home with news of the extraordinary traveller – 'Can this be the Christ?' Jesus speaks with his disciples about his true food: to do the will and work of his Father. He speaks of the harvest that has come so suddenly. Amazingly, the fields are already ripe for reaping. Others have sown, and now the disciples are to reap the harvest for eternal life.

By now the people of the town have come out to see Jesus. They beg him to stay with them. He does so, and many come to faith in him. From hearing the woman's testimony, they pass on to their own direct experience, sure now that he is the Saviour of the world. So already the harvest for eternal life is being gathered in, and the disciples then and now learn from the Lord that across the world the fields are beckoning.

Lessons at the Lakeside; Pictures of the Kingdom

Mark 4.1–2,26–34

Again he began to teach by the lakeside. A very large crowd gathered to him, so he got into a boat and sat there a little way from the shore, while all the crowd were on the land, reaching down to the water's edge. He taught them many things in parables, and as he taught them he spoke to them in this fashion . . .

'The kingdom of God is as a man who sows seed on the ground, then sleeps and rises as nights and days come round, and all the while the seed is sprouting up and growing, he knows not how. The earth bears fruit of itself, first the blade, then the ear, then the grain that fills the ear. But when the grain is ripe, he gets to work at once with the sickle, for the harvest has come.'

Again Jesus said, 'What can we compare the kingdom of God to? What parable can we use for it? We can compare it to a grain of mustard seed. When sown, the smallest of all the seeds that are sown on the earth; yet once sown, it springs up and grows bigger than all the other herbs, putting out great branches where the birds can shelter.'

A warm and pleasant place is the Lake of Galilee. The disciples have well remembered the characteristic scene as the Master sat in a boat just off the shore, and with his poetic words addressed the great throng seated on the hillside right down to the water's edge. It is a simple but effective arrangement. On the water he escapes the crush, and from the flat surface around him the melody of his voice resounds clearly up the slopes.

His teaching is a poetry of pictures and parables, here of plants and growth. Sensitive to the wonders of nature, he readily sees a likeness to human life and spiritual realities because he is so clear that all is in the hand and heart of the Father.

His pictures and stories illuminate the kingdom of God – announcing the new era of God's work was, after all, the core of his message. The parable of the growing seed suggests a role for human work for the coming of the kingdom – the seed is sown, the crop at length is reaped; but most of all, the parable brings out the mystery and miracle of God's power which gives life and growth. So, alert for our part, yet humble before the Creator and King, we are above all to trust in his power of new creation, knowing that it is surely at work night and day beyond all our understanding.

And the kingdom may take hold in something very small. As Jesus called one disciple at a time, visited one little town, healed one person, so we too must respect the potential of one encounter, one moment. The smallest of seeds grows into the greatest herb, with branches to shelter birds from far and wide. And many are those who will find their home in the kingdom grown mightily there from something very small, which yet enclosed the blessing of God.

Jesus Speaks to the Wind and Sea

Mark 4.35–41

> Later that day when evening had come, he said to them, 'Let us cross over to the other side.' Leaving the crowd, they took him with them in the boat, just as he was, and some other boats went with them. Then the wind got up into a wild tempest, and the waves pounded the boat till it was almost swamped. But Jesus was in the stern, asleep on a cushion. So they woke him, crying, 'Master, do you not care if we drown?'
>
> Waking up, he rebuked the wind and said to the sea, 'Hush, be still.' And the wind dropped and all was calm. 'Why do you fear?' he asked them. 'Do you not yet have faith?' But they trembled now with awe. 'Who is this,' they asked one another, 'that even the wind and sea obey him?'

Evening falls, and Jesus, exhausted from the day's teaching, finds the little boat still serviceable. They are able to leave the multitude on the shore and set out directly across the lake to seek quiet and renewal of spirit miles away on the far shore. The accompanying boats no doubt bring the rest of the disciples and close followers. In years to come they will remember vividly how Jesus fell into a deep sleep on a cushion in the stern of the boat.

Storms can rise suddenly on the Lake of Galilee. The wind may begin to blow furiously down the mountain passes and drive the waters into a wild tumult. And so it happens. The waves rear and crash into the boat. The disciples fear for their lives, but Jesus still sleeps.

In their panic they speak foolishly as they wake him – does he not care that they perish? He speaks first to the wild elements, bidding them hush and be still. When the wind abates, the waters soon fall calm again. The contrast is so great, the relief so profound, that it is a calm never to be forgotten. The Lord then speaks to them of the faith that overcomes fear. They, for their part, are trembling now with awe of the divine presence which they know in him.

The hostile wind and heaving waves, the human helplessness, the nearness of death – the scene is akin to many a situation when the heart is gripped by fear. At all such times, this recollection of Jesus can lead us also to find peace through trust in the power and wisdom of God the Father, Son and Holy Spirit.

14.

Patterns of Living in the Dawning Kingdom

Happiness Not Where the World Seeks It

Matthew 5.1–10

> Seeing the crowds, Jesus ascended the hill, and when he had sat down, his disciples gathered about him. Then he opened his mouth and began to teach them, saying:
>
> > 'Happy are the humble, for theirs is the kingdom of heaven!
> > Happy are those who mourn, for they shall be comforted!
> > Happy are the gentle ones, for they shall inherit the earth!
> > Happy are those hungering and thirsting for the good, for they shall be filled!
> > Happy are those who are kind, for kindness shall be done to them!
> > Happy are the pure in heart, for they will see God!
> > Happy the peacemakers, for they will be called children of God!
> > Happy those persecuted for what is right, for theirs is the kingdom of heaven!'

From all over Galilee and from beyond the borders, people were flocking to Jesus, many in hope of cures. In view of such a multitude, Jesus goes up to a height and his disciples gather about him. Is it a case of seeking a place of quiet in the mountains? That would not agree with the end of the teaching, where the crowds respond to what they have heard (7.28–29). Rather, then, we see Jesus seeking a practical arrangement for addressing disciples and crowd, as he did with the boat off the lake shore. He takes his seat as teacher on an eminence. His close followers sit round him, a shield from crowding, while the multitude spreads over the slopes below. Tradition locates the eminence near the lake, crowned now by the beautiful Church of the Beatitudes.

Jesus 'opens his mouth' – from the silence of the wise, the quiet of one who listens for God and meditates, he begins to preach, giving out the treasures entrusted to him. At once his words are like a melody, a poetic chant.

On many occasions he has proclaimed the dawn of the kingdom of God. Now he guides us how to be part of it. He holds up the happiness, the enviable bliss, of those who can thus enter the kingdom. Their characteristics, as he lists them, are in part contrary to what people might associate with happiness. As often, the teaching of Jesus has an edge to it.

Those enviably happy ones are humble ('poor in spirit'). Not that poverty has seized them as unwilling victims. Rather, they themselves have chosen an unselfish path, a life of service, caring nothing for the riches and honours of the self-regarding world. They gladly renounce such wealth for the Lord's sake, and walk humbly with him.

Even more surprising, these supremely happy ones 'mourn'. Not for them an insensitive jollity. Sadly aware of their own faults, they must also weep for the evil that stalks through the world, so brash, deceitful and cruel. But because of their tears and their gentle hearts, and their longing ('their hunger and thirst') for the kingdom of goodness, God will assuredly comfort them and show them the triumph of his kingdom.

Acting in kindness, they themselves will be blessed with the kindness of God. As 'pure in heart', they are sincerely devoted to God, open to him, wanting his will. So they will 'see God', being admitted to his near presence and the experience of his beauty. Already they enjoy the blessing of a vivid faith, walking with him, constantly aware of his reality, while superior persons, less devoted, fail in vision and in faith.

'Peacemakers', they have peace in their hearts and would harm no creature. But they also reach out with the power of peace. They are quick to make up quarrels. They turn the wrongs done to them into an opportunity to bless. They come between feuding parties to make peace. In this they are so in harmony with God's own desire that he owns them as his children.

To stay true to the good, true to the Lord, needs courage, for it will attract hostility. Enduring persecution, these faithful ones will be alongside their Lord and will share with him in the joy that transcends suffering.

Requirements beyond Natural Strength

Matthew 5.21–24,38–48

You have heard that it was said to people of old, 'You shall do no murder, and whoever commits murder shall be liable to judgement.' But I, I say to you, that anyone who rages against his brother or sister shall be liable to judgement. Indeed, anyone who calls his sister or brother *raka* (worthless] is in danger of the sentence of the court, and anyone who says, 'You blockhead!' is in danger of hell fire.

So if you are offering your gift at the altar, and there you remember that your brother or sister has something against you, leave your gift before the altar and go away; first be reconciled to them, and then come back and offer your gift . . .

You have heard that it was said, 'An eye for an eye and a tooth for a tooth.' But I, I say to you, Do not fight back at your attacker, and whoever hits you on the right cheek, turn the other to them also. And if anyone would go to law with you to take your shirt, let them have your coat as well. And if anyone presses you into service to go one mile, go with them two. Give to anyone who asks from you, and do not turn your back on anyone who wants to borrow from you.

You have heard that it was said, 'You shall love your neighbour and hate your enemy.' But I, I say to you, Love your enemies and pray for those who persecute you, so that you may be children of your Father who is in heaven. For he makes his sun rise on the bad and good alike, and sends rain on the just and on the unjust. For if you love only those who love you, what reward can you expect? Do not even tax-collectors do as much? And if you greet only your brothers and sisters, what are you doing more than others? Are not even the heathen doing as much? So then, you must be perfect as your heavenly Father is perfect.'

Even familiarity can scarcely veil the challenge of these words. Not only does Jesus call for attitudes far beyond the common morality; he also gives examples which are at the extreme. For should we indeed not resist an evil assailant? And should we not be wary of requests for gifts or loans? Does hell fire seem appropriate for one who calls his brother or sister useless or stupid? Or if a soldier of the occupying power requisitions us to carry his baggage for a mile, should we really offer to go a second mile?

Yes, these are provocative teachings, words to give us a jolt, and spoken with such authority, explicitly making a contrast with sacred or customary standards long accepted. Who can follow such a radical teacher? Certainly there is nothing humdrum here. It is a call to something extraordinary.

The theme resounding through these teachings is the call to love. Towards everyone we encounter we are to show this love – love in the sense of a constant good will, a set purpose of seeking the other's good. Within one's own circle (towards the 'brother or sister') this is difficult enough. The close contact and mutual knowledge can as well provide strain as affection. Rivalry and differences of temperament can make for bad temper and even ill will. But the love-command still applies beyond our circle. Towards aliens in race or religion, towards enemies, towards criminals, still the command applies – love positively, and for evil return good.

But there is an aspect of great significance which should not be overlooked: the pattern and the inspiration for such love is the mercy of God, his good will to all his creatures. Jesus is not so much teaching an ethic, a pattern for human relations, as calling us to live to please God and fulfil his purpose for us – to be as his children. It is that, insists Jesus, which entails this love in human dealings, love even for the unlovely. The ancient requirement was to be holy as God is holy, and Jesus gives it a new direction. The ideal shifts from ritual purity to love. To belong to the kingdom of God we should be 'perfect as he is perfect'. So we should fulfil his will for us, being wholly and consistently controlled by love, all in accordance with the divine example.

A huge requirement, put to us with uncompromising force! It seems overwhelming, way beyond us. But it is part of a new order, with its new possibilities, which will unfold further as the story of Christ unfolds. It is the way of the new kingdom, the era of God's new work and presence, of new birth and the gifts of the Holy Spirit. Here we are to live in his forgiveness, in humility and faith, in communion with the Father, manifest in Christ, and by the inspiration of the Holy Spirit. So we shall come to be formed by this love and live in accordance with it – the love flowing from God that means good for all his creatures.

Doing Good in Secret

Matthew 6.1–6

Beware of doing your charitable deeds openly for everyone to see, for then you have no reward from your Father who is in heaven. So when you give to the poor, do not trumpet it about as the hypocrites do in the synagogues and in the streets to get glory from other people. Truly, I say to you: they have had their reward. But when you give to the poor, do not let your left hand know what your right hand is doing. So your good deed will be done in secret, and it is your Father who sees in secret who will reward you.

And when you pray, do not be like the hypocrites. For they love to stand to pray in the synagogues and on the street corners for everyone to see them. Truly I say to you: they have had their reward. But you, when you pray, go into your room and when you have shut your door, pray to your Father who is known in secret, and your Father who sees in secret will reward you.

'To get glory from other people' – the motive of so much that is done. 'Hypocrites' (originally 'actors' and so people living a life of pretence, putting on a show) are still not hard to find. The prestige they may win is all the reward they are going to get. For the reward God gives comes to us as we do our deeds of kindness for his sake, in the reality of love. Our reward is to be close to him, for we have acted in harmony with his will.

All the more in personal prayer, our hearts must be set towards our heavenly Father, not towards human admiration The picture Jesus gives of a person standing with outstretched hands, praying out loud and long in a conspicuous place, fits that society where great prestige was accorded to piety and individuals observed set hours of prayer throughout the day. But no doubt in our more secular age there are still situations where we spoil our address to God, to truth, to beauty, by letting our eye stray towards the favours of other people.

Jesus does not deny the duty of witness, for that too is to be done only for God's glory, for the good which he wills. 'You are the light of the world,' he has already said (Matthew 5.14); 'let your light shine before others so that they may see your good works and glorify your Father who is in heaven' (5.16). Alongside secret acts of charity, all our words and dealings through the day can express thankfulness for God's mercy, our joy in Christ, a radiance of his love.

A Pattern for Prayer

Matthew 6.7–15

When you pray, do not rattle on as the heathen do, for they think they will be heard for the quantity of their words. Do not be like them, for your Father knows what you need before you ask him. But pray like this:

Our Father in heaven,
may your name be manifest in all its power,
your kingdom come,
your will be accomplished on earth as in heaven.
Give us our bread for the coming day,
and forgive us our sins
as we forgive those who sin against us.

And let us not come into the fiery trial,
but save us from evil.

For if you forgive others their offences, your Father will forgive you. But if
you do not forgive others, neither will your Father forgive your offences.

The prayer is worded as from a group – 'our', 'we,' 'us' – such as the two
or three who represent the community of the Lord and will be blessed
with his mysterious presence. All the same, it lends itself to individual
use, with its challenge to personal trust and to a forgiving spirit. But an
individual who says the prayer alone can readily be aware of the great
host that in the bond of Christ's fellowship lifts this prayer to the Father.

It begins at once with a word that expresses our relationship to God.
Here we are, speaking to the one who has given us our existence, who
knows and cares for us, and to whom we owe respect and love. Calling
to God might have been a groping in the dark, a wandering through cold
and endless years. But this 'our Father' places us in a precious knowledge
and loving bond, a position of confidence, a home in the vast universe.
Directly, we speak to almighty God in heaven – our Father!

The theme that then fills the first half of the prayer is so important that
it is expressed three times over. Our world is full of ills which in the end
only God can put right. Jesus has come to announce and indeed begin
that great work of God – a new creation, his new kingdom. Our part is to
pray for this work of God with all our heart. To pray like this, we must
believe that he can do it, and he alone can do it, also that he wills to do it,
and that there is nothing greater that can be desired, as we love all that
God has made and yearn for its healing and eternal blessing.

The first expression of the theme is familiar to us as 'Hallowed be thy
name.' The Greek here is a respectful way of asking that God glorify his
name, that is, make his divine power manifest and dominant. The same
thought is then expressed as the coming in of his new reign or kingdom,
the new world of his open and perfect rule: 'May your kingdom come.' A
third time the theme resounds as we pray that God should make his will
to be clearly effective, overcoming all hindrances, saving and blessing all
that he has made: may his will take effect on earth as in the perfection of
the eternal realm.

The second half of the prayer can also be regarded as a theme in threefold expression. This theme is our personal need. First it is expressed as the
need for bread. How little of all our bodily wants is asked for! Shelter and
clothing, for example, are not mentioned. No doubt 'bread' may cover food
and drink generally, but only enough for a day is asked for. Jesus sees life as
unfolding in trust of our Father, a day at a time, and he would have us be

content with little indeed. The familiar translation is 'Give us this day our daily bread', and here an almost unknown Greek word is translated 'daily'. But the picture may rather be of the portion that will be allotted in the evening or in the dawn for the coming day. Beyond this, Christians have sometimes found here a prayer for the heavenly bread, the meal of the Eucharist and the kingdom. The plainer meaning, however, is very eloquent, with its humility of desire and its faith in God's care.

Then comes our need for forgiveness. For Jesus it goes without saying that we are sinners, failing to render to God what we should. He has us ask our Father to forgive us our sins, but, as he often teaches, it will be a forgiveness that requires us to forgive the misdeeds and failings of others towards us. As the gospel unfolds, it is seen that Christ dies for our sins while we are yet unworthy, undeserving. But it remains necessary for us to believe in him, to open our hearts to him as our Saviour – and part of that openness, that receptivity, that faith, is our readiness to forgive.

Finally our need is seen against the prospect of a 'fiery trial' (or 'temptation'). The coming of the kingdom is a dangerous time. The old order will not give up without a struggle. For Jesus himself, and for many noble martyrs, there was already a fiery trial. But knowing our limitations, we pray that if it be possible this cup may pass from us, and, in any event, that God will rescue us from such evil.

There is an earnestness in this petition that we may not always have recognized. Just as there is a beginning of the new creation that we already experience in Jesus, so we have also to anticipate that final fierce conflict and testing. Again and again already we need to pray, 'Our Father, save us from this trial.'

There is a rounding off for the whole prayer familiar to us from church use and found, with variations, in a number of manuscripts. It ascribes all glory to God, and in its simplicity and brevity would be in keeping with the practice of Jesus and his disciples: 'For yours is the kingdom, the power and the glory, for ever. Amen.'

It is amazing how reluctant Christ's followers can be themselves to forgive. And so, at the end of the prayer Jesus tells us again that plain truth of forgiveness, vital as it is.

Learning from the Birds and Wild Flowers

Matthew 6.19–21,24–34

Do not hoard up for yourselves treasures on earth, where moths and all manner of creatures eat them away and thieves break in and steal them. But store up for yourselves treasures in heaven, where no moths or other creatures will eat them away, nor thieves break in and steal them. For where your treasure is, there will your heart be also . . .

No one can be slave to two masters, for either you neglect this one and favour that one, or are attentive to this one and disregard that one. You cannot be the servant of God and of mammon.

So I say to you: Do not worry about your life, what you will eat or what you will drink, or about your body, what you will wear. Is not life more than eating and the body more than clothes?

Look at the birds of the heavens – no sowing for them, no reaping, no gathering into barns! Yet your heavenly Father feeds them. Is not your price higher than theirs?

And can any of you by worrying add a single day to your life? And why worry about clothing? Just look at the flowers in the field. They do not labour or spin. Yet I say to you, even Solomon in all his finery was not arrayed like one of these. If God so clothes the wild flowers, which are there today and tomorrow are but fuel for the fire, will he not all the more clothe you that have so little faith?

So do not worry, saying, Oh what shall we eat, what shall we drink? Oh how shall we be clothed? These are things the godless worry about. Your heavenly Father knows you need all these things.

But seek first his kingdom and his good purpose and all these other things will be given you as well. So don't worry about tomorrow, for tomorrow can worry about itself. Today's trouble is enough to be going on with.

Words very familiar perhaps, yet when pondered freshly how astonishing! How far the world's way of living has drifted from the way insisted on by Jesus. Again and again he gives his radical call – to live simply, desiring above all the will of God, taking a day at a time in profound trust.

He points to the perishing of earthly stores. Thieves dig out the hidden gold; moths eat up the surplus clothes. He mentions another 'eating away' (not 'rust' as in some translations) and the picture may be of stored grain which is attacked by mice, worms, mould, and so on. But if our energy is directed rather to serving God, we build a treasure that endures – entering into the joy of being close to the Lord, a joy to be fulfilled in his eternal home.

Many who make some claim to serve God are at the same time servants of 'mammon' – money and its allure. But God asks for single-hearted devotion: 'with all your heart, and with all your soul and with all your strength' (Deuteronomy 6.5). Such devotion and genuine trust belong together. Both mark the person who knows the shining reality of God, the Creator and Father.

After the rains, early in the year, the bare hills of the Holy Land turn green and wild flowers spring up in abundance, including the red anemones which Jesus may mean here (hardly 'lilies'). East wind and sun soon wither them, and they may be cut to give rapid heat for the cooking pot. The saying about birds and the higher value of humans may be a humorous touch. There was a market price for birds and also for slaves or bondservants. People were the higher priced!

Jesus is not condemning wise foresight, but anxiety that shuts out God and only does harm. By anxious thought, he says, you cannot add to your 'lifespan' (rather than 'stature'). The beginning and end of our earthly life are in the gift of God our Father. Our extract ends with a note of tender sympathy. Jesus knows well enough the burdens of care which the common people carry every day.

You Will Surely Find Him

Matthew 7.7–8

> Ask, and it will be given you,
> seek, and you will find,
> knock, and it will be opened to you.
> For everyone who asks receives,
> and one who seeks will find,
> and to one who knocks it will be opened.

The little poem is worded tersely. Do not these promises need some qualifications? After all, there is a lot of asking that gets no answer, a lot of seeking that never finds, a lot of knocking on doors that never open. But this is wisdom of the kind that provokes meditation. The moment comes when the truth of it strikes us, and gives a wonderful encouragement in our reaching out towards God.

Behind the words lies knowledge of the love of God as our Father, a knowledge which Jesus has supremely. In all your needs turn to him, says Jesus. Have confidence that you will not be ignored or thrust away. He will answer in the way that is best.

And there is encouragement for those yet far from faith, though desirous of it. Only begin – ask, seek, knock, for if you truly desire, the door will be opened. More widely yet, the little poem can be taken to heart. To everyone in perplexity, in trouble, the Son of God, knowing the Father, speaks here: Ask, seek, knock. He will answer. You will find him.

The Narrow Entrance and Path

Matthew 7.13–14

> Enter through the narrow gate. For wide is the gate and broad the way leading to ruin, and many are those who go in there. But narrow is the gate and restricted the way leading to life, and few are those who find it.

At first sight it may seem that the requirements that Jesus lays on his followers are lighter than those of other teachers. In some ways they are, and it is true that the common people heard his preaching gladly and multitudes flocked to him. He does not, for example, specify duties of fasting, times of prayer and observances of ritual purity. But what he asks is the way of trusting God, in which forgiveness and love reach and pass the limits of what most people can contemplate, let alone achieve. Many therefore turn away when the cost of discipleship becomes apparent. And many indeed run after debased, worthless things dressed up to tempt them.

While the throngs hear Jesus gladly, he utters his warning that to follow him one must resist the flow of the multitude, the fashion of the shallow ones. The gate and way that open to true life are narrow, hard to traverse, hard even to find. Sacrifice, discipline, or dying to vain desires – these mark the hard way to life with God and the pure happiness found there. We are not to expect to see the crowds flocking that way. They prefer the easy and ready pleasures that in the end prove to be ruinous. So Jesus warns the would-be disciple of the serious decision that must be made at the outset, parting from the herd, from the trends.

The marketing people, so powerful in society today, want to favour the gate and the way where the multitudes are found. It is good for business. The churches are judged by the numbers they attract. This little saying of Jesus thus carries a much-needed message.

However, the question of how Christ will save these multitudes that hurry down the broad and false way remains with God – God for whom all things are possible (Mark 10.27).

Prepared for the Storm

Matthew 7.24–29

> 'Everyone therefore who hear these words of mine and does them shall be compared to a wise man who built his house on the rock. The rains poured

down, the floods came and the winds blew and beat on that house, but it did not fall, for it was founded on the rock. But everyone who hears these words of mine and does not do them shall be compared to a foolish man who built his house on the sand. And the rains poured down, the floods came and the winds blew and beat against that house, and it fell, and great was its fall.' Now when Jesus had finished all these words, the crowds were amazed at his teaching, for he taught them as one having authority and not as their scribes.

It is good if people come to hear the preacher. The crowd about Jesus has listened for a long time. Yet their patience has scarcely been tried, for they are enthralled by the wonderful and lively form of the teaching and by its freshness and authority. Yes, it is a great experience to hear Jesus, and he is glad they are keen to hear. But he wants something more. He wants them to do as he has taught, to put it all into practice.

Yet he does not appeal for such action without a parable. He pictures a wise man who built his house on good foundations, digging down to the rock. A foolish man, however, saved himself time and effort by laying his walls on the surface of sandy earth. When the heavy rains of winter fell and the torrents raced down the mountain gullies, the wise man's foundations held firm, but the house of the foolish man collapsed under the force of the winds. Jesus sees a time of great upheaval coming, a time of fierce trial and testing. The wise who have heeded and followed his teaching will be able to stand in the storm, but those who have built lives heedless of his counsel will see them fall with a sudden crash. As with our preceding extract, so here, he warns against the easy option. Better to dig deep, to heed and act on the challenging words. Something then is built which will withstand the storms that will surely come.

15.

Adventures as the Work of Jesus Unfolds

Disciples Sent Out to Preach and Heal

Mark 6.6b–13

Jesus was going round the villages preaching. And he called the twelve to him and began to send them out in pairs. He gave them authority over harmful spirits, and he told them to take nothing for their journey except a staff – no bread, no satchel, no money in their pocket. They should wear sandals, but, he told them, not a second tunic. 'Where you are received into a house,' he continued, 'stay there until you leave the district. If no one there will receive you or listen to you, shake the dust from your feet as you leave as a witness to them.'

So they went out and preached, calling for repentance. And they drove out many demons, and many sick people they anointed with oil and cured.

Caring for individuals in need as he did, Jesus could not proceed quickly through the numerous villages and settlements. But as his disciples have grown in experience, he now has confidence to send them out to expand his mission. Working in pairs they could reach many more people, while each could support and care for the other and each could add the contribution of his own particular gifts. In such work two are better than one.

Jesus endows his disciples with 'authority over the harmful/unclean spirits' – something of that authority and power so evident in himself, something of the victory of the in-breaking kingdom. But he was sparing indeed with human resources. They took no food, money or extra clothing. Their poverty was a sign of their dependence on God. It would also enable those they came to help to be helpers in their turn. Trust and friendship might readily follow from kind deeds of hospitality in the cause of the kingdom. Further, the disciples were to accept the guidance of God and to stay fast with the first homes to give them hospitality – they might well be the poorest! To accept other invitations might well prolong the visit unduly.

In places where they met only rejection of their mission, the solemn gesture of shaking the dust from their sandals was as a warning that the inhabitants were bringing on themselves dissociation from the kingdom. Perhaps they might still think again. The anointing of the sick with oil, not mentioned as a feature of the work of Jesus himself, was common in the early church. With proper faith it became a sign and carrier of blessing and life-giving grace bestowed by God.

Jesus Feeds the Multitude in the Wilderness

Mark 6.30–44

Then those Jesus had sent out gathered again to him and told him all they had done and taught. And he said to them, 'Come now to a secret place and rest awhile.' For many were coming and going, and they had no leisure even to eat. So they went away in the boat to a desert place apart.

But many saw them going and recognized them, and they ran there overland from all the towns and arrived ahead of them. When he came ashore he saw a great throng, and he had pity on them for they were like sheep that had no shepherd, and he began to teach them many things.

When it grew late, his disciples came to him and said, 'This place is a desert and it is already late. Send them away to go into the country and villages round about and buy themselves something to eat.' But he answered them, 'You yourselves give them something to eat.' And they answered, 'Are we to spend 200 denarii, buying bread to give them to eat?' So he said to them, 'How many loaves do you have? Go and see.' When they knew, they reported, 'Five, and two fish.' Then he ordered that all should be seated in parties on the green grass. So they sat in groups of hundreds and fifties. Taking the five loaves and the two fish, and looking up to heaven, he blessed and broke the loaves and gave them to the disciples to set before the people. The two fish also he divided among them all. And they all ate and were satisfied. And they gathered up fragments, twelve basketfuls, and what was left of the fish. And those who ate of the loaves were five thousand men.

Those sent out by Jesus (his 'apostles') now return to him to tell him of it all – the welcomes and rejections, the obstacles and the miracles. Jesus listens and then decides they need to withdraw for a while from the continuing stir and bustle resulting from the missions, and find rest and refreshment in solitude with God.

But even with the boat they could not escape the crowds. Their departure was seen and their destination anticipated. Word spread, and people ran so eagerly from the towns that, as Jesus came ashore, he could see a multitude already awaiting him in that usually deserted place. Just when it had seemed a time for essential withdrawal and rest, one of their greatest engagements with the multitude was about to unfold.

As Jesus had been quick to care for his disciples, so now he was moved with pity for the eager, questing crowd. He saw them as a wandering flock that needed a shepherd's care and guidance. So he taught them with such abundance and devotion that the hours slipped by, and it was the disciples who had to begin thinking of the lack of food in that desert place.

When Jesus commands that all should be seated in orderly companies, he is thinking already of a sacred meal such as those that took place before God in festivals at the temple, themselves a foreshadowing of the expected feast in the final kingdom of God. The arrangement was therefore precise, although the detail is not quite clear to us. As Jesus looks to heaven, he is raising his prayer and mustering all his faith. In blessing the bread he gives thanks to the Father, and he holds it and breaks it in the power of God. The breaking prepares for the giving and sharing, all likewise in the power of God. At the Lord's direction, the disciples serve as the distributors and mediators of the holy gifts. The gathering up of the fragments left over signifies reverence for the God-given food and also witnesses to the scale of the miracle. Indeed, the count of five thousand men, perhaps following the practice in pilgrim gatherings, has not included the number of any women and children.

The story was of great significance for the early Christians and is found in all four gospels. We are left with a vivid sense of the compassion of Jesus and the immense depth of his faith. The meal was an act of sacred fellowship, a sign of the kingdom of God linking with the ancient miracle under Moses in the wilderness and with the prophecies of the end time. It would come also to be seen as a foreshadowing of the Lord's Supper and its remembrance in the Eucharist. Christ's prayer and blessing, his breaking and sharing of the bread, the fellowship and life in God, the divine compassion and overflowing generosity – all would be known again in the sacrament of the sacrifice and victory of Jesus, known through all time and places until the end of time itself.

The Saviour Comes Over the Wild Waters

Mark 6.45–52

Then without delay he made his disciples get into the boat and cross over towards Bethsaida ahead of him, while he himself saw to the departure of the people. And after he had taken leave of them, he went into the hills to pray.

By nightfall the boat was well out on the lake, while he remained alone on the land. Towards dawn he saw them struggling to row against a contrary wind, and he came to them, walking on the lake. He would have passed them, but when they saw him walking on the lake, they thought it was a ghost and cried out, for they all saw him and were terror-struck.

But at once he spoke to them and said, 'Be of good courage. I am with you. Have no fear.' And he got into the boat beside them, and the wind dropped. They were utterly amazed, for they had not taken in the miracle of the loaves, their hearts having been closed to understanding.

Jesus insists on the immediate departure of the disciples across the lake, leaving himself to send the multitude on their way by land. Following the solemn meal (as we learn from John's gospel) there was a danger that a messianic fever would take hold of the people, leading to a political uprising, and hence his decisive action.

After his hours of prayer in the darkness and solitude, and with the sky lightening a little towards dawn, Jesus saw the boat struggling against a tempestuous wind. Having himself insisted on their departure, he is all the more concerned for them. Yet when he reaches them, walking over the lake, he 'would have passed by them'. We may understand this as part of the pattern of God's help – not always rushing upon us, but near, awaiting our call.

Though the cry in this case is one of sheer panic, Jesus answers them at once, speaks reassuringly, and climbs in to sit beside them in their danger. The tempest ceases, and the utter amazement of the disciples is linked in the story with their slowness to discern the divine power sent through Jesus in the feeding of the multitude.

The two miracles, then, are linked and to be pondered together. Out of the depths of his pity and concern, Jesus has called forth from his Father two exceptional miracles. These few hours of marvel and prayer in the lonely place and on the wild waters have been like an episode of transfiguration, a brief time when the glory of the Son of God was shown, before the humility, the vulnerability and earthly weakness of the Word-Made-Flesh became again his daily way.

Jesus the Divine Bread

John 6.28–35,40

They asked him, 'What must we do if we are to do the works of God?' Jesus answered, 'This is the work of God: believe in the one that he has sent.'

So they said to him, 'What do you do as a sign, so that we may see and believe you? What work do you perform? Our ancestors ate the manna in the wilderness, as it is written: he gave them bread from heaven to eat.' Jesus answered, 'Truly, truly I say to you: it was not Moses who gave you the bread from heaven, but it is my Father who gives you the true bread from heaven. For the bread of God is that which comes down from heaven and gives life to the world.' Then they said to him, 'Master, give us this bread for evermore.'

Jesus said to them, 'I am the bread of life. Whoever comes to me shall never hunger, and whoever believes in me shall never thirst . . . [v. 40] For it is the will of my Father that everyone who looks to the Son and believes in him shall have eternal life, and that I shall raise them up on the last day.'

Jesus is speaking with people who have returned from the feeding of the 5,000 and have found him already in Capernaum. He counsels them to set their heart, not on the food that perishes but on the sustenance that endures and nourishes to eternal life. They should 'work' for this, though at the same time it will be 'given' them by the Son of Man, the one 'sealed' (v. 27), attested by God.

But what is this work? So they ask, and the answer is profound. They are to believe in the one God has sent. Such is the 'work of God', the work he seeks from us. It means the turning of all our soul to Christ in trust, a faith that shapes all we are or do. And all the while he is there nourishing us with the sustenance of life with God, eternal life.

That sustenance is indeed the Word himself: 'I am the bread of life.' By faith we share – we 'eat' and 'drink' – that creative grace of God which goes beyond physical, transitory feeding, to nourish us in a life that will flourish still beyond 'the last day', the life with God when earthly things have passed away.

Jesus Confronts the Ritual Laws of Clean and Unclean

Mark 7.1–8,14

Now some Pharisees collected about him, together with scholars who had come from Jerusalem. They noticed that some of his disciples ate their bread with 'common' hands, that is, hands not ceremonially washed (the Pharisees themselves, and indeed Jews in general, do not eat without such special washing, following a tradition of the elders. And when they come from the marketplace, they sprinkle themselves as a purification before eating. And they have many other traditional practices such as the immersing of cups and jugs and copper bowls.) So the Pharisees and scholars asked him, 'Why do your disciples not live according to the tradition of the elders, but eat their bread with common hands?' And he said to them, 'Isaiah prophesied well of you hypocrites, as it is written [Isaiah 29.13]: This people honours me with their lips, but their heart is far from me, teaching as their doctrines mere human precepts. The commandment of God you neglect, and hold fast to human tradition . . . [v. 14] Then, calling the people together again, he said to them, 'Hear me, all of you, be clear: nothing that goes into someone from outside can defile that person. It is the things that come out of a person that defile them.'

Members of the strict religious party of the Pharisees, bolstered by a delegation of learned scribes from the great Jerusalem schools, make a formidable array of critical inspectors, closely watching the followers of Jesus. They set great store by their elaborate rules applying the ancient holy laws to every situation in present life. Scripture contained laws of ritually 'clean' and 'unclean' foods, and the Pharisees were concerned to avoid impurity resulting from contact with non-Jews and others who did not observe such laws – the population of the country was in fact very mixed. Ritual purification before eating seemed to them an essential precaution, and they were quick to find fault with disciples of Jesus who did not share their strictness.

But to their criticisms Jesus replies severely. He sees these fault-finders as preoccupied with human regulations while neglecting fundamental requirements of God. They are 'hypocrites', actors putting on a show, not near God in their hearts. The real impurity, he says, is the moral evil arising in a person's heart, mind and imagination. It is this evil, not the food that nourishes the body, that defiles the soul.

Here was a radical challenge to current religious attitudes and Mark (7.19) accordingly notes that Jesus has in effect pronounced all foods ritually clean. It would take some years and some struggles for Christ's followers to adjust to the revolutionary change. But the adjustment was made, and for the church the issue of the 'clean' and 'unclean' and the whole web of its regulation has long been left behind.

So now the passage speaks a warning against other ways in which well-meant human practices may lead us astray from the key requirements of God. Anything which inclines us to self-righteousness and censoriousness may become such a trap, leading us away from humility, kindness and faith.

A Trap for Jesus

John 8.1–11

> So they each went to his house, but Jesus went on to the Mount of Olives. Early next morning he came again into the temple. All the people gathered to him, and he took his seat and began to teach them. Then the scribes and Pharisees brought a woman caught committing adultery. Setting her in the midst, they said to him, 'Master, this woman has been caught in the very act of adultery. Now in the law Moses commanded us to stone such women. What therefore do you say?' They said this to test him, in order to find some charge they could bring against him.
>
> Jesus stooped down and began to write with his finger on the ground. But when they persisted in asking him, he raised himself and said to them, 'Let the one among you who is without sin be the first to throw a stone at her.' And he stooped down again and wrote with his finger on the ground. And they, hearing what he said, went away one by one, beginning with the eldest, till he remained alone, and the woman still in the middle.
>
> Then Jesus raised himself and said to her, 'Where are they? Has no one condemned you?' She said, 'No one, sir.' And Jesus said, 'Neither do I condemn you. Go your way, and from now on sin no more.'

Jesus has been teaching in the temple precinct since early morning and is in no sense sitting as a judge. But a group of religious experts confront him with an offender caught in the act. Hostile to Jesus, they hope to trap him into words that could be represented as blasphemy against the law of Moses. There was a tension between the harsh severity of the ancient law on adultery and the normal treatment of offenders in this later age (usually divorce and financial loss). Such tension would lead to dangerous disputes between religious partisans. The hopes of the would-be ensnarers were high as they put the clear-cut case, and indeed the accused woman herself, before the Master.

But he met their malicious intention with studied detachment. He neither looked at them nor spoke, being apparently absorbed in his writing on the ground. We wonder if such writing in the dust was a custom of his when teaching – an arrangement of key words as a plan for his discourse or a basis for a poetic utterance. The intruders would be disconcerted, not sure whether he was preparing some weighty answer to them. They pressed again for a response, and Jesus straightened up and faced them with his challenge – who was willing to be the chief witness and therefore executioner, himself pure and innocent? In Jesus something of the dread holiness and penetrating knowledge of

God is sensed. His words go deep, and as he looks down again to his writing, the adversaries are glad of the opportunity to slink away one by one.

His original hearers and his disciples are presumably still there, quietly in the background. As Jesus now speaks to the accused woman, who has remained motionless and solitary, he is not concerned to damn her, but to set her on the right path. The Son has not been sent to condemn the world, but that the world through him should be saved. And likewise to the individual then and now he speaks, with authority and kindness, the word of challenge and of hope.

The story was not a firm part of any of the gospels, though in style closest to Luke. We must be glad that somehow it was preserved, no doubt from early days, for it gives a precious glimpse of the Lord, formidable to the cruel and tender to the forlorn.

Jesus Crosses a Boundary

Mark 7.24–30

> Then he rose up from there and went into the region of Tyre and Sidon. He entered a house and did not want it known, but he could not escape notice. Directly, there came a woman who had heard he was there and who had a daughter possessed by an evil spirit. She came and fell at his feet. This woman was a Gentile, of the Phoenician people. She begged him to rid her daughter of the demon. But he said to her, 'Let the children be fed first, for it is not right to take the children's bread and throw it to the dogs.' She answered, 'Yes, sir, and yet the dogs under the table eat of the children's crumbs.'
>
> And he said to her, 'For this answer, go in peace. The demon has gone out of your daughter.' Then she went off to her house and found the child lying on the bed, and the demon gone from her.

Presumably for respite, Jesus passed out of Galilee and the rule of Herod Antipas, crossing the north-west border into the Roman-administered province of Syria. Along with some Israelite families, there would be a preponderance of Gentiles in that area. It was not yet his strategy to preach the kingdom outside the faith tradition of his own people, and he was desirous that his visit would pass unnoticed. When word spread and a Gentile Phoenician woman came and threw herself imploringly at his feet, he would be especially reluctant to respond. His healings were part of his proclamation of the kingdom, the in-breaking reign of God. The desired response of faith and understanding could not yet be expected in a Gentile population.

Like the prophets and gurus of several Eastern traditions, he therefore sets a test that would discourage the unworthy. His apparently harsh words she receives in humility, but also with persevering faith. Jesus at once accepts her and grants her prayer. His word is enough, and trusting him, she returns home to find her little girl well and at rest.

The vivid story still encourages those who meet a sharp obstacle on their path to Jesus not to turn back in indignation or dismay. Let the reality of the need and the yearning for his help still call out to him. Humility and faith will find his response of love.

The Secret of the Servant-King

Mark 8.27–38

Then Jesus and his disciples set out for the villages of Caesarea Philippi, and on the way he asked his disciples, 'Who do people say that I am?' They answered, 'Some say John the Baptist and others Elijah, and some say one of the other prophets.' Then he asked them, 'And you, who do you say that I am?' Peter answered him, 'You are the Christ.'

Then he strictly charged them that they should tell no one about him. And he began to teach them that the Son of Man must suffer many things and be rejected by the elders, and the chief priests and the scribes, and be killed, and after three days rise again. And he spoke the matter plainly.

Peter took him aside and began to remonstrate with him. But Jesus, turning about and seeing his disciples, rebuked Peter and said, 'Get behind me, Satan, for your mind is not on God's purposes but on those of mere human beings.'

And he called the multitude to him along with his disciples and said to them, 'Those who would come after me must deny themselves and take up their cross and follow me. For those who would save their life shall lose it, but those who lose their life for my sake and for the sake of the gospel will save it. For what does it profit you to gain the whole world and forfeit your soul? What indeed can you give in exchange for your soul? For whoever is ashamed of me and of my words in this unfaithful and wicked generation, of them will the Son of Man be ashamed when he comes in the glory of his Father with the holy angels.'

They are walking beyond Galilee to the north-east, heading for villages lying outside the Greek-style city by the springs of the Jordan, at the base of the mighty Mount Hermon. Jesus raises a sensitive question – his own role in the newly dawning kingdom of God, his God-given identity. His questions show that it is not something he has proclaimed or taught, and his reticence thus far has deterred them from asking him.

From the outset he has known that he must take a way abhorrent to human expectations and inclinations. The work the Father has given him, his role in the kingdom, is not what people will readily accept as the office of the expected Saviour. Rather than making claims about himself from the beginning of his ministry, his way has been to preach the God-centred reign, leaving his followers to discern gradually his own nature and destiny.

But now the time has come to take up the issue directly. The answers to his question show that the public perceive him as a great prophet sent to usher in the kingdom, while Peter (perhaps voicing the thoughts of all the disciples) goes a decisive step farther: 'You are the Christ' (meaning the Messiah, the Lord's Anointed). With this title comes the thought of the king who mediates the divine will, reigning with power as the representative of the heavenly King. This would mean the ending of the present empires and dominions. Especially among the heated and restless population of Palestine, this messiahship is political dynamite. No wonder Jesus has not thrust the title forward for himself.

But he does not reject it. Rather, he enjoins them sternly to tell no one about it. And then he begins to teach them plainly that it is his destiny to suffer and be put to death. He will do the Father's work not through blazing power, but through patience, poverty, humility. He will go to his death trusting the Father for the life that will lie beyond it.

Peter is not ready for this hard teaching. His protest revives that battle in the wilderness when Jesus rejected the false way to his kingdom. Peter is representing that 'Satan' (the Adversary and Tempter) and is strongly reproved, with any disciples minded like him.

The company on the way has grown to include a wider following. Jesus extends his teaching to them all. His destiny of self-sacrifice, he says, is necessarily the way also for those who would follow him. Open to pain and death in the cause of the gospel, such followers will find true life, a reality beyond all that the world of human ambitions can offer. For what gain is there in possessing the whole world and thereby losing your true life, your soul?

Twice here Jesus speaks of himself as 'the Son of Man'. In the way he uses this expression it takes on the sense of the Messiah who conquers through his self-sacrifice, and at the end of the world will return in open majesty.

The Shepherd Who Dies for His Flock

John 10.14–18

> I am the good shepherd, and I know my own, and my own know me, as the Father knows me and I know the Father, and I lay down my life for the sheep. Other sheep I have that are not of this fold. These also I must bring in. And they will hear my voice, so there will be one flock, one shepherd. For this reason the Father loves me: that I lay down my life so that I may take it up again. No one takes it away from me, but I lay it down of my own accord. I have authority to lay it down, and also to take it up again. It is a charge I have received from my Father.

From ancient times and in many lands the shepherd was an image applied to kings – in the first place to God himself, and then to those he appointed to embody his rule. It was an image of ruling, but with a dominant emphasis on caring.

In this chapter Jesus has spoken of the work of shepherding from various angles. He pictures first how sheep, often from several flocks, may be gathered into a fold – probably the courtyard of a house, protected by a stone wall and a hedge and entered by one gate under the eye of a gatekeeper. Jesus portrays himself as that gate (7.7). Genuine pastors of the sheep will enter through him, and through him the flock will pass safely between the open world and the enclosed place of shelter and rest.

Then Jesus applies the image differently: 'I am the good shepherd' – so different from the impostors, for he was for his flock to the extent that he will die for them. And with him there is the bond of knowledge. Just as a ewe amid all the spring symphony of bleating knows the voice of her own lambs, so sheep respond to the voice of their own shepherd when he calls his own out from a mixed collection. They will only follow him, and he knows them each one.

Such mutual knowledge binds Christ to his own, a profound love and belonging like that which unites Christ and the Father. It is seen above all in his readiness to die for them as the Father wills, his deliberate laying down of his life for them in trust of his receiving it again, according to the charge the Father has given him.

But, lest the image of the sheep fold should make for an exclusive spirit, Jesus speaks of his flock as extending to other folds where also his call will be heard and gladly recognized. Whenever his church makes boundaries around itself, this teaching will resound. For the laying down of this Shepherd's life, this life of the Creator-Word, is for no less than all creation.

Jesus Seen Briefly in Glory

Mark 9.2–9

Six days later, Jesus took Peter, James and John, and led them up a high mountain to a place of solitude. And there he was transfigured before them and his clothes became gleaming, intensely white as no cloth-dresser on earth could whiten them. And Elijah appeared to them, together with Moses, and they were talking with Jesus. Then Peter joined in, saying to Jesus, 'Master, it is good that we are here, for we can make three shelters, one for you, one for Moses and one for Elijah.' He hardly knew what he was saying, for they were filled with dread.

Then a cloud overshadowed them, and out of the cloud a voice spoke: 'This is my beloved Son. Hear him.' Then suddenly, as they looked round, they saw no one any more except Jesus standing alone with them. And as they were coming down from the mountain, he charged them to tell no one what they had seen until the Son of Man should have risen from the dead.

Soon after he has entrusted his disciples with the knowledge of his being the Messiah, Jesus takes the three foremost disciples up a remote mountain where, in solitude, they will be given further revelation. A mountain scene of divine presence in glory, cloud and voice from above – all is reminiscent of the story of the founding revelations given to Moses and the ancient people of God on Mount Sinai. But the heart of the present revelation is the disclosure of Christ's glory. Briefly, and to an intimate circle only, the divine glory of Jesus, the hidden Messiah, shines out. The voice from the cloud adds God's own testimony, confirming the meaning of the radiance. This is God's beloved Son, the bearer of the new kingdom, and he is to be revered and obeyed.

That the figures of Moses and Elijah appear and converse with Jesus shows that the old order is passing into the new. These masters of the old covenant – the lawgiver and the great prophet – join in witness to the Messiah of the new covenant. Both Moses and Elijah were depicted in sacred tradition as reaching towards the new kingdom, ready to come from heaven to serve anew. As for the shelters that the bewildered Peter has in mind, these relate to the booths of branches used in the Festival of Booths (or Tabernacles), the festival that was in part an anticipation of messianic glory and the dawn of the kingdom. Good Peter, there is more of wisdom and fitness in your words than you have thought!

Then suddenly the disclosure of the royal and divine presence is over, and the visitors from heaven have vanished. On the way down the mountain Jesus again enjoins secrecy, for among the general public his messianic role would be misunderstood, easily bursting into the flames of nationalism and armed revolt.

The revelation has been granted to a very few in the heart of the company of Jesus. In the time of his suffering and scorn, the hidden influence of that moment of glory will save them from final despair and prepare the way for the experiences of the resurrection.

Suffering comes before glory, but transfiguration here precedes both, giving grounds for hope. The brief but meaningful vision passes deep into the soul and sustains through many a dark hour.

16.

Scenes of Jesus

Jesus Indignant to See Children Turned Away

Mark 10.13–16

> People were bringing children to him that he should touch them, and the disciples rebuffed them. But when Jesus saw it he was moved with indignation and said to them, 'Let the children come to me. Do not turn them away. To such as these belongs the kingdom of God. Truly, I say to you: whoever will not accept the kingdom of God like a child can never enter it.' And he took them in his arms, and laying his hands upon them, blessed them.

Jesus was much grieved to see the children turned away by disciples, who no doubt were constantly protecting him from crowds eager for his words and hands of healing and blessing. His concern for the children is said to be without parallel in stories of great teachers in the ancient world. To appreciate his saying here about childlike acceptance of the reign of God, we may begin by picturing the faces of those children in our imagination, helped by recollection of children we have seen from societies that are poor and simple in comparison with the wealthier countries today. As they are brought near to Jesus, their eyes are wide with wonder, and shining with delight. The children are trusting and respectful, yet discerning, with a wisdom nourished by kindness and simplicity of life. To such wonder, wisdom and trust, the door of the kingdom readily opens.

How Hard for the Rich to Enter!

Mark 10.17–27

> Just as he was setting out on his way, a man ran up to him and knelt before him and asked him, 'Good Master, what must I do to inherit eternal life?'

Jesus said to him, 'Why do you call me good? No one is good except one, that is, God. You know the commandments: Do not kill, do not commit adultery, do not steal, do not bear false witness, do not defraud, honour your father and your mother.' He answered, 'Master, all these I have kept since childhood.' Jesus looked at him and his heart went out to him and he said, 'One thing you fall short of. Go and sell all you have and give the money to the poor, and you shall have treasure in heaven, and come, follow me.' He was sad at this saying, and he went away with a heavy heart, for he was a man of great possessions. Then Jesus, looking round about, said to his disciples, 'How hard it will be for those who have riches to enter the kingdom of God!' The disciples were astonished at his words. But Jesus said again to them, 'Children, how hard it is to enter the kingdom of God! It is easier for a camel to pass through the eye of a needle than for the rich to enter the kingdom of God.' They were utterly amazed, saying to one another, 'Then who can be saved?' Jesus looked at them and said, 'With humans it is impossible but not with God, for with God all things are possible.'

The man hastens to seize the opportunity before Jesus, so much in demand, is occupied with his journey. Deeply respectful to the great teacher, he kneels to him and addresses him as 'Good Master'. But Jesus, in his humility, does not want compliments and answers that only God is good. All the same, the man has no hesitation in stating that he has always kept the moral laws (Exodus 20.12–16; Leviticus 19.13) which Jesus quotes as he explores the nature of this enquirer.

So often Mark tells of the gaze of Jesus – three times in the present passage. And now, as Jesus looks at the man and into his soul, he is pleased to discern someone truly seeking God, someone who could be among his close followers. The one thing he lacks, says Jesus, is detachment from his possessions. He bids him therefore, 'Sell all you have, give to the poor, and come, follow me.' The challenge is, at that instant, too much for him. But though he goes away, he does so grieving. Perhaps he will in time find the way.

Then, with characteristic humour and memorable force, Jesus develops a general lesson, pressing home the severity of his teaching on wealth. A camel, he says, can more easily squeeze through the eye of a needle than a rich man get through the gate of the kingdom. The hearers react with consternation. All the more so since the wealthy liked to think of their prosperity as a mark of God's approval. What chance is there for anyone then?

The moral teaching of Jesus – as we see also in the Sermon on the Mount – has the effect of destroying complacency and self-righteousness. When all our virtues are reckoned up, we remain 'unprofitable servants' (Luke

17.10). Humanly speaking, it is impossible; we cannot earn a place in God's new creation. But there remains humility and trust, opening to the grace of God. With him all things are possible, even the salvation of our erring species. The terrible danger of wealth is that it commonly harms that very receptivity, the humility and trust in him which can receive his infinite mercy.

A Meditation of Jesus

Matthew 11.25–30

At that time Jesus, as he prayed, said, 'I thank you, Father, that you hid these things from the learned and wise and revealed them to the simple. Yes, Father, for so it pleased you. All things have been entrusted to me by my Father. And no one knows the Son except the Father, nor does anyone know the Father except the Son and anyone to whom the Son chooses to reveal him.

'Come to me, all you that labour and bear heavy loads
and I will give you rest.
Take my yoke upon you and learn from me
for I am gentle and humble in heart. And you will find rest for your souls,
for my yoke is easy and my burden is light.'

Jesus has been reflecting on the responses to his mission. The people as a whole have shown little inclination to change their ways. Jesus compares them to children he has seen in the streets playing at weddings and funerals, and when they piped happy music the others wouldn't dance, yet when they wailed like mourners neither would they join in the mourning. So this generation has accepted neither the grim warnings of John the Baptist nor the joyful gospel of Jesus.

Pondering further (and, according to Luke 10.21, rejoicing in the Holy Spirit) Jesus thanks his Father that the gospel has been received by the humble and simple, while from the elite, confident in their knowledge and expertise, the truth is hidden. So the Father has willed, and Jesus is thankful.

His meditation then moves into the depths of God's self-revealing. Though the nature and work of Jesus are little recognized, yet he reflects that all things have been delivered to him by his Father. As Son of God he represents the rule of God, being entrusted with lordship over all. He is truly recognized, truly known, at the heart of all reality. There the Father, and the Father alone, fully knows the Son, as the Son, and the Son alone, truly knows the Father, while into that communion he draws those who join themselves to him in humility and faith.

The will of the Lord, choosing those who are brought into that communion, does not dispense with a human response. So Jesus calls to the humble and the heavy-laden and offers them a welcome. He invites them to a way of gentleness and joy. Yes, there is a yoke, a discipline, but it is not a crushing burden of laws and intricate regulations. In this communion with God, the soul will find rest and healing, the love that is true happiness.

Who is My Neighbour?

Luke 10.25–37

> Then a scholar of the law stood up and, in order to test him, asked, 'Master, what should I do to possess eternal life?' Jesus answered, 'What is written in the law? How do you read it?' He replied, 'You must love the Lord your God with all your heart and with all your soul, with all your strength and with all your mind, and your neighbour as yourself.'
>
> 'You have answered rightly,' he said. 'Do this, and you will have life.' But wanting to justify himself, he asked Jesus further: 'And who is my neighbour?' Jesus answered in this way.
>
> 'There was once a man who went down from Jerusalem to Jericho and was attacked by robbers. They took even his clothes and beat him and went off, leaving him half dead. By chance a priest was going down that way, but when he saw him, he passed by on the other side. In similar fashion a Levite came to the place and saw him, and passed by on the other side. Then a Samaritan, travelling that road, came towards him, and when he saw him, he was moved with pity, and came to him and bandaged his wounds, having bathed them with oil and wine. Then he placed him on his own mule and brought him to an inn and looked after him. Next morning, he took out two silver pieces and gave them to the innkeeper and said, "Take good care of him, and if you spend more, I will repay you on my way back." Now which of these three do you think acted as neighbour to the victim of the robbers?' And he said, 'The one who showed him such kindness.' Jesus said to him, 'Go then, and act like that.'

This expert in the law of Moses does not ask his question from a desire to learn, but to draw Jesus into a debate where he might be caught in a difficulty. But the Master turns the question back to him. He answers well, combining the love of God taught in Deuteronomy 6.5 with the love for a neighbour taught in Leviticus 19, a combination sometimes used by Jesus himself. 'If you carry this out,' affirms Jesus, 'you will be saved.'

The scholar feels the need to justify himself for having asked a question which he himself can answer readily and well, so he presses further for a debatable issue – how far does this neighbourly obligation extend; who should be counted as a 'neighbour' and so entitled to such kindness? (It was commonly taught, for example, that Gentiles were not included, nor Israelites who were thought to be impious.)

Jesus does not accept the spirit of the question and so answers by telling a story that treats the topic from another angle. It is a story more forceful than argument. The setting is easily envisaged. The route eastwards from Jerusalem drops steeply for some 17 miles down the crumpled desert hills towards Jericho and the Dead Sea. Robbers can easily operate, hiding in the gullies and folds of this lonely wilderness, and confident of rich pickings from those who travelled the winding way to and from the capital city.

The priest and the Levite (one of the lesser temple ministers) should represent high standards of godliness, being servants of the Lord in his holy sanctuary. That they 'pass by' is, however, plausible, for the naked body may well be a corpse, a source of ritual defilement. The third person to arrive on the scene is at the other extreme in popular estimation, for the Samaritans are considered an impure race and not accepted in their claim to be followers of the law of Moses. They are indeed bitterly hated.

The outstanding kindness of this Samaritan is therefore startling. He does his utmost to help the sufferer regardless of status. We see him tear up his own garments to bind the wounds, having soothed and washed them with oil and disinfected them with wine. We see him give up his own mule to the wounded man and walk watchfully beside him. He makes him comfortable at the inn and pays for several weeks' farther care, obliging himself for any further expense. The lesson, in its story form, is of shattering power, as we trace again and again the behaviour of the three travellers. The wonderful kindness and mercy of God towards us calls us in our turn to a like-spirited kindness and mercy wherever the opportunity is before us. Here is not an obligation we can define and tick off when accomplished. In the end we recognize it as our response to God's mercy, which we can only give in the strength of that mercy, the strength of the Holy Spirit.

The One Thing Needed

Luke 10.38–42

> Further on their way he entered a village, where a woman called Martha welcomed him into her home. She had a sister called Mary, who sat down at the Lord's feet and remained there listening to his words. But Martha was distracted with many tasks, and she came straight up to him and said, 'Lord, don't you care that my sister has left me to do everything by myself? Tell her now to come and help me.'
>
> Then the Lord said to her, 'Martha, Martha, you are worrying and troubling about so many things, yet only one thing is needed. Mary has chosen that best part, and it is not to be taken away from her.'

We may suppose that a small circle of friends and neighbours sits around Jesus in Martha's home. Among them sits Mary, Martha's sister, an attentive disciple at the feet of the Master.

Left to Martha, then, the tasks of hospitality. Such care of guests is hard work, and when many things need attention at the same time the nerves easily get frayed. Mary's delight in the presence and words of Jesus is – in the circumstances – only an irritation to Martha. She bursts into the circle with frank indignation, which even includes Jesus in its heat. But that's a sign of their solid, underlying friendship.

When Jesus begins his reply, 'Martha, Martha', we catch a tone of gentle understanding and, again, an evidence of proven friendship. His reply then suggests that Martha is being overzealous in her care, and so is an easy prey to overwrought anxiety. He applauds Mary's decision to sit as a disciple, and he will not send her away.

It is a lively scene that we can readily enter into. Are we not, however, inclined to side with Martha? She is intent on practical kindness to the Lord on his tiring journey. She may think Mary has not chosen the best time for her devoted discipleship. Yes, we may sympathize with Martha. But here is the force of the story. It has something of an edge, something to provoke us to deeper consideration. The appearing of Jesus at the door is a precious opportunity – for some it seems an opportunity for practical service, for others an opportunity to listen and learn.

The work of Martha is valuable; it is indeed her service of love. But she is in danger of being dominated by her own ideas, her good intentions even. The attentiveness of Mary, on the other hand, stands for the Lord's chief requirement – receptivity to his will, a receptivity that means joy in his sheer presence, and openness to his guiding. It is a waiting before the Lord which, in the end, is the one thing that is needed.

God's Joy over One Sinner Who Repents

Luke 15.1–10

Now all the tax-collectors and other disreputable folk were gathering round him to listen to him. And the Pharisees and scholars were muttering among themselves, saying, 'This man welcomes sinners and even eats with them.' So he told them this parable.

'If one of you has a hundred sheep and loses one of them, will he not leave the ninety-nine in the wilderness and go to search for the one that is lost until he finds it? And when he has found it, joyfully he lays it over his shoulder. Then, when he gets home, he calls together his friends and neighbours, saying to them, "Be glad with me, for I have found my sheep that was lost." I tell you, in the same way there will be more rejoicing in heaven over one sinner who repents than over ninety-nine virtuous people who have no need to repent.

'Or again, if a woman has ten silver pieces and loses one of them, will she not light the lamp and sweep through the house and search every nook and cranny until she has found it? Then, when she has found it, she calls together her friends and neighbours, saying, "Be glad with me, for I have found the piece that I had lost." Just the same, I tell you, there will be joy among God's angels over one sinner who repents.'

It was a striking thing, how Jesus was so ready to befriend the disreputable. A stark contrast with the behaviour of the religious elite, who shunned fellowship with whole classes and occupations judged incompatible with the law of Moses. Associating with these classes would, they thought, bring contamination through their neglect of the food laws and other physical commandments.

In answer to their mumbling of condemnation, Jesus speaks his parables. In the first story, the man with a hundred sheep will not be poor, but he still has to mind his own flock. At the daily count he misses one animal and is so anxious to find and rescue it that he leaves all the rest in the wilderness-pasture. We may suppose that other sheep owners have undertaken to keep an eye on them. He finds the strayed one weak and weary in some hazardous place. Overjoyed, he makes the difficult way back with the sheep laid across his shoulders, its feet held over his breast. Once home, he invites others to celebrate the happy outcome with him.

So Jesus points to the joy of God over the saving of one sinner, a joy so keen that it seems greater than his pleasure in the many who never went astray. But we may hear a note of irony in the reference to the ninety-nine righteous who needed no repentance. There seems to be a warning here to those who judge themselves righteous and despise so many others.

The second story concerns a band of coins on the headdress of a poor woman, no doubt a small dowry which she is never parted from, day or night. When one of the pieces is missing, she lights the candle-lamp in her windowless room and vigorously sweeps over the floor with a palm-twig broom, listening for a clink on the stones. Again, such dedicated seeking, such joy in finding!

From both stories, then, we see the friendship of Jesus for the despised and outcast – which earned him such hostility from the strict followers of the law; we see that friendship as an embodiment of God's own cherishing of each person and his concern to save them when they have wandered from their true home. The depth of God's love and perseverance are shown in the joy which surrounds him in heaven, when the estranged one has come to a new mind and heart and the lost has been found.

A Father's Love

Luke 15.11–32

Jesus continued, 'There was a man who had two sons. And the younger one said to his father, "Father, give me now the share of the property that will come to me." So he apportioned his estate between them. Not many days later, the younger son turned the whole of his share into cash and went abroad to a distant country, where he went through all his money in reckless living. When he had spent it all, a severe famine came to that country, and he began to suffer. He found work with one of the citizens there, who sent him out to his fields to feed pigs. And he longed to fill himself with the carob pods which the pigs were eating, but no one would give him any.

'When he came to himself, he thought, "How many of my father's hired men have bread enough and to spare, while I here am dying of hunger! I will go back to my father and say to him, 'Father, I have sinned against heaven and before you. I am no longer fit to be called your son. Take me as one of your hired men.'" So he got up and came to his father. But while he was still a long way off, his father saw him and he was moved with pity. And he ran and embraced him and kissed him.

'And the son said to him, "Father, I have sinned against heaven and before you. I am no longer fit to be called your son." But the father said to his servants, "Go quickly and fetch the best robe and put it on him. And put a ring on his hand and shoes on his feet. And take and kill the fatted calf, and let us eat and make merry. For this my son was dead and is alive again, he was lost and is found." And they began to celebrate.

'Now his elder son was out in the field. And as he came and approached the house, he heard music and dancing. And he called one of the servants and asked what it meant. And he told him, "Your brother has come home, and your father has had the fatted calf killed because he has him back safe and sound."

'But he was angry and would not go in. And his father came out and pleaded with him. And he answered his father, "All these years I have worked for you and not once gone against your wishes. Yet you never gave me even a kid to have a feast with my friends. But when this son of yours comes along after wasting your living with harlots, for him you kill the fatted calf."

'And he said to him, "My child, you are always with me and all that I have is yours. But it was right to celebrate and be joyful. For this your own brother was dead and is alive again; he was lost and is found."'

The father anticipates his will and assigns all his property to his sons, the elder no doubt getting the greater share as customary. As long as the father lives, however, the yield of the estate is his. The younger son decides to sell his share and go abroad with the money, but again the purchaser will have to wait till the father's death to benefit from what he has bought.

The younger son accordingly departs to make his fortune in some more prosperous land. (The great majority of Jews in fact resided in the big Gentile centres outside Palestine.) However, he proves reckless and extravagant and squanders his resources. The advent of a severe famine sends prices rocketing, and he is soon in acute need. In Jewish eyes he could hardly sink lower than working for a Gentile with the ritually 'unclean' pigs. His wages are not enough to pay the inflated food prices, and he would gladly devour the pigs' food, but for the watchful overseers.

The father perhaps has often gazed up the way, thinking of his son. At any rate, he is quick to see and recognize the wasted, weary figure still in the distance. With no thought of the traditional dignity, he runs out to him and throws his arms around him. The son begins the speech he has thought out, but before he can beg to be taken on as a hired man, the father is already sending servants to fetch the finest robe, and the ring and shoes, symbols of the highest honour. The whole household, without delay, is to celebrate as for the greatest family occasion, with feasting, music and dancing. For the father has got back his beloved child, as though from the dead.

This is the happy high ground of the story. God's love for the unworthy, and his joy in their homecoming, has been given matchless expression. But the main force of the story, more sombre, is yet to come. The elder brother will not go in to the merry-making. He finds out from a servant what it all means, no doubt in more detail than is reported here. Again the father comes out to his son, the elder now who is consumed with envy and resentment, inventing grievances and putting the worst possible construction on his brother's folly abroad. 'Not just *my son*,' says the entreating father, '*but your own brother.*' Surely we must celebrate his coming back to life!

So through the parable Jesus appeals to those who begrudge his reaching out to 'sinners'. He goes out to these despised ones as does God's own love. He rejoices when he finds the lost as God himself rejoices. Will these begrudging, resentful 'elder brothers', censorious, self-righteous and unloving, will they continue to stay outside, nursing their grievances? God comes out to them also. Will they hear his entreaty and come in?

17.

Towards the Climax in Jerusalem

Premonitions: A Ransom for Many

Mark 10.32–34,45

> Now they were on the road, going up to Jerusalem, and Jesus was walking ahead of them, and they were filled with awe, and those who followed behind were fearful. Then he gathered the twelve again and began to tell them the things that were to happen to him. 'See now,' he said, 'we are going up to Jerusalem, and the Son of Man will be given up to the chief priests and scribes. They will condemn him to death and will hand him over to the Gentiles, who will mock and spit at him, flog and kill him. And after three days he will rise again . . . Truly, the Son of Man came not to be served but to serve and to give his life as a ransom for many.'

Soon they will be in Jericho, and then beginning the long and steep ascent to Jerusalem. Pilgrims to the Festival of Passover are already thronging up the way, and for them the anticipation is a happy excitement. But for Jesus and his followers there is the knowledge that they go to a place of acute danger. If most are inclined to shrink from it, Jesus himself is resolved; he walks purposefully in the lead, knowing of the perils ahead and what he must do. The disciples are awed at his resolve, and perturbed as the fateful journey is decisively begun. Those who follow behind them are afraid.

Soon Jesus finds an opportunity to speak to them about what lies ahead. He anticipates that the Jewish authorities will decide to do away with him, procuring his execution at the hands of the Romans who alone in that territory could sentence to death. Beyond the death he is confident of life and victory, in line with the prophecy of the Suffering Servant in Isaiah 53. The prophetic psalms also founded hope that the royal sufferer would not be left in the realm of death.

For the disciples, however, these insights are veiled. There are levels of knowing things, and these hard truths scarcely begin to sink in. Soon it is the question of their status in the expected kingdom that concerns them. There is indignation that the brothers James and John ask for the most favoured positions close to Jesus. He teaches that the one who would be great must take the lowliest position, serving the others in humility. As he speaks, it becomes clear why he will not evade the dangers in Jerusalem. He himself has come to serve, and at the very cost of his life. He has come to give his life as a 'ransom for many'.

The phrase gathers up ancient hopes of salvation and redemption, when the creative act of God will free people and the world from the chains of evil. The 'ransom' is not to be understood pedantically as a payment to captors, but poetically in the costly idea of faithful love. In the manner of the royal servant envisaged in Isaiah 53, so now Jesus will give himself to suffering and death to save the 'many'. The innocent one, beloved of God, will suffer for the salvation of all the world.

How this can be, perhaps it is the heart that most readily understands. Self-sacrifice for love's sake is a powerful thing. And when that love is the divine love, the sacrifice is the mightiest power for good in all the work of redemption.

Oh for Eyes to See the Son of David!

Mark 10.46–52

> So they came to Jericho. And as he was leaving Jericho with his disciples and a great throng, Bartimaeus, a blind beggar, the son of Timaeus, was sitting by the way. And when he heard that it was Jesus of Nazareth, he began to cry out, 'Jesus, Son of David, have pity on me.' And there were many rebuking him and telling him to be quiet, but all the more he cried out loudly, 'Son of David, have pity on me.'
>
> Then Jesus stood still, and he said, 'Call him.' So they called the blind man, telling him, 'Take heart, get up; he is calling you!' He threw aside his coat and sprang up and came to Jesus. Then Jesus spoke to him, asking, 'What do you want me to do for you?' And the blind man said to him, 'O Master, let me see again.' And Jesus answered him, 'Go on your way. Your faith has healed you.' And at once he could see again. And he followed Jesus on the road.

Leaving the warm oasis-town, Jesus faces a strenuous journey up and up the desert road to Jerusalem. It is probably early morning, before the heat of the day, and he moves briskly, along with his disciples and a large crowd, many of them no doubt on pilgrimage to the festival. Bartimaeus is already sitting at the wayside, depending on the charity of travellers. He can tell there is an unusual excitement in the approaching throng and someone tells him that Jesus is coming by.

Has he already heard of Jesus and longed for his help? Or are the scraps of news now given him enough to ignite the fire of hope and faith? At all events, he seizes the sudden and fleeting opportunity. The force and loudness of his cries, probably also the dangerous, revolutionary words 'Son of David', prompt people to try and shut him up – a person they probably look down on anyway. But Jesus hears something more in his voice. He hears the ring of faith. Bartimaeus has, in an instant, seen beyond ordinary sight. He has known the Lord, the Messiah, the only Saviour, and has committed himself wholly to him.

Jesus hears and stands still. The cry for pity, the cry of faith, has reached his heart. The miracle that follows is simply told, the detail of the story still sharp. And Bartimaeus, able to see again, will not leave his Saviour, but follows in his steps.

The story speaks to us of seizing the opportunity, not to be discouraged by negative voices. There is something that Jesus will do for us, if only we call to him with a whole heart, and with full trust. We should not put it off but seize the opportunity, when Jesus shows us his nearness, and indeed calls us to him, to speak our request.

The story speaks also of the wonder of faith. The blind beggar in Jericho had not had the chance to know Jesus which people had who were seeing and hearing him daily. But in the depth of his need, Bartimaeus met the mercy of the Lord. Faith was born, and blind though he was, he saw Jesus more clearly than most of the others did. Our littleness, our shortcomings, count for nothing if the spark of faith is kindled. Jesus looks for trust, and finding this in us, he will save us.

And then, like Bartimaeus, we shall follow him, in thankfulness setting our course in his footsteps. 'And he followed Jesus on the road' – the road of sacrifice.

Jesus Fulfils a Prophecy of the Royal Saviour

Mark 11.1–11

As they approached Jerusalem, near Bethphage and Bethany by the Mount of Olives, he sent two of his disciples, saying to them, 'Go on into the village that faces you, and just as you enter it you will find a tethered colt on which no one has yet ridden. Untie it and bring it. And if anyone says to you, "Why are you doing this?" answer, "The Lord has need of it and will return it without delay."'

So they set off and found a colt tethered beside a doorway out in the open street, and they untied it. Some of the people standing there said to them, 'What are you doing, untying that colt?' And they answered as Jesus had told them, and they let them alone.

So they brought the colt to Jesus. They laid their cloaks on the animal's back and Jesus sat on it. And many spread their garments on the path, while others spread rushes which they had cut from the fields. And those who led the way and those who followed after cried, 'Hosanna! Blessed be he who comes in the name of the Lord! Hosanna in the highest!'

So he entered Jerusalem and went into the temple. And when he had looked round at everything and evening was drawing on, he went out to Bethany with the twelve.

The details of how the young donkey was obtained, and the circumstance that he was as yet unridden, prepare us for a solemn enactment. Ancient customs of kingship and prophecies are evoked. The disciples and other supporters respond readily, improvising to represent the tradition of the deliverer who rides a strong young donkey covered with rich rugs along a sacred way. Links with prophecy are noted in the other gospels. Such a scene is foretold most clearly in Zechariah chapter 9, where Zion is to greet the entry of her king, humble on his young donkey and bearing divine salvation, bringing peace to all nations and the end of the weapons of war. And Psalm 118, always prominent in the festivals, gives the people apt words of acclamation: 'Hosanna! Save now!' in greeting to the royal Saviour, and cries of blessing for the king who comes in with all the support of the presence of God.

In enacting such evocation of prophecy, Jesus shows his conviction that the climax of his mission is at hand. Through his imminent suffering and its sequel, the new order – the kingdom of God – will shine in Jerusalem and to all the world. But while the simple prophetic drama shows his role as Messiah, the bearer of the kingdom, it also shows his rejection of a military nationalism, a rebellion against the Romans. He comes in peace and humility, and though it is still a dangerous act in the heated circumstances of the time, it is completed without rioting, or an intervention by the vigilant Roman garrison.

In Mark's account, it is on the next day that Jesus will clear the temple's 'court of the Gentiles' of the money-changers and sellers of animals for sacrifice. Again his action will call up prophecies of the coming kingdom – the zeal for God's house, the refiner's fire, and the traders gone, leaving the temple for the prayers of all nations.

The Grain That Has to Die to Bear Fruit

John 12.20–28

> Among the people going up to worship at the feast was a number of Greeks. They approached Philip who was from Bethsaida in Galilee and asked him saying, 'Sir, we should like to see Jesus.' Philip came and told Andrew, and Andrew went with Philip and they told Jesus.
>
> Then Jesus answered them, saying, 'The hour has come for the Son of Man to be glorified. Truly, truly I tell you: unless a grain of wheat falls into the ground and dies, it stays just a grain of wheat, but if it dies it bears much fruit. Anyone who loves their life loses it, but anyone who hates their life in this world will keep it safe into eternal life. If anyone would serve me, they must follow me, and where I am, there my servant will be also. Anyone who serves me the Father will honour. Now my soul is troubled, and what shall I say: Father, save me from this hour? No, for this I have come to this hour. Father, glorify your name.' Then a voice came from heaven saying, 'I have glorified it and also will glorify it again.'

These 'Greeks' may simply be Gentiles from one of the Greek-style cities, perhaps near Philip's town. Both the disciples who feature in this incident, alone among the twelve, have Greek names, perhaps an encouragement to the enquirers, who, like many other non-Jews, have a certain attachment to the Jewish faith. Together they bring to Jesus the request, but we are not told whether it led to a meeting. It would seem that the time has not yet come for the mission of Jesus to turn prominently to the Gentiles. The main force of the call still goes out to the Jewish people.

The significance lies in the making of the request – a prophetic significance. It has deep meaning for Jesus and prompts him to speak of the gravity of 'this hour'. His work of suffering to redeem all the world, the cross that will bear the glory of salvation – this his hour of destiny has come. The grain of wheat has to 'die' to bear fruit, and so it is for God's Son, and indeed for all who would follow him in devoted service.

Though the coming of this terrible hour brings dread – the troubling of soul foretold in the ancient psalm – Jesus is steadfast in asking that God's will be done, his purpose fulfilled. May God glorify his name, revealing his holy being victoriously through the coming sacrifice. Then the voice of God brings assent and comfort: already the obedient work of the Son has been glorifying God's name, and that work will be completed, accomplished.

And so the meditative thoughts continue, gathering up the meaning of all that Jesus has spoken and done. The challenge to respond is held out again, while there is still daylight: believe in this Jesus and you are drawn to the Father who sent him; look at this Jesus with sympathy of soul, and you have a vision of the Father.

Upheavals to Come: Keeping Watch

Mark 13

And as he was going out of the temple, one of his disciples said to him, 'See, Master, what great stones and what wonderful buildings!' But Jesus answered, 'Of all these great buildings, not one stone of them will be left on another. All will be overthrown.'

Then, as he sat on the Mount of Olives looking out over the temple . . . [v. 5] he began to say to them, 'Take care that no one deceives you. Many will come taking my name and saying, "I am the one", and they will lead many astray. When you hear of battles and news of war, do not be alarmed. These things must happen. For nation will rise against nation, and kingdom against kingdom. There will be earthquakes in many places and there will be famines. These things are the beginning of the labour pains . . . [v. 24] Then, after that affliction, the sun will be darkened and the moon will not give her light, the stars will be falling from heaven, and the powers that are in the heavens will be shaken. And then they will see the Son of Man coming in the clouds with great power and glory. And he will send out the angels to gather his chosen ones from the four winds, from the farthest bounds of earth to the farthest bounds of heaven . . . [v. 35] Keep watch, then, for you do not know when the master of the house will come. Evening or midnight, at cockcrow or in the morning, if he comes suddenly, he must not find you sleeping. And what I say to you, I say to all: Keep watch.'

As they leave the vast temple area, passing through the gate towards the Kidron Valley and the Mount of Olives, amazement persists. The main work of Herod's massive rebuilding has not long been completed. The great courts and their substructures resting on the sides and crest of the hill, the various buildings, porticos and walls, the colossal building stones exactly cut, the scale and beauty of the design – all amounts to one of the greatest structures the world has known. And a splendid view of the whole is afforded by the higher Mount of Olives.

So as they sit there and gaze back at the spectacle, Jesus develops his prophecy that soon all will become a ruin. Not only for Jerusalem does he foretell calamitous upheavals. Before the new world is born, there will be terrible birth pangs. The human and the natural forces will be caught up together in these throes. Wars, famines, distress of sun, moon and stars – such shaking of established orders above and below will be the prelude to the coming of our Lord in the fullness of his divine power to gather his own. And Jesus repeats the essential message for his disciples and all who will put their trust in him: keep watch, stay ready for this his coming.

But what will this message mean for disciples who live beyond the fulfilment of Jerusalem's ruin, disciples who have known famines, plagues and wars, earthquakes and meteorites, tsunamis and eclipses, terrible dislocations in their own lives and in the cosmic order? For, since the first Easter and Pentecost, have they not already known the Son of Man in his glory, have they not already been united with him? For such disciples, and through many generations, what is this watching for him as though he came from afar?

Surely the watching is in the receiving of these early gifts of his presence. From his death on the cross he has already returned to us. We are united to him in faith, in the bread and wine, in the fellowship of the Holy Spirit. He is with us by night and day. Yes, but still we may grow hard-hearted through worldliness; we may grow sluggish and faint in faith. As we truly love and worship him and work for him day by day, growing in knowledge of him, faithful in all adversity, seeing God's power and work in everything, so we 'watch' ready for that coming of our Lord in clouds and glory. So we are ready for the end of this world and the break of the eternal day.

An Act of Love for Jesus

Mark 14.1–11

Now the Festival of Passover and Unleavened Bread was only two days away, and the chief priests and doctors of the law were looking for a cunning way to seize him and put him to death. For they agreed that it should not be during the festival in case it caused a riot among the people.

And while he was in Bethany and reclining at a meal in the house of Simon the leper a woman came in holding an alabaster flask of very costly ointment. And she broke the flask and poured the oil over his head. But some of those present spoke indignantly among themselves, saying, 'Why has the oil been wasted like this? It could have been sold for over 300 denarii and given to the poor.' And they turned on her with anger.

But Jesus said, 'Let her alone. Why do you distress her? It is a good deed that she has done for me. For the poor you have with you always, and you can do good to them whenever you wish. But you will not always have me. She has done what she could. She has anointed my body beforehand for burial. Truly I say to you: wherever in all the world the gospel is proclaimed, what she has done will be told in memory of her.'

With only a few days to go before the great festival, tension in crowded Jerusalem and its vicinity is rising. The religious authorities planning the death of Jesus need to act quickly before the mood of the pilgrims gathers a force they cannot control. The opportunity comes when one of the twelve chief disciples approaches them with his treacherous offer to help them. But between those glimpses of the malevolent rulers and the traitor, Mark shows us an act of love for Jesus.

Among his friends in Bethany near Jerusalem, Jesus reclines at a meal in the house of a cured leper. Anointing with fragrant oil was a common custom at happy gatherings, but the act of the woman who enters now has deep significance. As an act of love alone it would in that situation be very precious – she is so wholehearted, not counting the cost, giving all. The flask has a narrow neck to eek out the expensive contents, but this she breaks and lets the oil pour out. Yes, such love in a world of ill-will and betrayal is very precious. But the anointing also fits the Messiah-King, the Lord's Anointed. And still more, it anticipates his death and burial, as he goes his way to die for the world's salvation.

They turn on her as recklessly extravagant, mean minds that cannot grasp the wonderful thing that she has done. But Jesus protects her and lets the distant light of the resurrection and its gospel touch her with glory.

Mark's account of her is rich enough. We may at some other time want to hear from John that she was Mary, the sister of Martha and Lazarus, both also present. And then we may wonder if, years before, she is the woman in Luke's story who in a similar way showed love for Jesus and found forgiveness of her sins. Is she now deliberately recalling that time, expressing anew her gratitude and devotion when, as she knows in her heart, the sign of love is especially needed?

But for now we rest in Mark's account, which calls us also to show ardent, unstinting love for our Lord, when the fashion of the world rejects him.

Jesus Bequeaths a Sign of Humility

John 13.1–16

Now before the feast of the Passover, Jesus, knowing that his hour had come and that he was to go from this world to the Father, having loved his own who were in the world, showed that love to the uttermost. For during supper, when the Devil had already put it into the heart of Judas Iscariot son of Simon to betray him, Jesus, knowing that the Father had given all things into his hands, and that he had come from God and was going back to God, got up from supper, laid aside his garments, took a towel and wrapped it around his waist. He poured water into a bowl and began to wash his disciples' feet, drying them with the towel he had round his waist.

When he came to Simon Peter, Peter said to him, 'Lord, do you wash my feet?' Jesus answered, 'You do not know now what I am doing, but afterwards you will know.' Then Peter said, 'You shall never wash my feet.' Jesus answered him, 'If I do not wash you, you have no part with me.' Simon Peter said to him, 'Lord, then not only my feet, but also my hands and my head!' Jesus replied, 'One who has bathed needs no further washing, but is clean all over, and you are clean – but not every one of you.' [Jesus said this, knowing who was to betray him.]

When he had washed their feet and put on his garments and reclined again, he said to them, 'Do you know what I have done for you? You call me Master and Lord, and you say well, for so I am. If I then, your Lord and Master, have washed your feet, you must be ready to wash one another's feet. For I have given you an example so that you also should do as I have done to you. Truly, truly I say to you: servants are not greater than their lord, and those who are sent are not greater than the one who sent them.'

Solemnly, the last sequence in the mission of Jesus is introduced. The imminence of the climax of agony and death is indicated in words of quiet depth and resolution: Jesus is fully aware that his time has come to leave this life and go to the Father, and he is set to carry through his task of love. Rejected, hated even by many, he devotes the remaining time to 'his own' who have believed in him. Two meanings are in the Greek words: he loves them 'to the end' and 'to the uttermost'. What he will do for them will be the supreme act of love. And most wonderfully, it will be found to be not only for his own, his faithful friends, but for all, taking away the sin of the world.

As they recline at supper, Jesus gets up and enacts a parable or prophetic sign. As the lowliest of servants, he washes the feet of all the company. It is a simple lesson in humility as the expression of greatness. It is a perpetual message to the church that is to be – its law of love. And yet more, it is the essence of the mission of the Son of God, about to be fulfilled on the cross. 'And during supper . . .' – in this one sentence John catches the height and depth of it: the divine majesty and simplicity, the glory shown in poverty, the might of God in humility.

Peter, as often, speaks out what the others feel. He is good-hearted, but must learn to accept what Jesus wills to give him, if he is to share in the life and work of his Lord.

The Father Known through the Son

John 14.1–10

Do not be ashamed. As you believe in God, believe also in me. In my Father's house are many rooms – if it were not so I would have told you – and I am going ahead to prepare a place for you. I will come again and bring you home to myself, so that where I am, there you may also be. You know the way to where I am going!'

Thomas said to him, 'Lord, we do not know where you are going, so how can we know the way?' Jesus said to him, 'I am the way, and the truth, and the life. No one comes to the Father except through me. If you had known me, you would have known my Father also. From now on you know him and have seen him.'

Philip said to him, 'Lord, show us the Father, and that will be enough for us.' Jesus said to him, 'Have I been so long with you, and do you not know me, Philip? One who has known me has seen the Father. How can you say: Show us the Father? Do you not believe that I am in the Father and the Father in me?'

The disciples are on the threshold of devastating events. Not only will their Master be cruelly taken from them; there will also be the shame of their standing apart through fear. Truly, their hearts will be in turmoil.

So the Lord speaks to his little flock gentle words of comfort, simple, yet as deep as anything that has ever been uttered. He calls them to the quieting of heart through faith, faith in God as they have known him, and in Jesus as their understanding of him now grows. In the terrible taking away they must see that he goes to his Father, and in that ample household will prepare a place for them. And when he goes, he will not just wait for them to make the journey on their own. Having made all ready, he will come to them again to bring them in safety and joy to their eternal home with him.

With gentle humour he assures them that in any case they know the way. Thomas expresses alarm like that of children suddenly left alone. So comes Christ's great reassurance: 'I am the way and the truth and the life' – the way to God, the truth of God, the life in God. In fellowship with Jesus, loving him, trusting him, we move ever closer to the Father, bound in God's faithfulness, nourished by God's life.

And just as nothing came into existence except through the Word, the Son, nothing has the light of salvation except through him. From the beginning of the world, all who have received that light have received it through him. As Moses, Elijah, Isaiah, Hannah, Ruth or David knew the Father through him. Likewise the humble and holy ones of many faith-traditions then and today have lived and been blessed through him.

In his time they join those who clearly know his name and his face, and they rejoice all the more in that knowledge.

And many are they who like Philip have been long with Jesus but have yet to know him. Before them lies the opening to living faith, where the Son is truly known as the outgoing of the Father, God as he forms and enters our lives

Last Teachings

John 14.15 – 16.23

> If you love me you will keep my commandments. And I will ask the Father and he will give you another comforter, to be with you for ever . . . [14.18] I will not leave you as orphans. I am coming back to you . . . [14.26] And the Comforter, the Holy Spirit, whom the Father will send in my name, will teach you everything and help you remember all that I have told you. Peace I leave with you. My peace I give to you. Peace such as the world cannot give, I give to you . . . [15.1] I am the true vine and my Father is the vine-dresser. Every branch in me that yields no fruit he takes away. And every branch that bears fruit he cleans by pruning to make it even more fruitful. You are cleansed already by the words that I have spoken to you. Remain in me as I in you. For as the branch itself cannot bear fruit unless it remains part of the vine, neither can you if you do not remain in me . . . [16.23] Truly, truly I tell you: if you ask the Father for anything in my name, he will give it you. Ask and you will receive and your joy will be complete.

The commandments given by Jesus are not so much laws as calls to faith and sacrificial love. It is love also which animates them as they are put into practice – love for Jesus himself. Till now he has been close to his followers, encouraging, strengthening and guiding them. Now that he is to be arrested and crucified, to whom shall they turn? He promises that he will come back to them. Not only will they see him as their risen Lord, but also his presence will continue with them powerfully in the form of the Holy Spirit. The Spirit will become for them another *paraclete*, meaning 'one called to their side as a strong helper'. In trials and imprisonment the

Spirit will be their advocate and intercessor. On the path of discipleship he will be their counsellor, showing them the meaning of Jesus, recalling all his words and deeds. Sent from the Father in the name of the Son, the Holy Spirit will enfold them in the divine reality, the very presence of God. So the 'peace' which Jesus now bequeaths is indeed a gift beyond all that the world can give.

The life of the disciples in God is then pictured in another way. From the vine so common in the Holy Land, prophets and psalmists imagined God's people as the vine he had planted and tended. But now we are shown 'the true vine' which is Christ himself, his followers being the branches. The Father's care ensures fruitfulness. The meaning is plain: the believers draw from Christ divine life, but only as they remain united to him. Taken as an image of the church, it shows the chief reality as Christ, with the Christ-life coursing through the whole organism. It is he who says, 'I am the true vine.' We can be members of the church only as members of him.

At this last supper, as Mark and the others tell us, Jesus shares the cup of 'the fruit of the vine' (14.25) and says, 'This is my blood' (14.24). And it will be especially in the holy communion of the Eucharist that church people will know themselves one with the living Christ, drawing from him the life of God.

When this promised time comes, the disciples will not be putting questions to Jesus as now they do. His guidance will be there for them through the Spirit. And they may be sure that prayer they make to the Father in the name of Jesus will be granted in his name – in prayer and answer he is the mediator. Such prayer arises from faith in the redeeming work of Jesus and it yearns that the Father's will alone be done.

Jesus Prays That They All May Be One

John 17

> When Jesus had said these things, he raised his eyes to heaven and said, 'Father, the hour has come. Glorify your Son, so that the Son may glorify you, for you have given him authority over all creatures, that he should give eternal life to all that you have given him. And this is life eternal, knowing you, the only true God, and the one you have sent – Jesus Christ . . .
>
> [v. 15] 'I do not pray that you take them out of the world, but that you keep them from evil. They are not of the world just as I am not of the world. Consecrate them by the truth. Your word is truth. As you sent me into the world, so I send them into the world. And for their sake I consecrate myself, so that they also shall be consecrated by truth.

'Not only for these do I pray, but also for those who will believe in me through their word, that they may all be one. As you, Father, are in me and I in you, may they also be in us, and the world will then believe that you have sent me . . .

[v. 24] 'Father, I desire that these you have given me may be with me where I am, so that they may see my glory, which you have given me, for you loved me before the founding of the world . . . [v. 26] And I made known to them your name, and will make it known, so that the love with which you have loved me may be in them, and I in them.'

Having spoken so many words directly to the disciples to prepare them for his impending death, Jesus now concludes with a meditative prayer to the Father which still gathers them in the place of comfort. The hour of the Passion has struck, and terrible as the events will appear to them, they are to know that in it all the love of the Father and the Son is at work, the glory of that love is revealed, and the gift of eternal life comes to those who will receive that revelation.

Jesus asks not that the disciples be taken from this world of violence, but that they be guarded from the temptation of its evil. Already they have a better homeland. They are in this world as though sent from beyond with a mission, and Jesus prays that they be kept true to God's mind and Spirit, dedicated, consecrated, living and working only for him amid all the worldly forces.

Such a mission is only possible in consequence of the mission of Jesus. So now, in the heart of this concluding act of prayer, he consecrates himself, making over his body, his life, to be a sacrifice for the world's salvation. Truth, like a power released from the cross, will take and hold them in God, the truth which is the divine faithfulness, the word of God, the grace given through the Son.

Their mission will be to speak the word of testimony to Jesus, calling for belief in him, and forming a chain of new believers to witness through the generations. If the believers are one in spirit, abiding in the love of Father and Son, their testimony will be truly convincing. The world will find salvation in believing it, accepting that Jesus is indeed the Son and Word sent from God.

Finally, Jesus utters his special wish, confident that it is acceptable to the Father: may these disciples given him by the Father be with him where he is, and here look upon the divine glory which the Father bestowed on him out of love before the beginning of the world. This will be their ultimate joy when they come at last to the Father's house. But the economical wording may include their present life: then Jesus desires their closeness to him already, and their faith illumined by vision. Even in this hour of his sacrifice may they in spirit be with him where he is, and behold even there the effulgence of his glory.

The Last Supper

Mark 14.22–25

> And as they were eating he took the bread and blessed and broke it and gave it to them and said, 'Take; this is my body.' And he took a cup and when he had given thanks he gave it to them and they all drank from it. And he said to them, 'This is my blood of the covenant – poured out for many. Truly I say to you: I will not drink again of the fruit of the vine until that day when I drink it new in the kingdom of God.'

Symbolic actions were an old tradition in the ministry of prophets and in ceremonies of worship. Still in the time of Jesus, people readily felt the solemn force in such actions. For them they were not just a dramatic way of teaching but bearers of a greater reality.

At this last supper, led by Jesus, all know that the bread conveys the reality of his body which is offered to God and broken in death. They know that the wine conveys the reality of his blood, given in death for the world's salvation, sealing the covenant of the new age. They know that the sacrifice which Jesus is about to offer is already present in this symbolic action.

And as they know also that, as they eat the broken bread and drink from the cup, they receive the salvation which he wins. It is awesome for them to identify so definitely with his sufferings, taking to themselves the breaking and the outpouring. But it is the sacrifice at the centre of the great salvation, and with the Lord Jesus they can already rejoice in the nearness of that day when they will feast together in the kingdom of God.

Mark's account is impressive in its economy. A fuller picture of how the tradition was preserved in the early days of the church appears in a letter of St Paul (1 Corinthians 11.23–25). The action of Jesus is there clearly seen to have founded a regular act of worship, whereby the bread and the wine will continue to convey the reality of his body and blood, maintaining the fellowship that centres on the glorious sacrifice and the communion of eternal life.

18.

The Death of the Messiah

Prayer and Betrayal in Gethsemane

Mark 14.26–42

When they had sung psalms of praise, they went out to the Mount of Olives. And Jesus said to them, 'You will all fall away, for it is written, "I will strike the shepherd and the sheep will be scattered." But after I am raised up I will go before you into Galilee.'

Then Peter said to him, 'Though they all fall away, I shall not.' And Jesus said to him, 'Truly I say to you: this very night before the cock crows twice you will disown me thrice.' But he insisted all the more, 'If I have to die with you, I shall not disown you.' And so said they all.

So they came to a place called Gethsemane, and he said to his disciples, 'Sit here while I pray.' And he took Peter and James and John with him. And he began to suffer horror and distress, and he said to them, 'My soul is very sorrowful, even to death. Stay here and keep watch.' And he went forward a little and fell on the ground and prayed that if it were possible the hour might pass away from him. And he said, 'Abba, Father, for you everything is possible – take this cup from me. Yet not what I will, but what you will.'

And he came back and found them sleeping. And he said to Peter, 'Simon, are you sleeping? Could you not watch one hour? Watch and pray that you be kept from temptation. The spirit is willing, but the flesh is weak.' And again he went away and prayed in the same words. And he came back again and found them sleeping, for their eyes were heavy. And they did not know what to answer him. And he came the third time and said, 'Do you still sleep and take your rest? It is enough. The hour has come. See, the Son of Man is betrayed into the hands of the wicked. Rise, let us go. See, my betrayer has come.'

Their last evening of fellowship ends with the singing of psalms. They probably sing from the sequences especially used at Passover time, Psalms 113 – 118. In that hour the words carry new depth of meaning.

So they set out and walk across the city to the east gate, while Jesus speaks of the loneliness of his coming ordeal, warning that they will be scattered. But there is hope too, for he speaks also of a time beyond, when he is raised up and the light of the gospel will break again over Galilee.

For Peter there begins a special trial of his faith. Midway he will sink very low, disowning his Lord three times. But wonderful indeed will be the end of Peter's story – most valiant, faithful disciple, an example for all time.

'Gethsemane' means 'Oil press', and we picture a grove of olive trees on the lower slopes of the Mount of Olives, a quiet retreat they know well. Peter, James and John were with him at the transfiguration and witnessed his glory, but now they witness the reality of his human suffering, the awful foreboding. As Jesus echoes the words of a psalm, he shows that he takes the destined path of the Servant-King. Throwing himself to the ground, he remains long in prayer. His companions hear only the theme of this communion before sleep overcomes them. If they would have kept vigil in prayer, it would have been a support to their Lord in this hard moment.

But no, he endures alone – until that other disciple comes out of the night with his kiss of greeting, the kiss that identifies his master to the high priest's men. So Jesus is seized and taken away, a prisoner in the hands of 'the sinners', the ruling elite who deserve the label they so readily apply to others.

Jesus Condemned before the High Priest

Mark 14.53–65

They led Jesus away to the high priest, and all the chief priests, elders and doctors of the law gathered there. Peter had followed at a distance right into the courtyard of the high priest and there he sat with the servants, warming himself at the fire.

Now the chief priests and the whole council were trying to find evidence against Jesus to have him put to death, but they did not find it. Many indeed bore false witness against him, but their evidence was not consistent. Then others stood up and bore false witness, claiming, 'We have heard him say, "I will pull down this temple made with hands and in three days I will build another made without hands."' But even so their testimony did not agree.

Then the high priest rose and stepped forward, and he asked Jesus, 'Have you no answer to make? What is it that these men witness against you?' And he remained silent and made no answer. The high priest questioned him farther and asked, 'Are you the Messiah, the Son of the Blessed One?' And Jesus said, 'I am, and you shall see the Son of Man sitting at the right hand of the Power and coming with the clouds of heaven.'

At this the high priest tore his robes and said, 'Need we seek farther witnesses? You have heard the blasphemy. What is your opinion?' And they all condemned him worthy of death. And some began to spit on him, and they blindfolded him and struck him, saying, 'Prophesy – who hit you?' And the guards took him away with blows.

Peter will fail his Lord, but at least his love has drawn him to shadow Jesus into the very den of the enemy.

We are used to legal proceedings long drawn out. But the condemnation of Jesus is accomplished with great dexterity and swiftness. All is cunningly planned with a view to avoiding public disturbance and securing his swift execution at the hands of the Roman authorities. The nocturnal trial is designed to stigmatize Jesus as abhorrent to Jewish piety, while he must also be caught in a charge that will merit the Roman death penalty. The two aims are difficult to combine in a society that could easily erupt against Rome. Subtlety and speed are essential.

Witnesses against Jesus are produced, but custom is strong that their testimony has to agree in detail, and the requirement proves hard to meet. A promising charge seems offered by words he is said to have spoken about the future doom of the temple and its replacement. But here again the witnesses diverge.

So the high priest resorts to confronting Jesus directly. He fails to get an answer regarding the allegations of the witnesses. The defendant rightly will not be drawn into comment on such a confusion. But when the high priest comes to the heart of the matter – the real identity of Jesus and his role in the kingdom of God – Jesus does not evade his question. He affirms that he is the Messiah the Son of God, and to leave no doubt about the scope of his meaning, he indicates his destiny to reign at the right hand of the Almighty, invested with all the power to effect God's kingdom. (The words of Jesus here take up vivid prophecy of God's Beloved Son from Psalm 110 and Daniel 7.13–14.) It seems to the high priest that this answer, coming from an unsuitable and disreputable person, is scandalous, a blasphemy, and his tearing of his robes makes a dramatic impact on the assembly, signalling utter horror and shame before God. So agreement is reached and the double aim achieved. Jewish piety is shown as scandalously affronted, and the offence can be presented to the procurator in a political light.

The earlier silence of Jesus before his accusers, and now his enduring of spitting, scorn and blows, remind us of his destined way, the way of the royal Servant of the Lord foretold in Isaiah 53. The Servant's way means his death, yet also, to the world's amazement, it will bring the forgiveness and healing of the multitudes.

When the Cock Crowed

Mark 14.66–72

> And while Peter was below in the courtyard, one of the high priest's maids came up. Seeing Peter warming himself, she looked at him closely and said, 'You too were with this Nazarene, this Jesus.' But he denied it, saying, 'I have no idea what you are talking about.' And he went out into the forecourt.
>
> The maid saw him there and began to say to those who stood near, 'This is one of them.' But again he denied it. A little later the bystanders began saying to Peter, 'Surely you are one of them, for you are from Galilee.' At this he swore with an oath, 'I do not know the man you speak of.' Immediately the cock crowed for the second time. And Peter recollected how Jesus had said to him, 'Before the cock crows twice, you will disown me thrice.' And he broke down and wept.

Jesus is in the hands of those who hate him. This incident of Peter's denial shows, alas, how weak is the support of those who love him. The light from the fire gives the maid a view of Peter's face. Brave as he is to be in the place of danger, he recoils from being linked to the arrested Jesus. Even so, he does not take himself right away. The persistent maid sees him again. He denies again, but remains in the space around the gate.

A cock will crow at fairly regular intervals in the night, and the time has come for its second crowing. As soon as Peter has for the third time made denial, vehemently swearing his ignorance of Jesus, the cock crows. Peter then recollects what Jesus foretold, and the good man breaks down in tears. His courage and loyalty will rise again and he will in the end follow his master most nobly to death. But this, his story, which surely springs from his own account, will ever be an encouragement to those who would give all for their Lord but falter, to their shame, on the way.

Jesus Condemned to Crucifixion

Mark 15.1–15

> First thing in the morning the chief priests, having made their plan with the elders and scribes and all the council, and having bound Jesus, led him away

and handed him over to Pilate. And Pilate asked him, 'You are the king of the Jews?' And he answered, 'You have said it.'

Then the chief priests made many accusations against him, and Pilate asked him again, 'Have you no answer to make? See how many charges they make against you.' But Jesus made no further answer, to Pilate's amazement.

Now it was a practice of the governor at the time of the festival to set free one prisoner at the people's request. In the prison were rebels who had committed murder in the uprising, among them one called Barabbas. When the crowd massed and began to demand that Pilate should now act according to his custom, he answered them, 'Would you have me set free for you the king of the Jews?' – for he knew that out of malice the chief priests had handed Jesus over to him. But the chief priests stirred up the crowd to demand rather the release of Barabbas. So Pilate said again to them, 'Then what shall I do with the man you call King of the Jews?' And they shouted back, 'Crucify him.' Pilate said to them, 'Why, what wrong has he done?' And they shouted all the louder, 'Crucify him.'

So Pilate, wishing to satisfy the crowd, set free Barabbas, and after having Jesus flogged, he handed him over to be crucified.

Early morning was the traditional time for judicial proceedings. So the chief priests are ready at daybreak. Their plan has been completed and approved by the council, and so they take Jesus to be judged by Pontius Pilate, the Roman governor, in the fortress overlooking the temple area.

To Pilate they put the messiahship of Jesus in a political light. They present the prisoner as a threat to Roman authority, a nationalist rebel aspiring to be ruler of the Jews.

The short answer of Jesus to Pilate's question seems to accept the designation 'King of the Jews', but with some reserve – he is not accepting the slant given by his accusers.

Against further charges he maintains silence. Such malicious twistings of his teaching are not worthy of reply. It is the silence of the royal figure foretold by the prophets: 'as a lamb led to the slaughter, as a sheep before her shearers, he opened not his mouth' (Isa. 53.7). So in his silence Jesus shows the patience and the majesty of the one ready to die for the sin of the world.

Pilate has had several sharp crises already in his time as governor, enraging the populace and the religious leaders, and for his part despising them. He sees through their hostility to Jesus but is chiefly concerned to get through the dangers of fanaticism over the time of the festival without an explosion. His custom of making a symbolic gesture, releasing one prisoner, chimes in with ancient ideals of the benevolent ruler who grants such amnesty at a time of celebration. Knowing that

Jesus has some popular support, he thinks this may be the answer – Jesus as the prisoner to be set free. But the crowd who have pressed excitedly up the hill may have come as supporters of Barabbas. At all events, it proves easy for the high priest's agents to orchestrate their tumult. Again and again they scream: 'Freedom for Barabbas, death to Jesus.'

Choosing Barabbas is something repeated to this day. The leader who appeals to instincts of aggrandizement, hatred and violence is preferred by the majority to the one who incarnates the searching demands of unselfishness, patience, faith and humility.

Pilate satisfies the powerful classes and their mob for the time being. He will survive in office a few more years before being called to account in Rome. For Jesus now, there is deeper entering into the sufferings of the prophesied Servant-Redeemer (Isaiah 50.6; 53.4). Deeper yet, but only for a few more hours, dear Lord, and then you will be at peace.

The Mocking and the Procession to Golgotha

Mark 15.16–22

> Then the soldiers led him away within the court of the governor's headquarters. And they called together their whole company. They dressed him in a purple cloak, and plaited a crown of thorns and put it on him. And they began to salute him: 'Hail, King of the Jews.' They struck him about the head with a reed and spat on him, and they knelt and worshipped him. When they had mocked him, they stripped him of the purple cloak and put his own clothes on him. And so they led him out to crucify him.
>
> Now a man called Simon from Cyrene, the father of Alexander and Rufus, was passing by on his way in from the open country, and they pressed him into service to carry the cross. And so they brought Jesus to the place Golgotha, which means 'The place of a skull'.

Jesus is now in the charge of the Roman soldiers who will carry out the sentence. They have some time in hand while the preparations are made, and they amuse themselves by mocking this one found guilty of setting himself up as king of the Jews. They are men recruited by the Romans from the many non-Jewish communities in Palestine – Jews being exempt from military service. From dynasties of Greek, Roman and other rulers they know something of a king who expresses heaven's will and power, a ruler who is divine. This unlikely 'king of the Jews', already wounded and weak, seems to them a good target for mockery. They put divine emblems on him in ridicule – the purple cloak and the circlet with sunrays, familiar on the emperor's coins and now mimicked with plaiting of twigs with long thorns, probably palm spines. Cruelly jesting, they kneel to the divine king, the God-man, Son of God. They do not know what truth they have stumbled into. They do not yet see that this day of humiliation and utter distress discloses the real divine glory.

They lead him out towards the place of execution, an eminence befitting a public spectacle, not far outside the city gate. Two other condemned men, comrades of the more fortunate rebel Barabbas, are included in the procession which winds through the city ways to the exit gate, placards stating the offences being carried in warning to others. The condemned men, as customary, carry their own cross, and it seems (from what is said of Simon) that it is only on leaving the city that Jesus no longer has strength to carry his.

And so it comes about that John's gospel states that Jesus carries his cross, while Mark tells of a passer-by coming in from the country who is compelled to carry it for him. Each writer has good reason for his focus. To John it is important to show Jesus, for all his low estate, as yet the Lord, giving his life of his own will, not overpowered and having it taken from him. Mark, from his particular circumstances, knows of the wonderful outcome of Simon's unwelcome duty. He surprisingly mentions the sons of Simon – Alexander and Rufus – surely because they are now believers known to the church Mark writes for. Their good mother (Romans 16.13) is like a mother to Paul, and their father may well be 'the dark-skinned Simon' (Acts 13.1) who helps launch the important first mission of Paul and Barnabas to the Gentiles. Cyrene is in North Africa, and Simon is perhaps one of those 'God-fearers', Gentiles linked to the Jewish faith, devout enough to make pilgrimage to Jerusalem. Suddenly he is stopped by a totally unexpected frustration, yet through it he will find Christ, the Lamb of God, and bring many to him.

Jests as Jesus is Crucified

Mark 15.23–32

> They would have given him wine mixed with myrrh, but he did not take it. Then they crucified him and divided his garments among them, casting lots to decide what each should have. It was about nine in the morning when they crucified him, and over him was fastened the placard showing the accusation, reading 'THE KING OF THE JEWS'. With him they crucified two bandits, one on his right hand and one on his left.

And those who passed by heaped scorn on him, wagging their heads and saying, 'Ha, you who would destroy the temple and build it again in three days, save yourself and come down from the cross.' So too the chief priests and scribes ridiculed him among themselves and said, 'He saved others, but he cannot save himself. Let the Messiah, the king of Israel, come down from the cross, so that we may see it and believe.' Those also who were crucified with him reviled him.

The drugged wine would have dulled the senses, but Jesus means to keep a clear mind. The hardened executioners follow their customary routine and are just as concerned to have their share of the meagre booty. The two rebels crucified with him are thought to make up an appropriate group – the rebel Messiah with warlike followers who have the coveted positions on his immediate right and left, as though his closest henchmen. All in a terrible irony, disclosing a travesty of justice.

The mention of the mingled wine, the gaming for the garments, the inclusion with the wrongdoers, and mocking that is so revealing of the spiritual and moral poverty of the perpetrators – all sustains the underlying dignity of the event – the Saviour's death for the world as prefigured in the prophetic depths of Psalms 22 and 69 and Isaiah 53. This is the dimension which saves us from a despairing grief, as we recall his words, 'Be of good cheer. I have overcome the world' (John 16.33).

Jesus Forgives

Luke 23.33–43

There they crucified him . . . and Jesus said, 'Father, forgive them for they know not what they are doing' . . . [v. 39] And one of the criminals who hung there with him railed at him, saying, 'Are you not the Messiah? Save yourself and us.' But the other answered, rebuking him, and said, 'Do you not fear God, seeing you are under the same condemnation? And we indeed with justice, for we pay the price of what we have done, but this man has done nothing wrong.' And he said, 'Jesus, remember me when you come into your kingdom.' And Jesus said to him, 'Truly I tell you: today you will be with me in paradise.'

As we shall read, the bearing of Jesus on the cross astonished and touched the centurion, the sergeant-major in charge of the execution. And Luke tells here of incidents which could turn any heart not wholly closed. Most immediately the forgiving prayer of Jesus is raised for the men who raise him on the cross. But it reaches out also for all who have a part in the crime, not seeing its enormity. From these lips, from this moment, what prayer could be more mighty? It is enough to create a new world.

Both bandits, Mark has said, deride Jesus, but it seems that his quiet acceptance of their mockery powerfully affects one of them, who rebukes his comrade and is touched with grace. He expresses faith that, beyond the cross, Jesus will come into his messianic glory. 'Jesus, remember me,' he asks. The reply of Jesus takes up the common conception that those close to God pass at death into his heavenly presence: this very day the repentant man will be with Jesus in paradise, the delightful garden that symbolizes joy in the nearness of God.

Jesus Binds Mary and John

John 19.25b–27

> Standing by the cross of Jesus were his mother and her sister, with Mary the wife of Cleopas and Mary Magdalene. So when Jesus saw his mother and the disciple whom he loved standing beside her, he said to her, 'Woman, behold your son!' And to the disciple he said, 'Behold, your mother!' And from that hour the disciple took her into his home.

The faithful women pictured here by the cross are an intimate, utterly devoted group, though the various gospel references do not identify them all beyond doubt. With the mother of Jesus is her sister, perhaps the Salome named in Mark's account and mother of James and John. (Mary wife of Cleopas, the Cleopas of Luke 24.18, may be the mother of James the Less and Joses.) The 'disciple whom he loved' is usually taken to be John, but is never named. At all events, the four women and the disciple represent a loving devotion to Jesus which weighs against the callousness of the soldiers and the scoffing world. Jesus speaks first to his mother. His words now must be few. 'Woman' is not disrespectful, almost 'Lady'. He says enough to commend to her the one who will now take care of her as a son. Then to the disciple he entrusts the care of Mary, care as for his own mother. The disciple at once gladly accepts the responsibility, so precious as his Lord's dying wish. Only to the one who has come closest to the knowledge and spirit of the kingdom would Jesus entrust her.

The Death of Jesus

Mark 15.33–40

When noon came, darkness fell over the whole land and lasted until three in the afternoon. And at that hour Jesus cried with a loud voice, *'Eloi, Eloi, lama sabachthani?'* which means, 'My God, my God, why have you forsaken me?'

On hearing this, some of the bystanders said, 'See, he is calling Elijah.' One of them ran and soaked a sponge in vinegar, put it on a reed and gave him a drink, saying, 'Now let us see if Elijah will come to take him down.'

Then Jesus uttered a great shout and breathed his last. And the curtain of the temple was torn in two from top to bottom. When the centurion, standing opposite, saw how he died, he said, 'Truly, this man was the Son of God.'

What connection this darkness may have with the sharply variable April climate (including storms and siroccos) is not considered. It is above all the mourning of earth and sky and all their creatures in the last hours of the suffering of their Lord.

The recollection of the words of Psalm 22 in the Aramaic language of Jesus (bringing us so close to him in this moment) clarifies the reaction of the bystanders, for they mishear his Aramaic words as calls for Elijah, the prophet expected to come from heaven as herald of the Messiah.

In the psalm the words begin a tremendous plea to the Lord who has not yet come to end the sufferer's ordeal. The horror of the suffering and the contrast to the expected mercy of God are graphically expressed, but all is prayer, the appeal of a sufferer who knows only one helper, only one Father-God.

The psalm is one of the closest prefigurations of the Passion, and in using its opening words to express his own last prayer, Jesus again shows that he fulfils the destiny of God's Son, even in this dark hour.

The centurion is astonished when the dying man utters a mighty shout. It sounds as the triumph-shout of praise, praise that the terrible task is done, accomplished, finished (as unfolded in John 19.30). Jesus now gives up his life, committing his spirit into the Father's hands – a final word being drawn from Psalm 31.5, according to Luke 23.46. The Gentile sergeant-major is the first to express wonder and conviction as he witnesses the work of Jesus accomplished.

The veil of the temple was a curtain screening the entrance of the 'Holy of Holies', the inmost shrine containing symbols of the presence of God. Only the high priest could pass behind it, and that only on the annual Day of Atonement. This rending from top to bottom therefore dramatically symbolizes the opening of the way to the divine presence through the death of Christ. Through his atoning sacrifice penitent believers will enter into fellowship with God.

The Burial of Jesus

Mark 15.42–47

> By now evening had come, and because it was the Preparation, that is, the day before the Sabbath, Joseph of Arimathea, a wealthy member of the council, who was himself eager for the kingdom of God, plucked up his courage and went to Pilate and asked for the body of Jesus.
>
> Pilate was surprised that he should be already dead. He sent for the centurion and asked him whether he was already dead, and having confirmed it from the centurion, he granted the body to Joseph. He then brought a linen sheet, and taking him down, wrapped him in the linen sheet. He laid him in a tomb which had been hewn out from the rock and rolled a stone against its entrance. And Mary Magdalene and Mary the mother of Joses saw where he was laid.

To the devout it was important that the bodies of the executed should be put away before the Sabbath began at sunset. But there is much more to Joseph's action. The bodies would have been unceremoniously disposed of anyway. Joseph, rather, is moved by heartfelt devotion. If he had once been cautious and discreet about his regard for Jesus, now he knows what he must publicly do. He steels his courage and goes into the governor's headquarters to make his petition. The centurion we know is already moved with awe at the moment of Jesus' death, and perhaps there is something about his report to Pilate which inclines the governor to be favourable.

So the acts of cruelty are now succeeded by acts of compassionate devotion. Joseph has the use of a newly hewn sepulchre nearby, one that he has ready for himself, says Matthew. The body would be laid on a ledge inside the rock-cave, and the small low entrance is now closed over by a great stone, probably the type shaped like a disk and rolled along a groove. The faithful women, who have been by the cross through all those dark hours, now see the kindness and have the blessed peace of knowing their Master is safely at rest.

19.

The Lord Is Risen

The Sun Rises on the First Day of the Week

Mark 16.1–8

> When the Sabbath was over, Mary Magdalene, Mary the mother of James, and Salome bought spices so that they might go and anoint him. Then very early on the first day of the week they came to the tomb as the sun rose. They were saying to one another, 'Who will roll away the stone for us from the entrance of the tomb?' for it was very large. And looking up, they saw that the stone was rolled back.
>
> Entering into the tomb they saw a young man sitting on the right side and wearing a white robe. They were terrified. But he said to them, 'Have no fear. You are seeking Jesus of Nazareth who was crucified. He is risen; he is not here. See, there is the place where they laid him. But go and tell his disciples and Peter that he is going before you into Galilee. There you will see him as he told you.'
>
> And they went out and fled from the tomb, for trembling and astonishment had overcome them. And they said nothing to anyone, for they were afraid.

Practical people might have said, 'Is it not too late to anoint the body after this lapse of time?' And they might have added, 'You are not strong enough to roll back the stone.' But these women, led now by Mary Magdalene, are intent only on doing what they can for love of Jesus. Hurrying through the early twilight, with veiled heads bowed, they are beginning to be troubled by the question of the stone. But as they come to the sepulchre and see it in the sunrise, they see the stone rolled away, exposing the small low entrance.

Only a little light penetrates the tomb, but they bravely enter, aware of an angel-figure in shining white. So it is revealed to them that Jesus is risen. The place where he was laid is empty. They are to tell 'his disciples and Peter', a gracious touch to comfort the good man who had fallen so low, 'You will see him again as he told you.' In some disciples that Galilean mission is to take wing again.

It is clear from textual evidence that Mark never continued his gospel beyond verse 8. It may be that illness or death intervened. So his wonderful work ends with this picture of the faithful women fresh from stumbling into the greatest of holy mysteries, and trembling with the dread of it. Peace and reassurance will come to them, for Jesus will come to them, and their brave and devoted love will have its reward.

No Ordinary Gardener

John 20.1–18

Early on the first day of the week, while it was still dark, Mary Magdalene came to the tomb and saw that the stone had been taken away from the entrance. So she ran and came to Simon Peter and the other disciple, the one Jesus loved, and said to them, 'They have taken the Lord away from the tomb and we do not know where they have laid him.'

Peter and the other disciple set off at once and made for the tomb. Both ran together, but the other disciple outran Peter and reached the tomb first. Stooping and looking in, he saw the linen cloths lying, but he did not go in. Following close behind him came Simon Peter, and he went straight into the tomb. There he saw the linen cloths lying, and the covering which had been on his head, not lying with the linen cloths, but rolled up in a place by itself.

Then the other disciple, who had reached the tomb first, went in also, and he saw and believed. [For till now they had not taken in the Scriptures foretelling that he must rise from the dead.] So the disciples went back home.

But Mary was standing outside the tomb weeping. And as she wept, she stooped down and looked into the tomb. And she saw two angels in white, sitting one at the head and one at the feet where the body of Jesus had lain. They said to her, 'Woman, why do you weep?' She said to them, 'Because they have taken away my Lord and I do not know where they have laid him.'

Saying this, she turned back and saw Jesus standing there, but did not know that it was Jesus. And Jesus said to her, 'Woman, why do you weep? Whom do you seek?' Thinking it was the gardener, she said to him, 'Sir, if it is you who have carried him away, tell me where you have laid him and I will take him away.' Jesus said to her, 'Mary.' She turned fully to him and said in Hebrew, 'Rabbuni', that is, 'My Master'.

Jesus said to her, 'Do not hold on to me, for I have not yet ascended to the Father. But go to my brothers and say to them, I ascend to my Father and your Father, to my God and your God.' So Mary Magdalene went and told the disciples, 'I have seen the Lord.' And she related to them all that he had said to her.

As we have seen in the preceding passage, Mark was able to introduce those dramatic developments early on the Sunday, and he showed a group of faithful women to the fore, naming first Mary Magdalene. But he could only make a beginning, before some adversity cut short his gospel.

Now John takes up the task. He appears to have more detailed knowledge and is inspired to bring out the primary role of one person, Mary of Magdala, someone without status, the woman Jesus had cured of grave disorders and who had ever after followed him to serve as she could (Luke 8.2), never deserting him (Mark 15.40,47). In John's account her women companions almost, but not quite, fall from view. Finding the stone removed from the tomb's entrance, she immediately fears the worst and hastens to alert Peter and that 'other disciple' (probably John, the son of Zebedee). They run to the tomb for all their worth – perhaps their alarm was tinged with an intuition of miracle. At all events, that other disciple sees the meaning of the linen cloths – no stealing of the body, but the Lord has risen, passing through the earthly bands.

Then, when the disciples have returned to the city, Mary is by now back at the tomb, still beside herself with grief that someone should have taken away her Lord. She looks in, sees the empty place and answers the angels' question without registering their presence, then does not recognize Jesus himself standing by her – neither his appearance, nor his voice. But then he speaks one word, her name Mary (Mariam), and it is enough to break through the wall of tears and desolation. Her immediate response, '*Rabbuni*', 'My dear Master', shows that in that instant she has made the immense journey from utter bereavement to the finding again, finding on the far side of loss, finding him in the miracle of his risen life.

We imagine that she throws herself at his feet and clasps them. But Jesus forbids such holding as he has not yet ascended to the Father. In this gospel this 'ascending' means the full journey of Christ from the limitations of this earth to his glory in heaven. This ascending, as also the giving of the Holy Spirit, will be accomplished this day, without precluding further appearances

Mary is to take the message to Jesus' 'brothers', that is, his disciples. The affectionate term reflects compassion and love. Their trials of recent days are understood, their failures put away. He sends assurance of his care and companionship in all that is to come.

The Blessing of Faith in the Risen Lord

John 20.19–29

> In the evening of that same day, the first of the week, when for fear of the
> Jews the doors were shut fast where the disciples had gathered, Jesus came
> and stood among them and said to them, 'Peace be with you.' And when he
> had said this, he showed them his hands and his side. Then the disciples were
> filled with joy to see the Lord. But Jesus said again, 'Peace be with you. As the
> Father has sent me, so I send you.' Then he breathed on them, saying to them,
> 'Receive the Holy Spirit. If you forgive the sins of any, they are forgiven them.
> If you declare them unforgiven, unforgiven they remain.'
>
> Now Thomas, that is, the Twin, one of the twelve, was not with them when
> Jesus came. So the other disciples told him, 'We have seen the Lord.' But he
> replied, 'Unless I see in his hands the mark of the nails and put my finger into
> the mark of the nails, and put my hand into his side, I will not believe.'
>
> A week later, his disciples were gathered there again and Thomas was with
> them. Though the doors were shut fast, Jesus came and stood among them
> and said, 'Peace be with you.' Then he said to Thomas, 'Reach your finger
> here, and see my hands, and reach out your hand into my side. And do not be
> unbelieving but have faith.' Thomas answered and said to him, 'My Lord and
> my God!' Jesus said to him, 'Because you have seen me, you have believed.
> Blessed are those who have not seen me and yet have believed.'

Bewildered and fearful, the disciples are gathered behind doors locked
and barred. It is the evening of the first Sunday of the Rising. Briefly
told is a momentous event that transforms the community of the disciples. The customary greeting of peace, twice repeated, has boundless
meaning on the lips of the risen Lord: on the trusting heart to bestow
fullness of life through the healing of God. Though he appears myste-
riously despite the closed doors, he is the same Jesus they have known,
and his risen body bears the marks of the nails and spear – yes, the same
Lord, and the Passion remains his eternal glory and the means of the
world's salvation.

The disciples, representing the church throughout all time, become
the continuation of Christ's mission on earth, 'sent' to extend and carry
through his work, yet only able to do this through his gift of the Holy
Spirit. As the Creator breathed his life into the first man, Adam, so Christ
breathes the divine life into the newly created ones, the children of the
Rising. Such are the disciples, his church, for all time. To forgive or retain
sins means a gift of authority, the power to maintain discipline in the
new community, a necessary power of exclusion or restoration. There is

no sharp definition of who has been given this authority. No doubt there will be a balance between the leaders and the body as a whole.

The story of Thomas re-emphasizes the identity of the risen Jesus with the crucified, and again shows the abiding importance of the Passion. Through the suffering on the cross, Thomas and all the believers to follow him are gathered into the divine salvation and know Jesus as their Lord.

The story of Thomas is indeed the last episode in the main part of this gospel (John 1 – 20), the culmination of that wonderful work of selection, arrangement and interpretation meant to help us to faith – to see in our hearts that Jesus is the Christ (Messiah), the Son of God, the one sent from God who is God reaching out, coming to us in humility and love. John longs for us to have this faith, so that, recognizing him in our hearts, we may have life in his name (20.30–31).

The Risen Lord by the Lake

John 21.15–25

When breakfast was over, Jesus said to Simon Peter, 'Simon son of John, do you love me above all else?' He answered, 'Yes, Lord, you know that I love you.' He said to him, 'Tend my lambs.'

Then he asked him a second time, 'Simon son of John, do you love me?' He answered, 'Yes, Lord, you know that I love you.' He said to him, 'Tend my sheep.'

A third time he said to him, 'Simon son of John, do you love me?' Peter was grieved that he asked him a third time, 'Do you love me?' 'Lord,' he said, 'you know everything. You know that I love you.' Jesus said to him, 'Feed my sheep. Truly, truly, I say to you: when you were young you girded yourself and walked where you wished. But when you get old, you will stretch out your arms, and someone else will gird you and carry you where you do not wish to go.' (This he said to show the manner of death by which Peter was to glorify God.) Then he said to him, 'Follow me.'

Peter glanced back and saw following them the disciple whom Jesus loved, the one who at the supper had leaned close to him and asked, 'Lord, who is it that will betray you?' So when Peter saw him, he asked Jesus, 'Lord, and what about this man?' Jesus answered, 'If it is my will that he wait till I come, what is that to you? Just follow me.' The report then spread through the company of disciples that this disciple was not to die. But Jesus did not say of him that he was not to die, but 'If it is my will that he wait until I come, what is that to you?'

It is this same disciple who bears witness to these things and wrote them down, and we know that his witness is true. And there are also many other

things that Jesus did, and if they were written everyone, I suppose that the world itself could not contain the books that would be written.

The main gospel of John was concluded at the end of chapter 20. But very soon a need was felt to make an addition, drawing further on the tradition of the risen Lord's appearances. In fact, the long story added as chapter 21 has much to teach the growing church.

Just how the change of scene from Jerusalem to Galilee took place we are not told, but it would be natural for the disciples to take an opportunity to be a while at the lakeside which held so many memories of those former days with Jesus.

A group of them are out fishing by night but without success despite great efforts. In the early dawn they see but do not recognize Jesus standing on the nearby shore. Following his advice they cast their net again, with wonderful result. So it will be with the mission of the church. If it is done as Christ directs, it will gather richly from the nations, and the net of unity will not break

The 'beloved disciple' (John, we think) is the first to realize the figure on the shore must be Jesus, but Peter is the one to rush through the shallows to the shore. They find Jesus has prepared breakfast for them, and he takes bread and distributes it, fish likewise. He is the presiding host in the act of sacred fellowship they know so well. After the meal comes the Lord's dialogue with Peter. The thrice-repeated question, answer and rejoinder puts away Peter's threefold denial. He is appointed the chief shepherd-leader of Christ's flock, but all on the basis and condition of his loyalty and devotion to his Lord. Jesus is sure of him. He will be a faithful witness to the end, though the end be crucifixion. This restoration of the fallen Peter will always be an inspiration to Christ's fallible but true-hearted disciples.

As for the beloved disciple (John), it seems that a misunderstanding about him in the early church has to be corrected. He is living to a great age, but Jesus has not said the end of all will come before he dies. It is John who bears his faithful witness in the gospel, a role different from Peter's, but also of the greatest significance.

Make All Nations My Disciples

Matthew 28.16–20

Then the chosen disciples went to Galilee, to a mountain that Jesus had appointed. And when they saw him, they fell down before him, though some of them were doubting. But Jesus came forward and spoke to them, saying, 'All authority in heaven and earth has been given to me. Go then and make all nations my disciples, baptizing them in the name of the Father and of the Son and of the Holy Spirit and teaching them to keep all that I have commanded you. And see, I am with you always, even to the close of the age.'

Matthew ends his gospel memorably with this account of the appearance of the risen Lord on a mountain in Galilee. This appointed mountain brings recollection of the mount that saw the anticipation of his glory, the transfiguration. Also of the Sermon on the Mount, and the Old Testament tradition of God's self-revelation at Mount Sinai.

Before the glory of Jesus the disciples fall down and worship, though some are bewildered and unsure. Yet to all, the confident and the doubters alike, Jesus gives the commission that is to be his church's task till the end of this world. Because through his Passion he is now raised to all authority on behalf of his Father, he is ready to command the taking of the gospel to all peoples, that they too may become his disciples, being baptized in the name – the power and the presence – of Father, Son and Spirit, and so joined to him and conformed to the way of life, the laws of the heart, that he has ordained.

And the scene ends with his marvellous words promising his presence and companionship in all aspects of this task, day by day and for ever. Nothing more is added. The end of the wondrous scene is not described. The promise of Jesus is the last word, the great word to sustain his disciples to the end of this world.

Transition to the New Form of Christ's Presence

Acts 1.1–14

In my first volume, dear Theophilus, I wrote of all that Jesus did and taught from the outset until the day that he was taken up, after he had given directions through the Holy Spirit to the apostles he had chosen. To these also he had shown himself alive after his Passion by many proofs, for he appeared to them over a period of forty days and spoke to them about the kingdom of God. And while he was in their company he charged them not to depart from Jerusalem, but to wait for the Father's promise. 'This promise,' he said, 'you heard from me, for John indeed baptized with water, but you will be baptized with the Holy Spirit in a few days' time.'

When they were all together they asked him, 'Lord, will you at this time restore the kingdom to Israel?' And he said to them, 'It is not for you to know times or seasons which the Father has appointed by his own authority. But you will receive power when the Holy Spirit comes upon you. And you will be my witnesses in Jerusalem and in all Judea and Samaria and to the farthest bounds of the earth.' And when he had said this and they were looking, he was taken up and a cloud received him from their sight. And while they were still gazing into heaven as he went, suddenly two men in white robes were standing by them. 'Men of Galilee,' they said, 'why do you stand staring into heaven? This Jesus who has been taken up from you into heaven will come again in the same way as you have seen him go into heaven.'

Then they returned to Jerusalem from the mount called Olivet which is near Jerusalem, just a Sabbath day's journey away. And when they had entered the city, they went into the upper room where they were staying, Peter and John, James and Andrew, Philip and Thomas, Bartholomew and Matthew, James son of Alphaeus, Simon the Zealot and Judas son of James. All these with one accord continued steadfastly in prayer, with the women, including Mary the mother of Jesus, and with his brothers.

This passage invites us to look back over the remarkable events from Easter morning on. Jesus had risen from the tomb and manifested himself from time to time to a variety of his followers. It was stressed that he was not a phantom, but the same Jesus, the Jesus who had died on the cross, able still to show the wounds in his hands and side, sometimes easily mistaken for a gardener or a wayfarer. He was often not recognized at first – eyes were held or hearts closed from knowing him. And he might appear or disappear in an instant, irrespective of the barriers of the material world.

These manifestations were a transitional phase in the life of Christ in his church. They brought comfort and reassurance after the shattering experience of Good Friday. Faith and courage were reborn and hearts were redirected to the great mission ahead. But when the manifestations had achieved their purpose, that mysterious 'physical' presence was withdrawn. Henceforth, to the end of this world, the disciples were to know him in the realities of faith, in the breaking of the bread, and in the constant gift of the Spirit. Raised again to the right hand of the Father, to the fullness of his heavenly glory and authority, Jesus Son of the Most High was with his people everywhere at all times, the very Life of his church. As we heard in our preceding passage, 'Lo, I am with you always' (Matthew 28.20).

With the opening of the Acts of the Apostles, Luke begins the second part of his great work embracing the gospel and the Acts, formally dedicated to Theophilus, probably a high Roman official keen to learn of Christ. Luke has already anticipated his account of the ascension at the end of his gospel, for it is the bridge between the two eras covered by his work: Christ on earth, and Christ ascended and given in the Spirit. Great artist that he was, Luke helps his readers to a sense of order in the manifold events. In Acts, though not in his gospel, he gives a picture of 'forty days' (evoking thoughts of great Old Testament revelations and sacred communions symbolically lasting forty days), a period for these extraordinary appearances of the risen Jesus, closing with the disciples' experience of seeing him taken up from them in the cloud of divine presence The picture passes over traditions of appearances in Galilee and focuses on the gathering of the disciples in faith and prayer in Jerusalem, awaiting the full endowment of the Holy Spirit that will inaugurate the church's mission. Luke's picture will be found so helpful that it will become embedded in the church's 'year', the annual cycle of worship built around Easter, Ascension and Pentecost (Whitsuntide). The church's mission to the ends of the earth now overshadows the older expectation of 'the kingdom restored to Israel', the traditional beginning of the messianic age and the new world. The disciples are not to stand gazing up as the ascension is completed, but to turn to the service of their Lord that will last till his coming again.

The nucleus of the church bravely keeps together in Jerusalem, and it is heartening to see that with the male disciples and the ever faithful band of women are now joined the family of Jesus – Mary and the 'brothers' – in full accord of prayer and fellowship.

20.

The Growing Community Living by the Spirit

The Outpouring of the Spirit

Acts 2

During the day of the Festival of Pentecost, they had all gathered together in one place. And suddenly there came from heaven a sound like the rushing of a mighty wind, and it filled all the house where they were sitting. And there appeared to them tongues as of fire, parting among them to rest on each one of them. And they were all filled with the Holy Spirit and began to speak in other tongues as the Spirit gave them something to proclaim.

At that time devout Jews from every nation under heaven were staying in Jerusalem. And when this sound was heard a great crowd came together, and they were astonished that each one could hear them speaking in his own language . . .

[v. 14] But Peter stood up with the eleven, and raising his voice, he addressed them thus: 'Men of Judea and all you who dwell in Jerusalem, know this and attend to my words. These men are not drunk as you suppose, for it is but nine in the morning. No, this is what was foretold by the prophet Joel: And in the last days, says God, I will pour out my spirit on all flesh, and your sons and your daughters shall prophesy, and your young men shall see visions, and your old men shall dream dreams . . .

[v. 22] 'People of Israel, hear these words: I speak of Jesus of Nazareth, a man shown to you by God through mighty works and wonders and signs, which God did among you through him, as you yourselves know. When he had been delivered up according to the set purpose and plan of God, you crucified and killed him by the hands of lawless men. But God raised him to life again, freeing him from the pangs of death, for it could not be that death should keep him in its grip. For David says of him [Psalm 16.10], ". . . You will not abandon my soul to the land of death, nor hand over your faithful one to suffer corruption". . . [v. 36] Let all the house of Israel therefore know for a surety that God has made both Lord and Christ this Jesus whom you crucified.'

Now when they heard this they were smitten to the heart and said to Peter and the rest of the apostles, 'Brothers, what shall we do?' Peter replied, 'Repent and be baptized every one of you in the name of Jesus Christ for the forgiveness of your sins, and you will receive the gift of the Holy Spirit. For the promise is held out to you and to your children, and to all that are far off, everyone whom the Lord our God calls to himself.'

And with many other words he testified and exhorted them, saying, 'Save yourselves from this crooked generation.' So those who received his word were baptized, and some three thousand were added to their number that day. And they continued steadfastly in the apostles' teaching and fellowship and in the breaking of bread and the prayers.

The ancient wheat-harvest festival, seven weeks after Passover, eventually became a celebration of the giving of the law on Mount Sinai. Known in Greek as 'Pentecost' (the fiftieth day) it attracted many pilgrims to Jerusalem from Jewish communities in many countries.

On this exciting day the little band of disciples experience a new Pentecost. The gift of God, superseding the law, is now his Holy Spirit, giving not set commandments but a living guidance and an enabling – indeed the very force of God's own life and the presence and power of Jesus Christ. This divine force is represented in the wind and fire, and the gift of it is granted to each disciple.

The impact of that power brings an emotional release and hence the 'speaking in tongues'. The long purpose of God is sensed as the ancient prophecy of Joel comes to mind. This foretold the end of an era and a new force of divine presence resulting in many ordinary people being filled with the word of God and seeing visions.

In the flow of the generally incomprehensible words, the 'tongues', the gathered crowd recognize here and there snatches of praise in their own languages, traditional hymns of the mighty works of God. It is all a sign of how the Spirit will enable the apostles to speak meaningfully of Christ from nation to nation to the ends of the earth. Peter seizes the opportunity of the awe-filled crowd even now to speak of Jesus, now made Lord and Messiah, that is, openly shown as such by his Father.

This festal day has been a climax of spiritual excitement, but the test of its worth will come in the conduct and faith evident in the succeeding days. Here the signs are good. There is faith that makes miracles possible.

There is mutual care and support with resources gladly provided to help the needy. There is steadfastness in worship, with daily visits to pray in the temple courts, also house gatherings where the holy communion of 'breaking bread' brings the life-giving experience of the body of Christ. Such a fellowship of believers cannot but grow.

Great Things Prepared through the Martyrdom of Stephen

Acts 7.54 – 8.1

When they heard Stephen's words, they were furious and gnashed their teeth at him. But he, being filled of the Holy Spirit, gazed up into heaven and saw the glory of God and Jesus standing at God's right hand. And he said, 'Oh, I see the heavens opened and the Son of Man standing at God's right hand!'

But they cried out with a loud voice and stopped their ears. Then they rushed at him and threw him out of the city and began to stone him. And the witnesses laid their cloaks down at the feet of a young man named Saul.

And as they were stoning Stephen, he prayed, 'Lord Jesus, receive my spirit.' Then he knelt down and cried with a loud voice, 'Lord, do not hold this sin against them.' And when he had said this, he fell asleep. And Saul was one of those who approved of their killing him.

Stephen is the first disciple to be killed for his witness to Jesus. He was one of a group of seven who were ordained by laying on of hands to support the ministry of the apostles. They were thus made associates of the apostles in preaching and healing and their duties in administration, especially poor relief.

Stephen's boldness in preaching and debate stirs antagonism and he is arraigned before the council and confronted by distorted witness. He makes a long speech in his defence, arguing that his opponents are following in the steps of the generations who rejected the prophets and resisted God's guidance. As he pointedly sums up his argument, their fury overwhelms the measured process of law. He is dragged outside the city and executed by stoning.

Those who gave witness against him have the customary responsibility of taking the lead in the stoning, and they have placed their cloaks in the care of a young supporter called Saul. Stephen's close following of his Lord, even to his last prayer for his persecutors, will bear its fruit, for this Saul will soon be changed into the great and valiant apostle Paul.

Philip Baptizes an Ethiopian Statesman

Acts 8.26–40

Then an angel of the Lord spoke to Philip and said, 'Rise and go south to the road that goes down from Jerusalem to Gaza, the desert road.' So he rose and went. And suddenly he saw an Ethiopian eunuch, who was in fact a chief minister of the *kandake*, the queen of Ethiopia, in charge of all her treasure. He had come to Jerusalem on pilgrimage and was now returning. As he sat in his chariot, he was reading aloud from the prophet Isaiah. The Spirit said to Philip, 'Go alongside the chariot.' So Philip ran up to him and heard him reading the prophet Isaiah, and he asked, 'Do you understand what you are reading?' 'How can I,' he answered, 'unless someone guides me?' And he entreated Philip to come up and sit with him. Now the place in Scripture that he was reading was this: 'He was led as a sheep to the slaughter, and as a lamb is dumb before the shearers, so he opens not his mouth. In his humiliation his rule was taken away. Who can declare his rank? For his life is taken from the earth.'

And the eunuch asked Philip, 'To whom, may I ask, does the prophet refer? Himself or someone else?' Then Philip opened his mouth and, beginning from this scripture, unfolded to him the gospel of Jesus.

And as they went on the way, they came to some water. 'See, here is water,' said the eunuch. 'What is to prevent me from being baptized?' He called for the chariot to stop and they both went down to the water, Philip and the eunuch, and he baptized him. And when they came up out of the water, the Spirit of the Lord caught up Philip, and the eunuch saw him no more and went on his way rejoicing. As for Philip, he appeared in Azotus, and passing on, he preached the gospel to every town until he reached Caesarea.

Philip is named next to Stephen among the seven ordained to support the apostles, and he too proves to be an effective evangelist full of the Spirit. When persecution scatters many of the believers from Jerusalem, Philip is soon found bringing the gospel fruitfully to the Samaritans, a population adhering to the law of Moses and looking for the Messiah, but despised and rejected by the Jews.

So the gospel begins to pass well beyond the original Jewish circle, and now Philip is guided to take a step further. He is prompted to take an unlikely direction, southwards from Jerusalem towards the desert. And here, sure enough, is the task that God has prepared for him. Eunuchs were employed in high office in many ancient countries, but Israelite law (Deuteronomy 23.1) excluded them from the worshipping community. The Ethiopian (modern Sudanese) must therefore have been somewhat restricted in his pilgrimage to Jerusalem, though he was a man of great devotion, probably one of the many Gentiles on the margin of the Jewish faith. The *kandake* was the Queen Mother, always the real power in that country, and he was her treasurer, a position of eminence and trust.

The chapter he was reading aloud in the Greek translation, Isaiah 53, while puzzling in some respects, is perhaps the most penetrating and revealing of all the scriptures that illuminate the death and rising of Christ – his sacrifice for the sin of the world and the salvation won by his 'intercession', his intervening. So the inspired Philip gladly 'opens his mouth' and, starting from this passage, unfolds the good news of Jesus. The good man eagerly takes the first opportunity to be baptized – wholly committed and blessed with grace, so that he is able to return home alone but joyful in his new faith. For now he is fully accepted. Jesus again has embraced the outcast, and another chapter of Isaiah has found fulfilment, for chapter 56 announces God's welcome for the eunuchs.

An Enemy Reborn to Become a Mighty Apostle

Acts 9.1–9,17–25

But Saul was still breathing threats and slaughter against the disciples of the Lord, and he went to the high priest and asked him for letters to the synagogues in Damascus, so that if he found any belonging to the Way, whether men or women, he might bring them bound to Jerusalem. Then as he journeyed and was drawing near to Damascus, a light from heaven suddenly shone about him. He fell to the ground and heard a voice saying to him, 'Saul, Saul, why are you persecuting me?' And he said, 'Who are you, lord?' And he answered, 'I am Jesus whom you are persecuting. But rise and enter the city, and you will be told what you must do.'

His companions on the journey stood speechless, for they heard the voice but saw no one. Then Saul rose from the ground, and when his eyes were opened he could see nothing. So they led him by the hand and brought him into Damascus. For three days he remained without sight and neither ate nor drank . . .

[v. 17] Then Ananias came and entered the house. Laying his hands on him, he said, 'Saul, my brother, the Lord Jesus who appeared to you on the road has sent me so that you may receive your sight and be filled with the Holy Spirit.' And at once it was as though scales fell from his eyes and he recovered his sight. Then he rose and was baptized, and when he took food his strength returned.

He stayed some time in Damascus, and without delay he began to proclaim Jesus in the synagogues, declaring that he is the Son of God. And all who heard him were amazed and said, 'Is not this the man who in Jerusalem ravaged those who called on this name? And did he not come here determined to bring them bound before the chief priests?' But Saul grew ever stronger in his task, out-reasoning the Jews of Damascus to prove that Jesus is the Messiah.

After a good while the Jews plotted to kill him, but their plans became known to Saul. They were watching the gates day and night to murder him, but his disciples took him one night and let him down over the wall, lowering him in a basket.

Saul, alias Paul, came from the thriving Greek-style city of Tarsus, near the coast of present-day south-eastern Turkey. He was at home in the Greco-Roman world and from birth held Roman citizenship. But his upbringing was that of a devout Jew, and indeed of the strict party of the Pharisees, and he studied zealously under the famous rabbi Gamaliel in Jerusalem. In such Jewish circles his name Saul (after the ancient king from the tribe of Benjamin) was used, but his similar sounding Roman name 'Paul' is preferred when he devotes himself to Christian mission in the wider empire.

We find him here still zealous for the law of Moses and its traditions. He takes the lead in harrying those belonging to the Way, that is, the way of Jesus. The high priest has powers extending to Jewish communities abroad, and Saul carries letters authorizing him to arrest and bring to trial in Jerusalem any Christians (probably fugitives from Jerusalem) that he may find in the Jewish circles in Damascus.

Struck down by the brilliant light, he knows it is a revelation from God, and asks, 'Who are you, Lord?' He hears Jesus address him, Jesus who is present in the persecuted ones, suffering with them. The three days of blindness without food or water are like days of death, a dying to the old life before rising to the new.

The new life, the filling with the Holy Spirit, the uniting with Christ in baptism – all come with the arrival of Ananias. This good man is a Christian disciple in Damascus. Knowing of Saul's original purpose, he was reluctant to obey the prompting to go to his help. But, pressed by the Lord, he sets off for Straight Street, finds Saul, and after kind words and the laying on of hands, healing and baptism follow directly.

Saul becomes a bold and effective preacher of Jesus as the Son of God and Messiah. So much so, that there are plots to kill him. After a daring escape by night over the great wall of Damascus, he heads for Jerusalem to meet the apostles.

Out from the Jews to the Gentiles

Acts 11.1–18

Now the apostles and believers who were in Judea heard that the Gentiles also received the word of God. And when Peter came up to Jerusalem, the circumcision party took issue with him, saying, 'You have visited uncircumcised men and eaten with them.' So Peter told them the whole story.

'I was in the town of Joppa, praying,' he said, 'and while in a trance I saw a vision, something like a great sheet coming down from heaven, let down by its four corners, and it came right down to me. I looked closely at it and saw four-footed animals, wild beasts, creeping things and birds. And I heard a voice saying to me, "Rise, Peter, kill and eat." And I said, "No, Lord, for nothing common or unclean has ever entered my mouth." But the voice came a second time from heaven: "What God has counted clean, do not call common" . . . And see, at that very moment three men arrived at the very house where we were staying, men sent to me from Caesarea. The Spirit told me to go with them and make no distinction between Jew and Gentile. My six companions here travelled with me and we entered the man's house. He told us how he had seen an angel standing in his house, saying, "Send to Joppa and bring Simon, surnamed Peter. He will speak words to you through which you and all your household will be saved."

I had hardly begun to speak when the Holy Spirit fell on them, just as on us at the beginning. And I remembered the word of the Lord, how he said, "John indeed baptized with water, but you shall be baptized with the Holy Spirit." If then God gave to them the same gift as he gave to us when we believed in the Lord Jesus Christ, who was I to stand against God?'

When they heard this they were silent, and then they glorified God, saying, 'So to the Gentiles also God has granted the repentance that leads to life.'

Peter has been involved in a radical development likely to be controversial. He has visited and baptized Gentiles, non-Jews. Returning to Jerusalem from the coastal towns of Joppa and Caesarea, he faces opposition from 'the circumcision party' – those holding strictly to the biblical laws of ritually 'clean' and 'unclean' foods, involving separation from Gentiles in table fellowship and hospitality.

Peter's actions involve such a turning point for the young church that the facts are gone over several times, with Peter in the end giving this careful report of it all. Moreover he has six companions who can confirm his account, making with himself a powerful sevenfold witness to the unmistakable way God led them into this radical departure, breaking with an old scriptural tradition.

Peter's report carries conviction, here in the heart of the church's Jerusalem headquarters. The stage is thus set for the missions of Paul and others to the Gentiles, though some aspects of the new orientation will still arouse sharp controversy and need all the prayer and love of Christ to settle in unity.

Planting in the Capital of Syria

Acts 11.19–26

Now those who were scattered because of the persecution that arose over Stephen had taken their way as far as Phoenicia, Cyprus and Antioch, speaking the word to Jews only. But some among them, men of Cyprus and Cyrene, on arriving in Antioch began to speak to Gentiles also, telling them the good news of Jesus. Moreover the hand of the Lord was with them and a great number believed and turned to the Lord.

When news of this came to the ears of the church in Jerusalem, they sent out Barnabas all the way to Antioch. Once he had arrived and seen the power of God, he rejoiced and exhorted them all to hold resolutely to the Lord, for he was a good man and full of the Holy Spirit and faith. And a great company was added to the Lord.

Then Barnabas travelled on to Tarsus to seek out Saul. And when he had found him, he brought him back to Antioch. And so it came about that for a whole year they met with the church there and gave instruction to many people. It was in Antioch that the disciples were first called 'Christians'.

Persecution of believers at the time of Stephen's martyrdom led to a scattering of them that proved to be a seeding in fertile ground afar. Antioch, capital of Syria and reckoned the third city in the empire, lay 300 miles north of Jerusalem. It had the imposing features of a Greek city, hardly ever again to be matched in world civilization. It had a strong Jewish community and was well situated for prosperity, but it had also come to have a reputation for depravity in some respects.

It may be that the men of Cyprus and Cyrene (capital of Libya) among the refugees from the Jerusalem church met fellow countrymen in Antioch who were Gentiles and they were led naturally to share with them 'the good news of Jesus'. But what a good contribution Barnabas made! Not only utterly positive about the welcoming of Gentiles into the faith, he was also inspired to seek out Saul who, for quite a number of years, had been back in his home area, no doubt maturing in his grasp of the faith and in experience of serving the gospel.

So Saul and Barnabas worked together for a valuable year, meeting believers in Antioch for worship and instruction. It was to be a very important base, from which missions would go out across the Roman world. 'Christians': what a good name for believers – people belonging to Christ, the Messiah, people defined by a life-forming devotion to him!

Overcoming a Controversy in the Church

Acts 15.1–5,22–29

But there were some who had come down from Judea and were teaching the brothers that unless they were circumcised according to the custom of Moses they could not be saved. And when Paul and Barnabas had no small disagreement and argument with them, it was decided that Paul, Barnabas and some others should go up to Jerusalem to bring the matter to the apostles and elders. Being thus sent off on their mission by the church, they passed through both Phoenicia and Samaria, telling of the conversion of the Gentiles and giving great joy to all the believers.

When they arrived in Jerusalem, they were welcomed by the church with the apostles and elders, and they recounted to them all that God had done through them. But some believers who belonged to the party of the Pharisees rose and said, 'It is necessary to circumcise them and charge them to keep the law of Moses' . . .

[15.22] Then the apostles and elders with the whole church resolved to choose some of their number and send them to Antioch with Paul and Barnabas. So Judas called Barsabbas, and Silas, leading men of the church, were chosen to go and carry the following letter:

The apostles and elders, brothers, to the brothers who are in Antioch, Syria and Cilicia – greeting! Since we have heard that men from our people have troubled you with their opinions and unsettled your minds without any authority from us, we have with one accord resolved to choose men to send to you with our beloved Barnabas and Paul who have devoted their lives to the name of our Lord Jesus Christ. We are therefore sending Judas and Silas, who will themselves tell you by word of mouth the same message that we write. For it has seemed good to the Holy Spirit and to our own understanding to lay upon you no greater burden than these necessary things, namely that you should abstain from meat that has been offered to idols and from blood and anything strangled, and from sexual immorality. If you keep yourselves from these things, you will do well. Farewell!

The scene again is the church in Antioch, where Paul (alias Saul) and Barnabas are still based. But much has happened since they began their work here together. First we hear that they were sent by the Antioch church to take alms to help believers in Judea in a time of famine. When back in Antioch, they were commissioned again through the prophetic word, this time to take the gospel to Cyprus and beyond (into present-day southern Turkey). Preaching first to Jews, then to Gentiles, they were sometimes near to death. But they were able to found a string of churches and return safely to resume preaching in Antioch.

But now come troublers from Judea, declaring that the Gentile converts in Antioch must be circumcised and so made Jews under the Mosaic law. It is deeply disturbing, and Paul and Barnabas are delegated to visit 'headquarters' in Jerusalem and have the matter resolved. There, too, opinions are divided, but in the end the decision is against the necessity for circumcision. But a proviso is made to ease the fellowship of all Christians at meals (including those that passed into commemoration of the last supper). All should abstain from certain things repugnant to devout Jews – from food that had been sacrificed in pagan worship (and commonly available in the markets), from blood of slaughtered animals and from sexual licence.

As Luke unfolds the story, we see the care of the church to preserve unity, with honest debate and reasoning, respect for the church authorities and for the guidance of the Spirit given through people recognized for their prophetic gifts and calling. His story shows a happy resolution of the controversy.

From the letter of Paul, written in the heat of the struggle, we see more complications and the persistence of the problem. But we also see how the struggle and distress that it brought to Paul and his converts bore fruit in the wonderful depth that developed in Paul's thought and teaching about the salvation which is not through law but through grace and faith.

Paul's Work in Corinth

Acts 18.1–11

After all this Paul left Athens and came to Corinth. There he met with a Jew called Aquila, a native of Pontus, recently arrived from Italy with his wife Priscilla, because the emperor Claudius had ordered all Jews to leave Rome. Paul joined them and being of the same trade he stayed with them and they worked together, for they were both tent-makers. And every Sabbath he spoke in the synagogue, seeking to persuade both Jews and Gentiles.

But when Silas and Timothy came down from Macedonia, Paul was moved to devote himself wholly to preaching, testifying to the Jews that Jesus was the Messiah. When they were set against him and shouted abuse, he shook out his cloak and said to them, 'Your blood be on your own heads! I shall not be responsible. From now on I will go to the Gentiles.'

So he left them and went to the house of a man named Titus Justus, a devout Gentile whose home was beside the synagogue. But Crispus, the superintendent of the synagogue, now came to believe in the Lord, and all his household with him. And many of the Corinthians, on hearing Paul, believed and were baptized.

Then one night the Lord spoke to Paul in a vision and said, 'Have no fear, but speak and do not be silent, for I am with you, and no one shall set on you to do you harm. For I have many people to claim in this city.' So he remained there for a further year and a half, preaching among them the word of God.

From his work in Antioch, Paul has set out with Silas on extensive missionary journeys in Asia Minor (present-day Turkey) and across to Macedonia and Greece. After many adventures, sufferings and successes, he has now arrived in Corinth, a bustling commercial centre in southern Greece. Living with Aquila and Priscilla, he plies his trade as 'tent-maker', perhaps making a range of goods from felted goat's hair, and speaking of the faith in the Sabbath gatherings of Jews and Gentile sympathizers, 'God-fearers', in the synagogue.

Some time later, with the arrival of his missionary co-workers, Silas and Timothy, he devotes himself fully to preaching. But opposition in the synagogue hardens and Paul now bases himself in a friendly household close by. A notable event is the conversion of the president or administrator of the synagogue and his family. In fact there is much opportunity for the Lord in this city, and Paul responds to guidance in a vision to make his stay in Corinth unusually long. His deep involvement with the growing church in this European and cosmopolitan city will be reflected in his letters to the Corinthians in all their passion and faith.

Paul's Witness in the World's Centre

Acts 28.11–16, 30–31

Three months later we set sail in a ship of Alexandria which had wintered in the island and had the 'twin brothers' [Castor and Pollux] as figurehead. Putting in at Syracuse, we stayed there three days. Then, sailing round, we came to Rhegium. A day later a south wind sprang up and next day we arrived at Puteoli, where we found Christian brothers and sisters and were urged to stay with them for a week. And so we came to Rome, where again believers, having news of us, came out as far as the Forum of Appius and the Three Taverns to meet us. At the sight of them, Paul thanked God and took courage.

When we entered Rome, Paul was allowed to have his own lodgings with the soldier who guarded him . . . Two full years he stayed in this rented lodging, and welcomed all who came to see him, telling them of the kingdom of God and teaching about the Lord Jesus Christ with all boldness, no one forbidding him.

An Egyptian corn ship, resplendent with its figurehead of the mythical twins Castor and Pollux and well rested after wintering in Malta, now carries Paul and his companions as far as its destination in Italy. The season is now favourable and they make good progress, passing along the east coast of Sicily and then up the western side of Italy to end their voyage at what is now Pozzuoli by the Bay of Naples.

Those bound for Rome make their way northwards overland and Paul and his friends are heartened to find Christians from the city have come 40 miles out to the Appian Forum and 30 miles to the Three Taverns to welcome them. Paul's situation of house arrest for two years (his case presumably not being heard for lack of accusers) is a sign of the onward march of the gospel through all tribulation. It makes a suitable place for Luke to end his present narrative, perhaps intending to add a third volume in due course.

21.

The Life of the Spirit

Nothing Can Part Us from God's Love in Christ

Romans 8.14–17,35,37–39

Those who are led by the Spirit of God are children of God. For it was not a spirit of bondage that you received, making for fear, but the Spirit that makes us children of God, able to say, 'Abba, Father.' This same Spirit bears witness with our spirit that we are children of God, and being children heirs, heirs of God and joint heirs with Christ, as we share his sufferings so that we may also share his glory . . .

[v. 35] What shall separate us from the love of Christ? Shall suffering or pain or persecution or danger or nakedness or peril or sword? . . .

[v. 37] No, in all these things we are more than conquerors through him who loved us. For I am certain that neither death nor life, nor angels, nor powers above, nothing that is and nothing that will be, no force, no height, no depth, nor any other creature shall be able to separate us from the love of God which is in Christ Jesus our Lord.

We may think of Paul as writing to the church in Rome while he is working in Corinth about the year 57. He writes to prepare the ground for a visit he hopes to make after his forthcoming journey to Jerusalem. From Rome, granted the support of the Christians there, he will be able to undertake mission westwards to Spain.

His letter for the most part is an account of the gospel as he understands it, set out thoughtfully so that the Roman believers may share his vision and be at one with him in the great tasks that may lie ahead.

A chief theme is the nature of the life in Christ, not an enslavement to law but a life led by and filled with God's Spirit. As the believers are united with Christ in his death and resurrection, the grace and power of

God at work through the Spirit puts them in the position not of slaves to a master but of children towards a loving parent. Into the very love that binds Jesus to the Father they too are drawn. And in every need the Spirit helps us, pleading for us in yearnings beyond words, while all things are made to work together for our good as we are drawn into the true love of God – our destiny.

Reflecting on all this, Paul is inspired with winged words of testimony to this love of Christ, faithful, enduring, triumphing over all the sufferings of this world. Whatever assails us in life or death, nothing will separate us from that love and its glorious fulfilment in the eternity of God.

God's Foolishness?

1 Corinthians 1.17–31

For Christ did not send me to baptize but to proclaim the gospel, but not with skilful argument lest the cross of Christ should be emptied of power. For the meaning of the cross is foolishness to those set on their own ruin, but to us who are on the way to salvation it is the very power of God. For it is written, 'I will destroy the wisdom of the wise, and the understanding of the clever I will reject.' Where is the wise person, where the learned? Where is the great debater of this age? Has not God made foolish the wisdom of this world ? For since in the wisdom of God the world through its own wisdom does not know God, it pleased God through the folly of the gospel to save those who believe. For Jews ask for proof by miracles and Greeks demand wisdom, but we preach Christ crucified, to Jews a stumbling-block and to Gentiles nonsense, but to those who hear the call, both Jews and Greeks, he is Christ the power of God and the wisdom of God. For God's foolishness is wiser than human beings and God's weakness is stronger than human beings.

For consider your own call, my brothers and sisters. There are not many wise people among you in the world's eyes. Not many mighty, not many of noble birth have been called. But God has chosen things the world counts folly to put to shame those that purport to be wise. And God has chosen what the world counts weak to put to shame things that boast strength. Yes, things that are lowly in this world and despised God has chosen, things that counted for nothing, that he might bring to nothing the things that dominate, so that no creature should boast in the presence of God.

But he has given you life in Christ Jesus, who came to us as the divine wisdom, setting us right, sanctifying and redeeming us. As it is written, 'Let the one who would boast boast in the Lord' [2 Corinthians 10.17; Jeremiah 9.23–24].

Paul worked hard to establish the church in Corinth, residing there as we have seen for quite a long period. Now, a few years later, he is visiting the church in Ephesus and is troubled by reports that the Christians across the water in Greek Corinth are dividing into factions. In particular, a learned and brilliant missionary from Alexandria, Apollos, has been teaching there, and his skilful presentations have inclined some Christians to disparage the relatively plain and basic teaching they received from Paul. The unity of the church is threatened by partisanship and an attitude of superiority adopted by some who have acquired more sophisticated beliefs – in supposedly higher wisdom.

Paul, himself a learned man and profound theologian, is not setting himself against dedicated thought and learning. He deplores the lack of humility. Too easily we succumb to the vanity that lurks in human wisdom and we relish a fancied superiority over others. We become critics who even boast in the presence of God. So in Corinth there is harm to the unity of Christian love and a danger that the essential truth of the gospel may be 'emptied' – disparaged and disregarded in the quest for a prestigious wisdom.

Paul therefore calls his children in the faith back to Christ the crucified who is the power of God and the wisdom of God. In this Christ God has granted us to live, finding peace in him and the holiness that is harmony with him, and so the life of true freedom.

Differing Gifts, from the One Spirit

1 Corinthians 12.4–13

There are indeed varieties of gifts, but it is the same Spirit. There are varieties of service, but the same Lord. There are many kinds of work, but all of them, in every person, are the work of the same God. In each one is given a manifestation of the Spirit for a good purpose. One may be given through the Spirit the word of wisdom, another the word of knowledge through the same Spirit, another faith through the same Spirit, another gifts of healing through the one Spirit. Another may be given power to work miracles, another the gift of prophecy, another the distinguishing between good and bad spirits, another kinds of ecstatic speech, another the ability to interpret them. But in all of them one and the same Spirit is at work, allotting the gifts to each person as he wills. For just as a body is one yet with many parts, and all the parts, many as they are, form one body, so it is with Christ. By one Spirit we were all baptized into one body, whether we were Jews or Greeks, slaves or free, and we were all given to drink of the one Spirit.

The concern for unity sounds again and again as Paul continues his letter with matters he has been asked about. In the variety of work done in the fellowship and worship of the church there is no place, he says, for attitudes of superiority or jealousy. The one God is working in our work; the one Spirit imparts the particular gift to serve his good purpose in building up the church. As Paul mentions examples, we have an impression of many lively Christians contributing from their differing gifts. One member gives wise counsel; another speaks of God from the knowledge of genuine experience. One is a rock of faith when others waver. Another has the word of healing, while another has light from God on some present problem. One can discern spirits, able to judge the value of claimed inspirations. Another speaks in 'tongues', when deep emotion releases utterance outside the normal frame of language, and another has the gift of sensing its meaning. In all such different endowments there is no ground for pride or jealousy. For each has what the one Spirit has given for the good of the one body of Christ. In baptism they were made parts of this body and given the Spirit as a life-giving drink.

Yet there may be something to add. Paul's prophet-soul may be inspired now with the thought of something flowing from God that surpasses the gifts he has mentioned. We must read on.

The Supreme Gift

1 Corinthians 13

Though I speak in the tongues of earth and heaven but have no love I'm just a sounding gong or clanging cymbal. And if I have the gift of prophecy and understand all mysteries and all knowledge but have no love, I am nothing. And if I give all my goods for the hungry or give up my body to be martyred in flames but have no love, it profits me nothing.

Love is patient and kind. Love does not envy. Love is not boastful or prated up, does not act rudely, is not selfish or quick to take offence, does not harbour grievances or rejoice at wrongdoing, but delights to hear of good. Love is forgiving, always full of faith and hope and endurance.

Love never ends. But if there are prophecies, they will pass away; if there are tongues, they will cease; if there is knowledge it will fall away. For we know in part and we prophesy in part, but when the whole is revealed, what was only in part will be put away. When I was a child, I spoke like a child, I felt like a child, and I thought like a child. Now that I am a grown man I have left behind the ways of a child. Now we see poor reflections in a mirror, but then we shall see face to face. Now I know in part but then I shall know as fully as I am known. But now these three remain – faith, hope and love, and the greatest of these is love.

Paul continues his letter to the effervescent Christians in the effervescent cosmopolitan port of Corinth, and is himself inspired to add to what he has written about the Spirit's charismatic gifts, admirable as they are, yet needing to be governed by humility and desire for the blessing of the whole fellowship. They are all in vain, he says, without love (*agape*). He has in mind Christlike love, love which flows from Father, Son and Spirit into those who become part of Christ's body. He gives a moving description of this love and especially praises its enduring nature. When the inspired tongues have finished their outpouring, when the wondrous learning and teaching have been overtaken by fuller revelation, when our visions give way to the reality of God's face, love will remain, being of the very essence of God's will and work and eternal being.

And even now in this earthly life, while we see many good things falling away as their time is past, we have the continuing joy of faith, hope and love. And of these the greatest, the purest and most enduring gift of God's heart, is love.

The Strength of Weakness

2 Corinthians 11.21–31; 12.7b–10

Yet what they boast of – I speak rashly – I can boast of too. Are they Hebrews? So am I. Are they Israelites? So am I. Are they children of Abraham? So am I. Are they servants of Christ [I speak madly]? I more so, with far more labours, far more imprisonments, with blows beyond counting, often close to death. Five times the Jews gave me the forty lashes less one. Three times I was beaten with rods, once I was stoned, three times I was shipwrecked, a night and a day I was adrift at sea. I have been constantly on journeys, facing danger from rivers, danger from robbers, danger from my countrymen, danger from Gentiles, danger in towns, danger in the open country, danger at sea, danger from false friends, enduring toil and hardship, nights without sleep, hunger and thirst, often without food, suffering cold and exposure. And beside such bodily perils, anxiety for all the churches weighs on me daily. For who is weak, and I am not weak? Who is made to stumble, and my heart does not burn? If I have to boast, I will boast of things that show my weakness. The God and Father of the Lord Jesus (blessed be he for ever] knows that I do not lie . . .

[12.7b] And so that I should not be too elated by the abundance of the revelations given to me, I was given also a thorn in the flesh, an envoy of Satan, to assail me, for fear I should be too elated. I begged the Lord three times that this should leave me, but he answered me, 'My grace is sufficient for you, for my strength is made perfect in weakness.'

All the more, then, I will glory in my weakness, since there the strength of Christ will rest upon me. So for Christ's sake I am glad of weaknesses, injuries, necessities, persecutions, distresses, for when I am weak, then I am strong.

What has occasioned this passionate outburst? It seems that Paul has recently revisited the Corinthian Christians, hoping to build on his earlier ministry there. But he has been rebuffed. Delegates from circles in Jerusalem have been there to oppose Paul's teachings on the Jewish law. To this end they have disparaged his authority as a leading apostle. Not one of the twelve, he would easily be portrayed as a latecomer, his teaching not authoritative. So the mood of the Corinthians turned against Paul. Now back in Ephesus, he has to write to restore both his credentials and also the right way for this largely Gentile church.

Deeply troubled, he writes, as he says, like a fool or a madman, because he has to seem to brag of his service for Christ. To boast also of wonderful revelations given him, as though he was caught up to the highest heaven. But he has also been given 'a thorn in the flesh', some painful ailment to keep him from undue elation over his visions. (The Satan or 'Adversary' is thought of here as the angel responsible for testing the faithful with sufferings.)

As this pain remains, he has learnt from the Lord that in the very weakness he will know the grace and power of the divine presence. So he can even be glad of such sufferings since they occasion richer experience of that holy presence abiding over him, that overshadowing of the Lord's beauty, strength and grace.

It may well be that those scholars are right who believe that several surviving fragments of Paul's correspondence with the Corinthians were joined by the collector of all his letters to make our 'Second Letter to the Corinthians', and that chapters 1 – 9 reflect the situation after our passage. Thus it appears that a reconciliation will follow the bitter period. Paul is to have joy again in these his children in Christ, these young Christians of Corinth.

Clothed with Christ

Galatians 3.23–29

But before this faith came, we were kept under guard by the law, confined until the faith should be revealed. The law was thus our guardian minding us for Christ, when through faith we should be set right with God.

But now this faith has come, we are no longer under a guardian. For through faith you are all children of God in Christ Jesus, since all you who were baptized into Christ have been clothed with Christ. There is now neither Jew nor Greek, neither slave nor free, neither male nor female. For you are all one in Christ Jesus. And if you are Christ's, then you are children of Abraham, the heirs that were promised him.

Paul's letter is to the groups of converts in various towns in the province of Galatia in Asia Minor (modern Turkey). His founding work there is being undermined by visits from his opponents. They seek to bring the new Christians under the law of Moses, and to that end they belittle Paul's status.

Over several centuries, with the nation suffering conquest, dispersion and subjugation, this law and its interpreters came to have the dominant role in Jewish religion and life. Jews who became Christians, especially those from the Jerusalem area, found it very hard to take a new view of it.

So we find Paul battling hard to keep his non-Jewish converts free of that old law, free to be servants of Christ. He teaches that the law has completed its work in its allotted time, like a 'tutor', a guardian who had to mind and control the young. He insists that since Christ is the true seed of Abraham – the descendant who fulfils the covenant promise God made to Abraham – then all baptized Christians, being one with Christ, are also the seed of Abraham and fully children of God, irrespective of gender, class and the Jewish–Gentile divide. If through trust in the Lord Jesus we are united with him, part of him, clothed with him, what more do we need to relate us wholly to God? Not by the yoke of the law but by faith we are justified, that is, put right in God's eyes through our faith in the Son of God who lived, died and rose again for us.

The Spirit's Law of Love

Galatians 5.13–16 – 6.18

For you, my brothers and sisters, were called to freedom: only do not use your freedom as a chance for self-indulgence. Rather, through love be servants to one another. For the whole law can be summed up in one saying: 'You must love your neighbour as yourself.' But if you bite and maul one another, take care that you are not destroyed by one another! What I say is, walk by the Spirit, and then you will not satisfy selfish cravings . . .

[5.22] Now the fruit of the Spirit is love, joy, peace, patience, kindness, goodness, faithfulness, gentleness, self-control. Against such there is no law!

And those who belong to Christ Jesus have crucified their selfish nature with its passions and desires . . .

[6.14] But far be it from me to glory in anything but the cross of our Lord Jesus Christ, through which the world has been crucified to me and I to the world. Being circumcised or not being circumcised is nothing. What matters is a new creation. Peace and mercy be on all who walk by this rule, and on the Israel of God! From now on let no one trouble me, for I carry the marks of Jesus branded on my body. The grace of our Lord Jesus Christ be with your spirit, my brothers and sisters. Amen!

Reaching out to those who have moved away from him, Paul twice here calls them his *adelphoi*, 'brothers' – used comprehensively, 'brothers and sisters (in Christ)'. He has written of their freedom from the law of Moses, but he knows that some make a virtue of licence, satisfying every inclination. So he speaks of the new service the Christian enters, a disciplined and devoted life of godly love towards others, a life of 'the fruit of the Spirit'. Only by the Spirit's divine power animating us, bringing us the life that flows from Christ's work, can we bear this fruit. The first fruit in Paul's list is indeed love (*agape*), and the rest simply unfold it. There is the characteristic joy, however hard the service; there is the humility and faithfulness so evident in Christ; and there is at the end the note of the discipline required – self-control.

Through the cross we die to the world's concerns for self-importance and pleasure and enter a new world, the new creation, where the divine love is all. The scars Paul carries from all he has suffered in his service of Jesus are like the brand marks in the Roman world which showed who was a slave's master or a devotee's god. Those who attack him must reckon with his master, Christ. But the last word in Paul's outspoken letter is given to the grace of our Lord Jesus Christ and the bond of Christian love.

A Prayer to Know the Depths of Christ's Love

Ephesians 3.14–21

To this end I kneel and pray to the Father from whom every family in heaven and on earth is named. I ask that he, out of the riches of his glory, may grant you to be strengthened with power through his Spirit deep within you, and that Christ may dwell in your hearts through your faith. Then, being rooted and grounded in love, may you be strong to grasp with all God's people the sheer breadth and height and length and depth of Christ's love, knowing it though it is beyond knowledge. And so may you be filled more and more with all the fullness of God. Now to him who through his power at work in us is able to do far more than all we ask or think, to him be the glory in the church and in Christ Jesus to all generations for ever and ever. Amen.

This letter may have been sent to a number of churches and certainly has a rather general character. All the more readily, then, should Christians of any place or time think of the great prayer in our passage as rising for them. The Father of all fathers, the Source and Creator of all families, will hear in his compassion and grant that inner strengthening and growth which is an essential part of the Christian way. So, through the Spirit, Christ dwells in their hearts, and more and more they come to experience the immensity of his love, great beyond everything of this world.

More and more we are given of the riches of God. We come to see and trust in his care, which goes far beyond what we are able to pray for or even imagine. And so we live for his glory and praise, rejoicing in his goodness shown in the church and in the unfailing nearness of Jesus.

And Again I Say, Rejoice

Philippians 4.4–8

> Rejoice in the Lord always, and again I say, rejoice! Let your gentleness be shown to everyone. The Lord is near. Let nothing make you anxious, but in everything, by prayer and supplication with thanksgiving, make your requests to God. Then the peace of God which passes all understanding will guard your hearts and minds in Christ Jesus. And now, my brothers and sisters, whatever things are true, whatever things are honourable, all things that are good, all things that are pure, all things that are lovely, all things encouraging, if there is anything of beauty, if anything worthy of praise, dwell on these things.

On one of his missionary journeys, Paul had been led to cross from Asia Minor to Macedonia, north of Greece, and the first church he founded, his first in Europe, was some 10 miles in from the coast at Philippi. As he writes to them now, he is suffering imprisonment (just where and when is debatable). They have been anxious for him and he has been touched by the thoughtfulness prompting the practical help they have sent.

Suffering himself, he can give encouragement to all who suffer. As always, the example of Jesus is before him, the Lord who stripped himself of his glory and humbled himself as a servant, even to death on the cross

(Philippians 2.5–8). If this mind is in us, it will be possible in all times of distress still to 'rejoice in the Lord' – and that is the key. In the Lord, in Christ Jesus, united to him, we can put away anxiety and ask God's help with it all, yet giving thanks. And then the wonderful peace of the Lord beyond all words and understanding will stand guard over our hearts and minds, keeping away the enemies of fear and worry. Not by forced effort but naturally from being in Christ Jesus, we think thankfully of things that are good and true and beautiful. The clamour of the world, with all its folly and evil, moves away. We live in the first light of a new world.

Hidden with Christ in God

Colossians 3.1–4,12–17

> So if you have been raised with Christ, seek the things that are above, where Christ is, seated at the right hand of God. Set your mind on such things above, not on things that are on the earth. For you died, and your life is now hidden with Christ in God. When Christ who is our life appears, then you also will appear with him in glory . . . So put on, as God's chosen ones, his own, his beloved, put on compassion, kindness, humility, gentleness and patience. Be forbearing with one another, forgiving when you have a grievance. Just as the Lord forgave you, so you must forgive. And over all these garments put on love, the bond that will complete your clothing. And let the peace of Christ have rule in your hearts, for this is our calling as parts of one body. And ever be giving thanks.
>
> Let the word of Christ dwell among you richly, as you teach and exhort one another with all wisdom, singing psalms and hymns and spiritual songs from hearts thankful to God. And whatever you do, in word or deed, do all in the name of the Lord Jesus, giving thanks to God the Father through him.

Another great letter that Paul writes from his imprisonment. It is addressed to the church at Colossae, some 100 miles inland from coastal Ephesus (and so in present-day central-southern Turkey). News has reached him of a cult growing among the Christians there, in which the unique role of Christ is obscured, and superior merit is arrogantly attached to a system of ceremonial practices. So he writes to set out the significance of Christ in the salvation of the universe, and also to insist on the conduct that should mark the Christian life.

Paul teaches that those who are Christ's have died and risen with him. In that death they put off the worldly nature, and in that rising they put on the garments of Christ's ways – humility, a forgiving spirit, love – as symbolized in the immersion of baptism.

The life of this 'new' person can be said to be 'hidden with Christ in God' – united with Christ and wholly given to God. The desires and thoughts and values that now fill the mind are from 'above', pleasing to God, inspired by him, not by the sinful world. It is a way of lowliness and sacrifice that proves to be the way to glory, as will be revealed when Christ's own splendour is manifest.

Christ's word is the gospel of his teaching and life, but lying within it is the divine presence. As his disciples meet together for study and spiritual nourishment, learning together and praising God, the word dwells in and among them richly, preparing the harvest of fruits of the Spirit. In all the teaching, in all the living, Christ is to be at the centre, all being done in his name and gathered up in thankful praise of the Father through him, the Son who alone truly reveals him.

22.

Messages for the Churches

Eyes Fixed on Jesus

Hebrews 12.1–2; 13.20–21

> We too, then, being surrounded by such a great cloud of witnesses, should
> throw off every encumbrance and the sin that so easily clings to us, and
> keenly run the race that lies before us, our eyes fixed on Jesus, the founder and
> finisher of our faith. He, for the joy that was set before him, endured the cross,
> despising the shame, and has taken his seat at the right hand of the throne
> of God . . . [13.20] Now may the God of peace who brought from the dead
> our Lord Jesus, that great shepherd of the sheep, by the blood of the eternal
> covenant, make you perfect in every good work to do his will, working in you
> what is pleasing in his sight through Jesus Christ, to whom be glory, for ever
> and ever. Amen.

The oldest manuscripts head this letter of exhortation just 'To Hebrews',
and when all is considered the writer must be regarded as unknown,
though evidently learned and more skilful in Greek and eloquence than
any other in the New Testament. It is good to have so substantial a contribution of Christian thought to set alongside those of John, Paul, and the
rest. Those addressed seem to be Jewish Christians in or near Rome,
knowing well and trusting the author, who wishes to brace them against
falling back from their faith in a time of hardship and discouragement.
The letter sets out the utter superiority of Christ and his work. The salvation he brings is as substance to mere shadows that have preceded it.

In our extract the theme is perseverance in the faith. A survey of the
Old Testament saints of faith has just been given, showing how they
endured and acted in hope of something yet to come. Christ has realized these hopes, and now Christians who have begun to experience that

fulfilment must be all the more dedicated and persevering towards the final completion. They must look away from all distraction and keep their gaze on Jesus, who so faithfully went his way through suffering and the cross, to take his eternal place of cosmic rule in the glory of God.

This earthly life is a way for us to traverse with the commitment and discipline so evident in athletes and their races. Through Christ's once-for-all sacrifice we have forgiveness and access to the Father. But still there is the way to go, and a work of God in us to complete our remaking. So this great prayer is offered: may he be ever working in us according to his will, through Jesus Christ, to whom be the glory for ever.

Receive the Word and Act Accordingly

James

[1.19b] Let everyone be swift to hear, slow to speak and slow to get angry, for human anger does not yield the goodness God requires. So put away all filthiness and upsurge of wickedness, and humbly welcome the implanted Word that is able to save your souls. Yet be doers of the word, not just hearers, deceiving yourselves . . .

[1.26] If any consider themselves religious but do not bridle their tongues, they deceive themselves; their religion is a sham. Religion that is pure and undefiled before our God and Father is this: to visit orphans and widows in their time of trouble, and to keep oneself undefiled by the world . . .

[4.13] Come now, you who say, 'Today or tomorrow we shall go to such and such a town and spend a year there and trade and make money', yet not knowing what tomorrow will bring – what after all is your life? You are but a mist seen for a little while and then vanishing. You ought rather to say, 'If the Lord wills, we shall live to do this or that' . . .

[5.13] When any among you suffer, they should pray. If any have cause for joy, let them sing praise. Are any among you ill? Let them call for the elders of the church to pray over them and anoint them with oil in the name of the Lord, for the prayer offered in faith will save the sick and the Lord will raise them up. Any sins they may have committed will be forgiven. Confess your sins, then, to one another and pray for one another, so that you may be healed. A good person's prayer has great effect . . .

The sermon-like letter of a certain 'James' is full of down-to-earth wisdom, with quite a few echoes of our Lord's 'Sermon on the Mount'. The evidence does not settle whether or not (as came to be believed) this James is the brother of Jesus who became leader of the church in

Jerusalem. In any case, the practical, blunt counsel that is given has a special value.

The gem of our extract is the saying about the 'implanted Word'. The teaching about Jesus and the way of discipleship, as we receive it with ready hearts, becomes planted within us, a living seed that will give wonderful fruit. Understood more deeply, this 'word' is the Lord himself, the expression and outgoing love of God. Planted in our hearts, nurtured with humility and love on our part, this living 'Word' will indeed save our souls, filling all our life with the light and grace of God.

The advice about illness encourages the practice of anointing. Here penitence, faith and prayer play their part, and also the joining together of church members in their loving concern. And not least, the oil itself contributes. It opens our imagination and represents the kindly fellowship of all living things.

New Birth and Living Hope

1 Peter 1.3–9

> Blessed be the God and Father of our Lord Jesus Christ! In his great mercy he has given us a new birth into a living hope by the resurrection of Jesus Christ from the dead. It is an inheritance nothing can destroy or defile, kept unfading for you in heaven. By God's power you are guarded through faith for a salvation ready to be revealed at the end of this age. In this you have much joy, though now for a little while you may be distressed in various trials to test your faith, which is more precious than perishable gold that has to be tested by fire. So your faith will come to praise, glory and honour at the revelation of Jesus Christ. Without having seen him you already love him. You trust in him even though you do not see him, and you are filled with a joy glorious beyond words, for you are receiving the goal of your faith – the salvation of your souls.

We may think of Peter sending his message of encouragement with the secretarial help of Silvanus (5.12), also called Silas, who assisted Paul. Thus the warm and abundant ideas are expressed in accomplished Greek. Probably writing from Rome ('Babylon', 5.13), the apostle addresses churches in several areas of Asia Minor where there is persecution.

He has no doubt about the gift of God already received – new birth through the resurrection of Jesus Christ, a cause of inexpressible joy and the beginning of salvation. But it is a new birth into a living hope, a transforming hope, combined with faith. Such hope has a sure grasp on the perfection still to be fully revealed.

In fact it is a recurring theme: God's saving work has yet to be fully known and seen. The present, meanwhile, includes great sufferings, testing faith like the furnace which purifies and proves gold. Peter warmly commends the followers of Jesus who, without having seen him (as Peter has, in life and in the resurrection), yet love and trust him.

Love, trust and joy in the Lord – such are the graces which will bear us through the fearsome times of suffering.

God is Love

1 John 4.7–21

> Beloved, let us love one another, for love is from God, and everyone who loves is begotten by God and knows God. One who does not love does not know God, for God is love. The love of God was shown among us when God sent his only Son into the world, so that we might have life through him.
>
> The essence of love is not that we loved God, but that he loved us and sent his Son to be the means of forgiveness for our sins. Beloved, if God loved us so, we also ought to love one another. No one has ever seen God, but if we love one another, God dwells in us and his love is completed in us. We know that we dwell in him and he in us when he gives us of his Spirit.
>
> And we have seen and can testify that the Father sent his Son to be the Saviour of the world. Whoever acknowledges that Jesus is the Son of God, God dwells in him and he in God. So we know and believe the love that God has put in us. God is love, and those who dwell in love dwell in God, and God dwells in them. Love is completed in us when we have confidence regarding the day of judgement, for even in this world we have become like him. There is no fear in love, for perfect love drives out fear. Since fear has dread of punishment, those who fear are not complete in their love.
>
> We love because he loved us first. But if any say, 'I love God' and yet hate their brother or sister, they are lying. For those who do not love the brother or sister they see, how can they love God whom they do not see? So we have this commandment from him, that those who love God must love their brother and sister also.

This letter (a kind of homily) is closely related to the Gospel of John, and it is good to have further expression of great themes found there. Those addressed are not specified. The letter remains open for any church with a need for this particular teaching, strong especially on the Word as having truly become flesh, truly human.

The thoughts in our passage revolve around love (agape, unselfish love as in Christ). Most fundamentally, John teaches that God is love, and that this love was shown supremely in the sending of his Son into the world to gain our forgiveness and give us eternal life.

From God's love arises our love, and our knowing or communing with God is a sharing in the divine love. Sharply, then, John rebukes those who do not act in love (goodwill and kindness) towards their fellows, and it is when the love is lacking for those especially near, fellow Christians, that the clash with the professed faith is most discordant. The claim to be loving God is then nothing but a lie.

'Those who dwell in love dwell in God.' It is true that these wonderful words follow on thoughts of faith and apply to those who acknowledge Jesus as the Son, the one who in the deepest sense is 'of God'. But when all is considered, the words still carry the truth that those who practise unselfish love, *agape,* are closer to God than they may know. Already they dwell in him. As they could not live but for God, so also they could not love but for him.

Buy from Jesus Gold from the Furnace

Revelation 3.14–22

> And to the angel of the church in Laodicea write: These are the words of the Amen, the faithful and true witness, the beginning of God's creation. I know your ways, and how you are neither cold nor hot. I wish you were cold or hot. But because you are lukewarm and neither hot nor cold, I will spit you out of my mouth.
>
> For you think to yourself, 'How rich I am, how prosperous! There is nothing I lack.' You do not see that you are a wretch, pitiable, poor, blind and naked. So I advise you to buy from me gold refined in fire so that you may become rich, and white garments to clothe you and keep you from the shame of your nakedness, and ointment for your eyes so that you may see.
>
> Those I love I reprove and chasten. Show zeal, then, and repent. See, I stand at the door and knock. If you will hear my voice and open the door, I will come in to you and eat with you, and you with me. To the one who conquers I will give a place to sit down with me on my throne, as I myself conquered and sat down with my Father on his throne. Let anyone who has an ear listen to what the Spirit says to the churches.

A Christian brother and visionary named John is on the little island of Patmos (Patina). Very likely he is suffering exile with hard labour for his faith. One Sunday, 'the Lord's Day', he is given visions and messages for the churches, especially seven churches in the province of Asia (part of Asia Minor, now Turkey). This material is full of strange symbols and images, many echoing earlier Jewish revelatory books, and often difficult if not impossible to interpret. Yet the book speaks to Christians under persecution and carries a strong message of God's certain work to destroy evil and establish his new creation.

There is a particular message for each of the seven churches (addressed to their angels as their representatives). In the word to Laodicea, Christ describes himself as the Amen and the Beginning (*arche*); like the Father, he is the Last and the First, eternal and supreme. He is also the ultimate martyr ('witness') and his faithfulness ever shines as an example to his followers who suffer.

This church is a victim of its own wealth, gained from black wool and banking. (After an earthquake in AD 60 the town was able to reconstruct without funding from the empire.) They are condemned for being only lukewarm in faith and for complacency, unable to see their spiritual poverty. This tepidity is abhorrent to the Lord, who counsels the church to get white robes and his fire-tested gold – treasures of the Spirit – rather than be content with worldly riches from trade and financial dealings. The one who conquers has stood fast in persecution and will be given a place of honour beside Christ in his kingdom.

The image of Jesus knocking to come in remains eloquent. Weak and half-hearted as comfortable Christians may be and in danger of alienation from God, yet Christ loves them and knocks at their door like the lover at night in the Song of Solomon (5.2), and if it is opened to him will come in for a reunion of great joy.

When All is Made New

Revelation 21.1–8

> And I saw a new heaven and a new earth, for the first heaven and the first earth had passed away and the sea was no more. And the holy city, new Jerusalem, I saw coming down out of heaven from God, prepared as a bride adorned for her husband. And I heard a great voice from the throne saying, 'See, the dwelling of God is with humankind, and he will dwell with them, and they shall be his peoples, and God himself will be with them. And he shall wipe away every tear from their eyes, and death shall be no more, neither shall there be mourning, nor dying, nor pain any more. For the former things have passed away.' And the one who sat on the throne said, 'See, I make all things new.'

And he said, 'Write, for these words are faithful and true.' And he said to me, 'It is accomplished. I am the Alpha and the Omega, the beginning and the end. I will give to the thirsty water without price from the fountain of the water of life. Those who overcome shall inherit these things, and I will be their God and they shall be as my children. But as for the cowardly and unfaithful, the vile, the murderers, the libertines, sorcerers and all dealers in deceit, their lot shall be in the burning lake of sulphur which is the second death.'

Visionary John continues his account of revelations given him to brace the churches against terrible persecution. He has told of fearsome upheavals as God puts an end to the forces of evil. And now he has a crowning vision to relate. He sees the whole cosmos made new, delivered from the old chaos-troubles symbolized by the raging ocean, which is now no more.

Jerusalem in the ideal is where God and his worshippers live together in peace. Come down in perfect beauty from heaven, this new Jerusalem is the centre of a world where there is no more suffering and God himself has wiped away his people's tears.

The vision has taken shape in the situation of bitter suffering where steadfast believers face torture and death for holding to their faith. So this revelation expresses a fierce challenge and at the end has a stark, unrelenting, indeed merciless quality, matching that crisis. Those who overcome and conquer are those who, resisting passively, are yet unyielding against the persecutors. They inherit the new world and drink the water of eternal life. But John sees those who give way condemned with the wicked in the judgement of the dead. He sees them go to a 'second death and thrown into the lake of burning sulphur'.

We reflect on the stark contrasts of this vision, allowing for its dire situation, but having to relate it to other revelations and inspired teaching. We reflect that most good people are not consistently saintly, and most wrongdoers are not wholly evil. Believers commit sins of weakness and untruth while wrongdoers on occasion show kindness. We should indeed hear from prophet John that, contrary to appearances, evil will certainly be conquered, and that God calls us to a faithfulness like that of Christ himself. But we hold on also to John's message that God will make all things new. Long and bitter may be the way for the despisers of God and of good, but in the end, in the wondrous mercy of the Lord who is Alpha and Omega, all will be made new, all will be well.

Sometimes people say they cannot believe in God because of the state of the world. But scripture after scripture has shown God himself as anything but content with the world as it is. In Christ he dies to change it. And still his name is yet to be hallowed, his glory to be manifest, his reign come. And God's own words ring in the prophet's ear: 'Behold, I make all new.'